The Language of Canon Law

OXFORD STUDIES IN LANGUAGE AND LAW

Oxford Studies in Language and Law includes scholarly analyses and descriptions of language evidence in civil and criminal law cases as well as language issues arising in the area of statutes, statutory interpretation, courtroom discourse, jury instructions, and historical changes in legal language.

The Legal Language of Scottish Burghs: Standardization and Lexical Bundles (1380–1560)
Joanna Kopaczyk

"I'm Sorry for What I've Done": The Language of Courtroom Apologies
M. Catherine Gruber

Dueling Discourses: The Construction of Reality in Closing Arguments
Laura Felton Rosulek

Entextualizing Domestic Violence: Language Ideology and Violence Against Women in the Anglo-American Hearsay Principle
Jennifer Andrus

Speak English or What?: Codeswitching and Interpreter Use in New York City Small Claims Court
Philipp Sebastian Angermeyer

Law at Work: Studies in Legal Ethnomethods
Edited by Baudouin Dupret, Michael Lynch, and Tim Berard

Speaking of Language and Law: Conversations on the Work of Peter Tiersma
Edited by Lawrence M. Solan, Janet Ainsworth, and Roger W. Shuy

Confronting the Death Penalty: How Language Influences Jurors in Capital Cases
Robin Conley

Discursive Constructions of Consent in the Legal Process
Edited by Susan Ehrlich, Diana Eades and Janet Ainsworth

From Truth to Technique at Trial: A Discursive History of Advocacy Advice Texts
Philip Gaines

Discourse, Identity, and Social Change in the Marriage Equality Debates
Karen Tracy

Translating the Social World for Law: Linguistic Tools for a New Legal Realism
Edited by Elizabeth Mertz, William K. Ford, and Gregory Matoesian

Conceptions in the Code: How Metaphors Explain Legal Challenges in Digital Times
Stefan Larsson

Deceptive Ambiguity by Police and Prosecutors
Roger W. Shuy

Legal Integration and Language Diversity: Rethinking Translation in EU Lawmaking
C.J.W. Baaij

Legal Translation Outsourced
Juliette R. Scott

Shallow Equality and Symbolic Jurisprudence
Janny H.C. Leung

Strategic Indeterminacy in the Law
David Lanius

Confronting the Death Penalty: How Language Influences Jurors in Capital Cases
Robin Conley Riner

Language and Legal Interpretation in International Law
Anne Lise Kjaer and Joanna Lam

The Language of Canon Law

JUDITH HAHN

OXFORD
UNIVERSITY PRESS

OXFORD
UNIVERSITY PRESS

Oxford University Press is a department of the University of Oxford. It furthers the University's objective of excellence in research, scholarship, and education by publishing worldwide. Oxford is a registered trade mark of Oxford University Press in the UK and certain other countries.

Published in the United States of America by Oxford University Press
198 Madison Avenue, New York, NY 10016, United States of America.

Library of Congress Cataloging-in-Publication Data
Names: Hahn, Judith, 1978– author.
Title: The language of canon law / Judith Hahn.
Description: New York, NY : Oxford University Press, 2023. |
Series: Oxford studies in language and law | Includes bibliographical references and index.
Identifiers: LCCN 2022029899 (print) | LCCN 2022029900 (ebook) |
ISBN 9780197674246 (hardback) | ISBN 9780197674260 (epub)
Subjects: LCSH: Canon law—Language. |
Canon law—Interpretationa dn construction. | Law—Language.
Classification: LCC KBU160.H34 2023 (print) | LCC KBU160 (ebook) |
DDC 262.9—dc23/eng/20220924
LC record available at https://lccn.loc.gov/2022029899
LC ebook record available at https://lccn.loc.gov/2022029900

DOI: 10.1093/oso/9780197674246.001.0001

Printed by Integrated Books International, United States of America

Contents

Preface and Acknowledgments ix

1. Introduction 1
   1.1 The Language of the Church and of Its Law 1
      The Gospel, Message, and Mission 1
      Law in Service of the Gospel Message 2
   1.2 Canon Law on Language 4
      In Service of the Gospel Mission 4
      Ecclesiastical Language Crimes 6
      Solicitation and Threat 7
      Lying under Oath 8
      The Sacramental Seal 10
      Defaming Speech 10
      Language in Penal Law 12
   1.3 Part of the Law and Language Debate 13
      Linguistics and Legal Studies 14
      Learning from Legal Practice 15
      Theology and Canon Law Studies 16
      Scope of My Study 19

2. The Function of Language in Law 23
   2.1 Purposes of the Law 23
      Creating Social Cohesion 23
      Influencing Behavior 24
      Exchanging Information 26
      Concealed Purposes 26
   2.2 Law as Communication 27
      Sending Legal Messages 29
      Receiving Legal Meaning 30
      Making Legal Meaning 31
      Communal Meaning 32
      The Media of the Law 33
      The Silence of the Law 34
   2.3 The Sacramentality of the Law 35
      The Language of Magic 36
      Ritual Speech 38
      Law as a Matter of Belief 39
      Legal Speech Acts 41

Classes of Illocutions 42
Legal Illocutions 44
Status Function Declarations 48
Deontic Powers 50
Sacramental Speech 52
Ex Opere Operato 54
True Communication 55

3. Idiosyncrasies of Legal Language 59
3.1 The Grammar of the Law 59
Gender Issues 60
Passive Constructions 60
Challenging Syntax 61
Expressing Commands 65
3.2 The Terminology of the Law 67
Common Terms as Legal Terms 68
"Lending" and "Loaning" 69
"Possession" and "Property" 70
Changing Meaning 72
Technical Terminology 74
3.3 Legal Terms, Foreign Words 76
Borrowed Terms 76
Canon Law Latin 79
Language Training 81
Canon Law Jargon 82
Neologisms 84
3.4 Indeterminate Terms 86
"Grave Necessity" 86
"Just Cause" 88

4. Comprehension Difficulties 91
4.1 Ambiguity of the Law 92
Lexical Ambiguity 93
"Fideles" as Legal Subjects 94
Syntactic Ambiguity 97
4.2 Transfer Problems 99
"Annulment" Terminology 99
Substance and Accidents 101
A Grin without a Cat 102
4.3 Blending Literary Genres 103
Theological Trimmings 104
A Custom Commercial 106

5. Challenging Legal Incomprehension 109
5.1 Exclusivism and Elitism 109
Language Weapons 111
Linguistic Distinction 113
Preventing Legal Heresy 114
5.2 Endorsing Plain Language 116
Avoiding Useless Precision 116
Simple Structure and Style 118
Modernizing Legal Speech 119
5.3 Plain Canon Law? 120
Simplifying Constructions 121
Replacing Outdated Terms 122
Challenging Law Latin 124
Intelligibility over Distinction 125
Comprehension over Tradition 126
Supporting Equal Comprehension 127

6. A Global Law and Its Language 129
6.1 Linguistic Relativity 130
Perceiving Reality via Language 130
Relativity of Legal Concepts 132
Cultural Conflicts in Global Law 135
6.2 Strong and Weak Language Theories 136
Language and Cultural Borders 137
Reconstructing Meaning 138
6.3 Legislation for Multi-Language Groups 141
Legal and Linguistic Colonialism 141
Structures of Dominance 143
Multi-Language Approaches 145
Creating Multi-Language Law 146
Drafting in Foreign Languages 147
Multi-Language Canon Law 149
Literalistic and Free Translations 151
Intermediate Approaches 153
Achieving Legal Equivalence 155

7. Interpreting the Law 157
7.1 Plain and Proper Meaning 157
No Meaning without Context 158
Challenging "Plain" Meaning 160
Open Texture of the Law 162

7.2 A Matter of Interpretation 163
(Re)constructing Meaning 164
Purposeful Interpretation 165
Textualist Approaches 166
Intentionalist Interpretations 167
Relevance of the Author 168
The Death of the Author 170
Canons of Construction 171
Blending Interpretation Rules 173
Borders of Interpretation 175
Multi-Language Interpretations 176
7.3 Competent Interpreters 177
Binding Interpretations 178
Authentic Interpretations 179
Interpretive Legal Development 181
Controlling Meaning 182
A Neoconservative Agenda 183

8. The Language of Legal Action 185
8.1 Hearings and Testimonies 186
Complex Dialogues 187
Fair Questioning 189
The Right to Silence 190
Privileges in Evidence Law 192
Witness Competence Rules 193
Oral Hearings, Written Acts 194
8.2 Adjudication Language 196
Existential Decisiveness 196
Oral Debate, Written Verdict 198
Unassailable Speech 199
The Language of Verdicts 200

9. Conclusion 203

Bibliography 207
Index 225

Preface and Acknowledgments

Writing a book is as much a reclusive task as it is not. While I certainly tend to retreat from public life whenever I am in the middle of a writing process, I am very aware of those many individuals who have supported me and contributed to the working process up to this point and have allowed me to complete the book. I cannot mention all of the individuals to whom I owe encouragement and inspiration but would like to name at least some without whom I would probably never have had the idea to write a book on the language of canon law.

Being part of a lively campus university is a tremendous help when undertaking an interdisciplinary study, as it makes it much easier to cross paths with scholars from other disciplines, such as linguists. I am particularly pleased to have made the acquaintance of Stefanie Dipper, professor of computer linguistics at Ruhr University Bochum, quite early on when I started working in Bochum in 2010. I will never forget her famous and infamous inaugural lecture "*Ente Apfelmus*" ("Duck Applesauce"), which was not only hilariously funny but also provided one impulse for me to start thinking about the relevance of linguistics for canon law. I also look back with much gratitude upon my time as a fellow at the Käte Hamburger Center for Advanced Study in the Humanities "Law as Culture" at the University of Bonn in 2015 and 2016, during which I was fortunate enough to meet renowned and enthusiastic scholars of law and language as well as of law and literature, including Lawrence Solan, Sabine Meyer, and Joachim Harst.

As a longtime member of the Faculty of Catholic Theology at Ruhr University Bochum, and now a new member of the Faculty of Catholic Theology at the University of Bonn, I am extremely fortunate to have belonged to two inspiring colleges of theological scholars. I am grateful to my colleagues for their enormous collegiality and enduring support. The exceptional community spirit which exists in Bochum has in many ways been highly conducive to my academic career. It is the same spirit which has now taken me to Bonn. In particular I would like to thank Andrea Hartwig, who handled all the administrative affairs for my chair over the past years so that I could easily retreat from time to time to write my books.

My German speaking skills I owe above all to my parents. My mum was very strict when it came to grammar and style, something for which I am most thankful (now). And I was lucky enough to have the most wonderful German teacher at school, "Frau Müller," whom we all feared and revered at the same time. I know my German grammar well entirely thanks to Ms. Müller, who was a genuine grammar crack, although she would most certainly not approve of this expression. So I feel secure whenever I am operating in German, but less so when writing in English. However, as I left school with an embarrassingly poor knowledge of English, my ability to speak it reasonably well today is something I owe above all to my friends and fellow students at Heythrop College back in 1999–2000. Above all, I am grateful to Sarah, Mark, and Mark for their friendship and the patience they showed when listening to me and correcting my mistakes over and over again. I am most grateful to Robert John Murphy for improving my writing skills in English and for supporting me by carefully proofreading many of my manuscripts over the last couple of years. As ever, he was also an indispensable help with this study. I needed his language skills and linguistic expertise to publish a book on language; that is an interesting twist, I find.

As always I dedicate this book to my family, the people I enjoy speaking to the most.

1
Introduction

1.1 The Language of the Church and of Its Law

Recent years have seen many questions being raised with regard to the Roman Catholic Church and its current state. In the German church, as in many other local churches, the abuse scandal has triggered debates not only on sexual abuse in religious institutions as such but also on moral teaching and sexual ethics, the roles attributed to women and men in the church, the participation of laypeople in decision-making, church leadership, and the training for church offices. The debates have been intense to say the least. They all appear to be connected in some way. They revolve around the core issue of whether the church in its earthly institutional structure is managing to communicate its message of faith, hope, and love to present-day individuals authentically, or if the institution in its real shape tends to distort the Gospel message instead.

The Gospel, Message, and Mission

As many reservations are rooted in doubts about whether the church is still a medium that is communicating the Gospel message, it is not surprising that communication itself—and with it the language of the church—has become a topic of debate in its own right. In Germany, this debate was started in 2016, initiated by the Catholic consultant and author Erik Flügge, who, in his book on the language being used in church, maintained that the church was currently doing a miserable job in communicating its message.[1] As the debate widened, it started to draw in journalists, theologians, and church officials alike. It addresses the highly critical question whether the church needs to reform its "sound" to have a chance of being heard by modern individuals. In particular, Flügge criticizes the church's "jargon of concern," which it mostly uses in pastoral situations, exposing it as the fake and shallow sound of sympathy and as an attempt to lull listeners into some kind of feel-good atmosphere without offering them any serious content. His book is a tough critique of typical pastoral "sounds." While the church has a serious message to convey, Flügge suggests that it is hindering

[1] See Flügge, *Der Jargon der Betroffenheit*, Munich, Kösel, 2016.

The Language of Canon Law. Judith Hahn, Oxford University Press. © Oxford University Press 2023.
DOI: 10.1093/oso/9780197674246.003.0001

itself from successfully imparting it by using the wrong tune. Flügge's critique is harsh and hurtful, as it does strike a chord. It is clearly now high time for the church—and also for theology as the academic endeavor of understanding the church—to think about how it speaks about religious matters, about the church, its message—and its law.

In contrast to Flügge's diagnosis on pastoral jargons, canon law—the body of laws, legal principles, and legal institutions of the Roman Catholic Church—is seldom accused of a "jargon of concern." Quite the contrary, whenever canon law comes into play, the church tends to be accused of sounding harsh, merciless, and anti-pastoral. The church obviously uses several jargons, all of which give it a different tenor. From a theological point of view, it is essential to devote greater attention to these different sounds. This is because the debate about church language is not simply a linguistic issue, but ecclesiologically vital. Ecclesiologically speaking, the church itself is at stake. It is not only a messenger of the Good News, but is grounded in the message itself.[2] It is the message which passes on the incarnation of Christ. The incarnation as an act of communication through which Christ communicated with the world[3] is the existential reason for the church and bestows it with its main purpose, namely, of passing on the Gospel message.

Law in Service of the Gospel Message

My discipline, canon law studies, revolves around the matter of Roman Catholic canon law. Ecclesiologically speaking, canon law is therefore concerned with the issue of how the law contributes to the church fulfilling its function of passing on the Gospel message. Canon law studies is indebted to Klaus Mörsdorf for examining the relation between the communications of the church and the law of the church and for expounding what this connection conveys about the law itself.[4] Mörsdorf referred to "word" and "sacrament" as the two pillars on which the church rests and which constitute the two ways of passing on Christ's communication. In spreading the Good News, the church passes on the incarnation in the form of words. This is also a legal act, as Mörsdorf discovered, as spreading the Good News is only possible effectively when it is accomplished with power, that is with the authority to preach and teach as given to the church and its members by Christ himself. This power and the obedience that it demands of those who

[2] E.g., Pontifical Council for Social Communications, "Pastoral Instruction *Communio et progressio* on the Means of Social Communication," May 23, 1971, especially no. 11, *Acta Apostolicae Sedis* 63 (1971), 597–598.

[3] For a theological and linguistic interpretation of the incarnation, see Tran, "Marlo's City of Words," in idem/Werntz, eds, *Corners in the City of God*, Eugene, OR, Cascade Books, 2013, 59–61.

[4] See Mörsdorf, "Wort und Sakrament als Bauelemente der Kirchenverfassung," *Archiv für katholisches Kirchenrecht* 134 (1965), 72–79.

perceive the message is one fundament of the law, as Mörsdorf contended. So according to him, the law of the church is grounded in the word—the Word that is Christ himself and the power to pass on the word that Christ entrusted to the church.

Sacraments are those symbolic acts that make the word tangible. They are likewise given to the church by Christ, and serve as ways in which Christ lives on and continues to act in his church. When it comes to how the sacraments function, Mörsdorf discovered parallels between the ways in which the sacraments and the law take effect. He saw a kinship between legal and sacramental acting, as they both stand for an invisible reality which becomes tangible through the act itself. Mörsdorf called this the "sacramental root of the law."[5] One of his examples, the imposition of hands, is part of sacramental rituals, but was also part of legal rituals, as in the ancient practices of electing a king. So evidently, the act of imposing hands as a symbolic resource of ancient Jewish law was established as part of Christian religious practice within the sacraments. This reveals the proximity of law and sacrament; I will return to this connection in chapter 2, section 2.3. Mörsdorf drew on symbol theory to understand the parallels better. The law and the sacraments both rely on symbols which represent an invisible reality. This is done with the help of symbolic words and gestures which render this reality effective in the here and now. The reality so symbolized and effectuated can be a legal reality or a religious reality, for instance, an act conveying God's grace to the receivers of a sacrament. According to Mörsdorf, this parallel reveals that both the church's sanctifying mission and its law are based on the symbolic representation of Christ here on earth through words and actions, and this representation has an essentially legal quality to it.

As the church—as a symbolic representation of the Word itself, which is Christ, and his mission of passing on his message in word and sacrament—is all about words, speech, and communication, it is therefore of paramount importance for the church to think about its language. A first step is to ask how the church speaks and communicates with its members and with society when it preaches and teaches, celebrates its faith, or makes legal utterances. The tune is evidently different, as I have suggested, when the church speaks pastorally or conveys a legal message. This difference and the irritation that it causes among many Catholics might be one reason why many church members at present tend to ignore the legal communications of the church. Canon law is currently challenged by a major problem of acceptance among many local Catholics.[6] Nevertheless, it has to be noted that the church as an institution relies on its legal structure and also relies on the law as one major medium of communication with

5 Original quote, "sakramentale[n] Wurzel des Rechtes," ibid., 77.
6 See Hahn, *Foundations of a Sociology of Canon Law*, Cham, Springer Nature, 2022.

the church members. As a complex institution which is dependent on law, the church is reliant on successful legal communications. From an ecclesiological point of view, it is therefore of vital interest to learn more about the legal communications of the church and the language of canon law.

1.2 Canon Law on Language

Speaking about the language of canon law is an endeavor that requires the adoption of several perspectives. My study is primarily concerned with the issue of how the church uses language in the context of its legal communications. However, the language of canon law can also be approached by scrutinizing language as an *object* of canonical regulations. To this end, I use the next section to give a short overview of how the law of the church relates to language issues. In doing so, I admittedly take on somewhat of a reverse perspective. While my study is primarily about the language of the law, I want to devote the next section to studying the *law on language*. Reversing the perspective is not a capricious endeavor. Indeed, I find this step helpful for gaining a better understanding of two aspects of the canon law and language debate. First, by delving into the substantive law of the church to discover an example of how it deals with language, I want to offer non-canonist readers a chance to get a clearer grasp of the law of the church. For non-canonists, the legal order of the church is an alien and often slightly bewildering matter. Studying how the law deals with language provides a glimpse into this world of religious law, which is foreign to most modern thinkers. Second, examining how the law responds to language issues also helps to provide at least some explanation why canon law studies has so far failed to afford canon law and language the academic significance that it deserves. As substantive law as the main subject of canonical studies focuses on language merely through a very narrow lens, canon law studies still has some way to go before it learns that language issues are actually at the heart of legal issues. Devoting some thought to how the law references language might therefore provide us with a first idea of where to start studying the language of canon law.

In Service of the Gospel Mission

Most interestingly, the law of the church is very aware of the fact that language is a necessary precondition for the church in pursuing its mission to spread the Gospel message throughout the world. Language consequently plays a recurring role in many norms of the law, among them ecclesiastical constitutional law which, while mostly relying on territoriality for the organization of local churches, acknowledges language as being one criterion for the establishment of personal parishes (see canon 518 CIC/1983). There are four topics which stand out with regard to language issues when studying the norms of the current Code of Canon Law of 1983 (hereinafter abbreviated as CIC/1983): language as content of the ecclesiastical ministers' education; language issues in the editions and translations of official texts and ecclesiastical documents in canonical media law; the employment of interpreters and translators in the administration of sacraments or in adjudication; and language crimes as sanctioned in ecclesiastical penal law.

Language is a prerequisite for pastoral ministry, making language training an essential element of the ministers' formation. Accordingly, the regulations on priestly formation prescribe the training of priest candidates in those languages they need for their later pastoral ministry (see canon 249 CIC/1983). This is especially important for candidates who intend to serve in foreign churches. It has to be part of their education "that they learn the language of the region and understand its institutions, social conditions, usages, and customs" (canon 257 §2 CIC/1983). The Code refers not only to language training but also includes cultural learning, thus pointing to the close connection between language and culture. In addition, Latin still plays a key role in priestly formation (see canon 249 CIC/1983), not least due to the traditional function of Latin for the celebration of the Eucharist even though canon law today acknowledges vernacular languages for liturgical purposes (see canon 928 CIC/1983). This has resulted in Latin becoming increasingly insignificant for the liturgy since the Second Vatican Council.

Besides these educational contexts, language as a topic of canon law plays a major role in ecclesiastical media law with respect to the publication of key religious and theological texts and for the translation of biblical or liturgical texts. Before they can be cleared for publication, Bible editions and their vernacular translations require the approval of the Apostolic See or the respective bishops' conference (see canon 825 §1 CIC/1983). Ecumenical translations of the Bible into vernacular languages require the permission of the bishops' conference (see canon 825 §2 CIC/1983). Liturgical books may be published only by the Apostolic See (see canon 838 §2 CIC/1983). The Apostolic See also oversees their vernacular translations in concordance with the local bishops' conferences (see canon 838 §3 CIC/1983). Reprints of liturgical books and their vernacular translations must be examined to ensure they agree with the approved editions before publication (see canon 826 §2 CIC/1983). Catechisms need the approval of the local ordinary (see canon 827 §1 CIC/1983), and prayer books also require his permission (see canon 826 §3 CIC/1983). When used for teaching in schools, Bible editions and books on theology, canon law, ecclesiastical history, and moral matters require the approval of an ecclesiastical authority (see canon 827 §2 CIC/1983).

A third topic that raises language issues as a subject of canon law is whenever the law relates to the service of interpreters and translators. This happens in relation to the administration of sacraments when the service of interpreters is employed for confessions (see canon 990 CIC/1983; see also canons 983 §1 and 1386 §2 CIC/1983) and marriages (see canon 1106 CIC/1983). And it also happens in ecclesiastical adjudication, where trained linguists are required to participate in judicial hearings (see canon 1471 CIC/1983) or to translate the case files into foreign languages (see canon 1474 §2 CIC/1983).

Hence, summing up the previous findings, one may note that canon law relates to language in several respects. It acknowledges language skills as social and cultural skills, which serve as essential prerequisites for the church fulfilling its mission of spreading the Gospel message successfully. This is a realistic assessment but also a fairly instrumental view of language. In this context, we also get a first glimpse of the omnipresent Latin as the language of the church, which in its function as the language of canon law will reappear as an issue in the course of my study. In ecclesiastical media law, the focus on language is slightly different even though evidently similarly narrow. Here, language is above all subject to control. The ecclesiastical authorities attempt to maintain control of the translations of key doctrinal and disciplinary texts because they fear the translations might distort the original meaning. A similar concern seems to lie behind the rules which relate to the service of interpreters and translators. The control of meaning in church with regard to processes which tend to alter meaning, such as translations or interpretations of texts, is an issue that will reappear repeatedly throughout my study on the language of canon law as well.

Ecclesiastical Language Crimes

One major issue where language evidently plays a leading role in canon law is with regard to so-called language crimes, as forensic linguist Roger Shuy termed offenses committed through language.[7] The term describes crimes or torts which are committed by speaking. All legal orders know such offenses. Classic examples are, as summarized by law and language scholar Peter Tiersma, "bribery, conspiracy, perjury, threat, and solicitation."[8] These crimes, as Tiersma wrote together with fellow law and language scholar Lawrence Solan, "are about

[7] See Shuy, *Language Crimes*, Malden, MA, Blackwell, 1996.
[8] Tiersma, "The Judge as Linguist," *Loyola of Los Angeles Law Review* 27 (1993), 270.

illegal speech acts,"[9] as they use speech to perform an illegal action. Language crimes, as the authors note, are always based on an agent's ill intent to change the world through speech, thus referring to the illocutionary effect of speech acts; I will return to a discussion of the illocutionary function of speech in more detail in chapter 2, section 2.3. They are acts which, according to speech act theory, represent "things we do in saying something,"[10] to quote legal philosopher John Austin's famous phrase. By using words which defame, insult, or express the untruth voluntarily, these acts are what they express, namely, defamations, insults, or perjury. Some language crimes also depend on their effect on the hearer, thus referring to the perlocutionary effect of speech as those acts concerning that "what we bring about or achieve *by* saying something."[11] Threatening someone, as Tiersma and Solan contend, requires the person addressed by a threat uttered to truly perceive that utterance as a threat.[12] As many language crimes sanctioned by secular law are also sanctioned by canon law, some in a similar and others in a different way, I want to provide some examples of regulations which show where secular law and canon law meet and where they diverge. By studying the similarities and idiosyncrasies of the canonical regulations, the specific character of canon law as a legal order of a religious community becomes somewhat clearer.

Solicitation and Threat

A useful example for showing differences and similarities is the crime of solicitation that consists of suggesting or requesting that another person commit a crime, thus often including language as the means of soliciting the third party to engage in criminal action. It does not appear in canon law as an individual offense but in a specific context. Here, it describes a crime committed by priests in administering the sacrament of penance, which consists of them soliciting a penitent to enter into sinful sexual acts with the cleric or another person (see canon 1385 CIC/1983). So solicitation plays a role as a crime under canon law but is not regulated individually as a solitary offense. Instead, it is connected with the idea of a priest approaching a penitent with sexual intentions, thereby becoming the so-called crime of solicitation (*crimen sollicitationis*). This crime, as absurd as it

[9] Tiersma/Solan, "The Language of Crime," in idem, eds, *The Oxford Handbook of Language and Law*, Oxford, Oxford University Press, 2012, 340; see also Oğlakcıoğlu/Schuhr, "Verbotene Sprache," in Felder/Vogel, eds, *Handbuch Sprache im Recht*, Berlin, Walter de Gruyter, 2017, 527–546; an interesting overview of texts as crimes, with a focus on the genre of blackmailing letters, is given by Sabine Ehrhardt; see Ehrhardt, "Texte als Straftat und im Straftatkontext," in Felder/Vogel, eds, *Handbuch Sprache im Recht*, Berlin, Walter de Gruyter, 2017, 547–566.

[10] Austin, *How to Do Things with Words*, Oxford, Oxford University Press, 1962, 108.

[11] Ibid.

[12] See Tiersma/Solan, "The Language of Crime," in idem, eds, *The Oxford Handbook of Language and Law*, Oxford, Oxford University Press, 2012, 340.

may sound when hearing of it at first, is in fact a phenomenon which reappears now and then, particularly in cases of clerics spiritually abusing adults. Here, the offenders use a pastorally fragile situation such as confession to solicit a penitent into sexual action. Hence, the example of solicitation in canon law alludes to the fact that ecclesiastical sanctions are most concerned with sex—clerical sex as a violation of clerical chastity mostly—and with the sacraments as key actions of the church, the validity and effectiveness of which the law is most concerned to protect.

Another language crime which shows comparable similarities and idiosyncrasies in church is a crime connected with threat. An act of threatening somebody verbally or with gestures, directly or indirectly, can be a crime according to most legal orders in certain circumstances, such as robbery or blackmail. In a similar way, threatening in canon law is not an offense in itself but is mentioned as part of a sex crime, as a cleric threatening somebody with or forcing them to perform a sexual act is to be justly punished, not excluding his dismissal from the clerical state (see canon 1395 §3 CIC/1983). So canon law, again, focuses on clerics as offenders and on specific clerical sex crimes, which the church understands as incompatible with the clerical obligation of celibacy, so that they may justify dismissing a cleric from the ranks of the clergy.

Lying under Oath

Perjury—the crime of lying under oath—is punishable in most secular legal orders and also in canon law. Canon 1371 §3 CIC/1983 reads, "A person who, in asserting or promising something before an ecclesiastical authority, commits perjury, is to be punished with a just penalty." The term used in the authentic Latin text of the canon is *periurium*, which, like its English translation, reveals pitifully little about its meaning. This nondefinition makes perjury particularly interesting for forensic linguists, not only because it is a crime committed by speaking (falsely) but also because its meaning is a matter of terminological debate. In American scholarship this has led to debates on whether perjury, as regulated in 18 US Code § 1621, is restricted to making statements that are literally false or whether it also includes those statements that are literally correct but are meant to mislead the hearers. The US judicature tends to understand perjury as making literally false statements only. In the famous precedential case *Bronston v. United States*,[13] the defendant was charged with perjury for giving a literally correct answer to a question posed to him under oath, which was obviously meant to

[13] The United States Supreme Court, "Bronston v. United States," decided January 10, 1973, *United States Reports* 409 (1973), 352–362.

mislead the questioning creditors' committee. When questioned about whether he *has* any bank accounts in Swiss banks, the defendant truthfully denied this. However, the question "Have you ever?" he answered by saying, "The company had an account there for about six months, in Zürich," while omitting to say that he had also personally had an account there for a while. In the end, the perjury charges were dropped with the argument that the defendant was literally telling the truth. There is nevertheless reason to view this interpretation by the US Supreme Court critically, not least because it encourages those obliged to tell the truth to make literally correct but deeply misleading statements—the technique of sticking to what might be understood as true in a literal sense was employed successfully by President Bill Clinton in the Lewinski hearing, as Lawrence Solan has shown.[14] Besides the pragmatic problem of encouraging smart individuals to give deceitful testimony in official hearings, there is also a linguistic concern arising from the literalistic narrowness of this understanding of perjury. Tiersma and Solan rightly point out that this approach suggests that speaking truthfully is about uttering the literally correct words, without taking into account that speech when viewed through the lens of linguistic pragmatics is a more complex phenomenon.[15] We have to ask ourselves if we understand "lying" more as a literal phenomenon or rather as a broader strategy for depriving questioners of the truth. History sometimes seems to point in the literal direction. Tiersma mentions Isolde's successful ordeal of the hot iron after stating that she had never been in any other man's arms than those of her husband and that pilgrim (Tristan in disguise) who had carried her from the boat to the shore.[16] This was literally true, even though not exactly the information that her husband would have liked to receive. Today, with a more complex idea of communication in mind, we might wonder how she got away with it. For canon law, the same question arises. Here, we are obliged to ask whether *periurium* is only intentionally telling the literal untruth or if the term also covers acts which intentionally mislead the listeners. I am unaware of any adjudication or literature that discusses this problem.[17] So to the best of my knowledge, it is an open question to be debated by canonists. For an institution as concerned with the truth as the church, it is somewhat surprising that as yet nobody has examined what actually constitutes telling an untruth.

[14] See Solan, "The Clinton Scandal," in Cotterill, ed, *Language in the Legal Process*, Basingstoke, Palgrave Macmillan, 2002, 180–195.

[15] See Tiersma/Solan, "The Language of Crime," in idem, eds, *The Oxford Handbook of Language and Law*, Oxford, Oxford University Press, 2012, 348–353.

[16] See Tiersma, *Legal Language*, Chicago, IL, The University of Chicago Press, 1999, 12.

[17] In her study on the oath in Bible and law, Irina Kreusch in this sense defines perjury as telling the untruth voluntarily, yet without touching on the problem of what "telling the untruth" actually is; see Kreusch, *Der Eid zwischen Schwurverbot Jesu und kirchlichem Recht*, Berlin, Duncker & Humblot, 2005, especially 265.

The Sacramental Seal

A typical ecclesiastical language crime is violating the sacramental seal (see canon 1386 CIC/1983), a crime unique to the church. The law states the seal to be inviolable, connecting this with the legal consequence of forbidding any acts that might be suitable for conveying knowledge gained in confession to a third party, "it is absolutely forbidden for a confessor to betray in any way a penitent in words or in any manner and for any reason" (canon 983 §1 CIC/1983). So the norm primarily sees "words," either written text or speech, as possible media for disclosing information gained in confession to others, but also other means of communication like signs, for instance. Whatever is suitable for transporting the message is regarded as a way of violating the sacramental seal. The same prohibition that binds the confessor also applies to interpreters and others who gain knowledge of sins from confession (see canon 983 §2 CIC/1983). The explicit mention of interpreters in the norm is particularly interesting from a law and language point of view, as it shows the act of confession to be an act of communication, in which a mutual understanding between confessor and penitent is key. If this understanding is obstructed due to the lack of a common language, interpreters can be employed to enable mutual understanding. This whole act of communication is then protected by the law as a situation of utmost confidentiality. This protection is ensured by threatening, with sanctions, anybody who breaks this confidentiality. The confessor who directly violates the sacramental seal, that is by directly repeating content from the confession, incurs an ipso facto *latae sententiae* excommunication, the lifting of which is reserved to the Apostolic See, whereas if he only indirectly violates the sacramental seal, that is by using signs or suggestions, he is to be punished justly according to the gravity of the deed (see canon 1386 §1 CIC/1983). The latter penalty may also be imposed on interpreters or others who disclose knowledge gained from confession (see §2). Most interestingly, a new norm, canon 1386 §3 CIC/1983, was added to these norms more recently. It threatens to punish those who use technical devices to record what is said in a real or simulated confession or disseminates the recording in social media. If this is done by clerics, they risk dismissal from the clerical state.

Defaming Speech

Another typical language crime penalized in canon law is a specifically religious version of defamation, which is blasphemy. Canon law threatens any Catholic with a just penalty who publically, in speech, writing, or another media, "utters blasphemy, or gravely harms public morals, or rails at or excites hatred of or contempt for religion or the church" (canon 1368 CIC/1983). Adding to this, canon law also explicitly penalizes public incitement against church authorities, threatening an individual with an interdict or just penalties who "publicly incites hatred or animosity against the Apostolic See or the ordinary because of some act of ecclesiastical office or duty, or who provokes disobedience against them" (canon 1373 CIC/1983). This complex of norms protecting the Catholic faith and the Catholic authorities from insult are typical crimes of religious institutions. Yet related regulations do still appear at least in some secular legal orders. The German Criminal Code, for instance, still criminalizes the public defamation of religions and religious communities if this act "is capable of disturbing the public peace" (section 166 Criminal Code). The Criminal Code speaks of *beschimpfen*, "insulting" or "badmouthing," religious content or religious organizations in a way that seems likely to pose a threat to public peace—notwithstanding whether the insult does indeed disturb any peace. In this respect, the regulation is highly abstract and highly indeterminate, which contributes to the debates on abrogating it. As the regulation also conflicts with the principle of secularity and with the basic right of freedom of speech, it is hotly debated and challenged. Yet it still exists and is responsible for at least a small number of convictions every year. So, interestingly, some secular legal orders continue to carry relicts of language crimes with a religious focus.

But there are also language crimes in canon law that have no parallel in secular legal orders due to their particularly religious nature. Two examples of ecclesiastical crimes without any parallel in modern secular law are heresy and apostasy. Heresy is "the obstinate denial or obstinate doubt after the reception of baptism of some truth which is to be believed by divine and Catholic faith"; apostasy is "the total repudiation of the Christian faith" (canon 751 CIC/1983). Whoever commits these crimes is punished with a *latae sententiae* excommunication, which ipso facto befalls the offender upon committing the crime (see canon 1364 §1 CIC/1983). In the first instance, the denial, doubt, or repudiation of faith usually happens internally, within the individual rejecting her or his faith. This act only becomes a crime when heretical or apostatic views are uttered audibly, as canon law defines a crime as an act of "external violation" (canon 1321 §4 CIC/1983) of a law or precept. Therefore, heresy and apostasy are language crimes committed through speech alone.[18] To accomplish the offense it is necessary that the utterance be witnessed by somebody. A heretical or apostatic statement unheard by anybody is an attempted offense only (see canon 1330 CIC/1983) and remains unpunished (see canon 1328 §1 CIC/1983). This shows that canon law has learned, even though not fully, that law is about external matters. Whereas the internally committed denial, doubt, or repudiation of faith is regarded as a

[18] See Lüdicke, "Canon 1364," in idem, ed, *Münsterischer Kommentar zum Codex Iuris Canonici* (suppl. sheets 35, November 2001), 4–5, no. 3.

sin, these deeds become legally relevant only when they are communicated to others.

Language in Penal Law

Studying speech as incriminated in the church allows outside observers to understand a lot about the church and its law. Many crimes revolve around clerics and their discipline. This points to the fact that canon law, as Klaus Mörsdorf saw it, is primarily a law of the "leading church,"[19] a church led by clerics. The law expresses this focus on clerics clearly in the way that canon 207 §1 CIC/1983 defines the church by alluding to its members, stating, "By divine institution, there are among the Christian faithful in the church sacred ministers who in law are also called clerics; the other members of the Christian faithful are called lay persons." The emphasis of the law is on clerics, while "the others," the vast majority of church members by number, are of lesser interest. Penal law considers them as potential offenders, for instance, by committing perjury before an ecclesiastical authority, but pays them less attention in comparison to clerics. The law of the church promotes a top-down view of ecclesiastical society. It starts at its clerical top and then works its way down to the laypeople at the bottom of the hierarchical pyramid. While the 1983 reform of the Code devoted some thought to making the law more a law of the whole church and one less in line with Mörsdorf's "leading church," the spotlight on clerics is still manifest. It is also striking to see how much attention is paid to sexual issues with regard to clerical discipline and celibacy. In this light one may find the sex abuse scandal that has been rocking the church for years now to be no lamentable coincidence but the systemic result of an institution criminalizing autonomous adult sex and turning a blind eye to other forms of violent sex. With its long tradition of protecting the church and its mission—its preaching and teaching, and its liturgies and sacraments—from human wrongdoing, the law of the church still tends to revolve around the protection of the institution and less around the well-being of its members. The crime of solicitation, with its focus on the protection of the sacrament of penance and less on protecting individuals harassed by priests, may serve as an example. The absolute protection of the sacramental seal where confidentiality knows of no exception is another example. As core elements of the church's mission, word and sacrament are of particular legal concern, which is also evident in canonical penal law. Language crimes such as heresy and apostasy expose that concentration. In this context, language appears to be so threatening

[19] Original quote, "leitende Kirche," Mörsdorf, *Die Rechtssprache des Codex Juris Canonici*, 2nd edn, Paderborn, Ferdinand Schöningh, 1967, 18.

to the faith that speaking heretically or apostatically deserves the utmost ecclesiastical punishment, *latae sententiae* excommunication, which befalls the speaker ipso facto upon uttering the heresy or apostasy publicly. When uttering speech that threatens the faith of the church, the law strives to silence the speakers by condemning them to the gravest stigma that the community has to offer.

My observations on language crimes in canonical penal law most certainly fail to deliver a full picture of the law of the church. However, as I want to suggest, they are in fact rather well suited for giving a first impression of how canon law perceives the world. Compared to state law, it is a narrow lens through which to view reality. Yet it is helpful to take note of this lens to understand the frame of my study. Studying the law on language as a glimpse into this religious legal universe prepares the scene for my study to examine the language of the law.

1.3 Part of the Law and Language Debate

Having mentioned how the law deals with language issues, my study will not penetrate any more deeply into the canonical regulations on language matters. This is because I am absorbed less with the issue of how the law regulates language matters and more with the language of canon law itself—with the way language *matters* for the law. Studying the language of canon law is an endeavor that merits scholarly attention in its own right. Yet, fortunately, studies in this field are not an isolated endeavor. They strongly relate to the *law and language* debate examining the various aspects and implications of the law's dependence on language. This debate is particularly vibrant in the United States and in the Anglo-American legal cultures and has grown in importance for legal and linguistic scholarship over the past twenty years.[20] Lawrence Solan and Peter Tiersma have identified reasons why law and language became an influential topic during that time. They inter alia identified an increasing interest in the law among nonlegal disciplines as one reason underlying the rise of law and language as an interdisciplinary endeavor.[21] So scholarship on law and language is not the exclusive domain of legal studies and linguistics but involves literature studies, communication studies, translation studies, sociology, ethnology, and anthropology. I want to add that theology, religious studies, and religious legal studies should also have their share in this debate. This multidisciplinary setting renders the subject of law and language a most interesting but also highly complex field.

[20] On the history of law and language scholarship and its aims and topics, see Vogel, "Rechtslinguistik," in Felder/Vogel, eds, *Handbuch Sprache im Recht*, Berlin, Walter de Gruyter, 2017, 209–232; Mattila, *Comparative Legal Linguistics*, 2nd edn, London, Routledge, 2016, 5–21.

[21] See Solan/Tiersma, "Introduction," in idem, eds, *The Oxford Handbook of Language and Law*, Oxford, Oxford University Press, 2012, 1.

Linguistics and Legal Studies

From a linguistic point of view, Dietrich Busse names two main areas of law and language research.[22] One area is linguistic studies, which analyses the style of legal language either with a focus on the comprehensibility of the law or with a focus on translation and interlanguage legal communication. Another area focuses more on legal communication itself, such as studies on the communication between courts and other legal institutions with legal subjects. Their focus is on oral communication more than on legal texts, and more on the institutional aspects of legal language than on individual communication. Yet, as I said, law and language is not an exclusively linguistic domain. While it needed the law and language movement to motivate legal scholars to subject the linguistic characteristics of the law to closer scrutiny, legal scholarship has always concerned itself with language issues, as legal *interpretation* is inextricably entwined with language issues. Interestingly, for a long time, this was not really seen as a linguistic issue but as a standard problem of the law to be solved by legal methodology and application theory. Legal hermeneutics is therefore a field in which linguistic issues played a role even before other disciplines started thinking about them. Yet it is a field so intrinsic to the law that it was taken as self-referential and legal scholars seldom related it to the broader twentieth-century debate on linguistics.[23] This has changed slowly but steadily over the past couple of years, not least due to the interpretation problems arising from the challenges to the law as a result of globalization and its effects on both culture and language. One recently discussed example is the spread of Anglo-American-style contract law across the globe. Contracts between multilanguage partners today are not only often composed in English but also tend to take on the specific style of Anglo-American Legalese, including its tendency to draft long and wordy contracts compared to the usually more concise versions used in civil law traditions, as legal scholar Claire Hill has observed, thereby adopting "the style's pathologies and excesses."[24] I can relate very well to her observation from my experience signing the contract which enabled me to publish this very book. This effect of "Americanizing" global law has many cultural implications, including challenges related to language.

It was not least as a result of the *law and economics* debate that legal scholarship acknowledged that language issues were presenting the law with questions

[22] See Busse, "Rechtssprache als Problem der Bedeutungsbeschreibung," *Sprache und Literatur* 29 (1998), 25.
[23] See Goodrich, "Legal Hermeneutics," in Craig, ed, *Routledge Encyclopedia of Philosophy*, vol. 5, London, Routledge, 1998, 506–510.
[24] Hill, "Why Are Non-US Contracts Written in US Legalese?," in Freeman/Smith, eds, *Law and Language*, Oxford, Oxford University Press, 2013, 461.

that went beyond the problem of mere interpretation. As with other successful "and" research areas that started in the United States, like *law and society* and *law and literature*, law and economics has proven to be sensitive to linguistic matters and has contributed largely to the law and language debate, as Solan and Tiersma have stressed.[25] The same can be said about law and society and law and literature, fields where legal scholarship meets sociology, anthropology, communication, cultural, and literature studies. Books like legal scholar Richard Posner's *Law and Literature*,[26] now available in a third edition, have contributed greatly to emphasizing the importance of language for the law. Over recent years *law and the media* has become an issue as well.[27] Law and legal topics are covered by the news, and they are also popular subjects for TV shows, as proven by highly successful current shows like "Better Call Saul." Now, forensic scholars are even discussing the existence or nonexistence of the "CSI effect," a phenomenon which is allegedly inducing jurors to develop exaggerated expectations about forensic evidence and to demand watertight proof for a conviction.[28]

Learning from Legal Practice

The law and language debate has also profited from the practical discourses on the application of the law, involving judges, juries, and lawyers who work at the intersection of common language and the specialized language of the law. Forensic linguists such as Roger Shuy and Malcolm Coulthard have shared their experience of serving as linguistic expert witnesses in trials[29] or have discussed the intricacies of dealing with recorded evidence in court.[30] In recent years, forensic linguists have contributed greatly to better understanding the effect of question techniques on the answers of witnesses in formal interviews.[31]

25 See Solan/Tiersma, "Introduction," in idem, eds, *The Oxford Handbook of Language and Law*, Oxford, Oxford University Press, 2012, 1–2.

26 Posner, *Law and Literature*, 3rd edn, Cambridge, MA, Harvard University Press, 2009.

27 E.g., Hans, "Law and the Media," *Law and Human Behavior* 14 (1990), 399–407; Amatrudo, "The Consumption of Legal Language," in Freeman/Smith, eds, *Law and Language*, Oxford, Oxford University Press, 2013, 386–399.

28 For an overview of empirical findings on the matter, see Podlas, "The 'CSI Effect,'" in *Oxford Research Encyclopedia of Criminology*, August 22, 2017, DOI: 10.1093/acrefore/9780190264079.013.40.

29 E.g., Shuy, "To Testify or Not to Testify?," in Cotterill, ed, *Language in the Legal Process*, Basingstoke, Palgrave Macmillan, 2002, 3–18.

For an excellent introduction into forensic linguistics, see Coulthard/Johnson, *An Introduction to Forensic Linguistics*, Abingdon, Routledge, 2007.

30 E.g., Coulthard, "Whose Voice Is It?," in Cotterill, ed, *Language in the Legal Process*, Basingstoke, Palgrave Macmillan, 2002, 19–34.

31 E.g., Johnson, "*So* . . . ?," in Cotterill, ed, *Language in the Legal Process*, Basingstoke, Palgrave Macmillan, 2002, 91–110.

The debate on how to communicate legal ideas to legal "lay" people who do not speak Legalese inspired lawyers to think about what would constitute a clear and intelligible legal language. Legal scholars like Bernhard Black have campaigned to make *plain language* obligatory for consumer contracts.[32] Forensic linguists like Gail Stygall have shown that one main obstacle when immigrating into the United States is the lack of transparency in application forms that individuals without a profound legal education, and particularly nonnative speakers of English, find very difficult to understand.[33] Solicitor Mark Adler became famous for his efforts to improve legal language. His book *Clarity for Lawyers* is now available in its third edition and provides advice and even drafting techniques for lawyers in an attempt to train them to use understandable—*plain*—language when writing legal texts.[34]

In Anglo-American legal literature, the problem of communicating the law to legal laypeople has also resulted in a broad range of contributions examining how best to go about jury instruction.[35] Following this, many US states have taken action to improve jury instructions by shifting to instructions in plain language. Instead of traditionally instructing a jury to convict a defendant only in the case of a proof "beyond a reasonable doubt," they now, for instance, refer to a proof "that leaves you with an abiding conviction that the charge is true." Instead of speaking of a civil judgment following the "preponderance of the evidence," many juries are now instructed to find a decision that is "more likely than not."[36]

Theology and Canon Law Studies

A second intellectual development that Solan and Tiersma identified as being responsible for the rise of law and language "is the tremendous foothold that linguistics has taken in the intellectual world."[37] For philosophy and the humanities, this foothold even coined a term, and we speak of it in terms of a paradigm shift, calling it the "linguistic turn." This paradigmatic turn has also left its mark on

[32] See Black, "A Model Plain Language Law," *Stanford Law Review* 33 (1981), 255–300.

[33] See Stygall, "Textual Barriers to United States Immigration," in Cotterill, ed, *Language in the Legal Process*, Basingstoke, Palgrave Macmillan, 2002, 35–53.

[34] See Adler/Perry, *Clarity for Lawyers*, 3rd edn, London, The Law Society, 2017.

[35] E.g., Charrow/Charrow, "Making Legal Language Understandable," *Columbia Law Review* 79 (1979), 1306–1374; Tiersma, "Reforming the Language of Jury Instructions," *Hofstra Law Review* 22 (1993), 37–78; Heffer, "'If You Were Standing in Marks and Spencers,'" in Cotterill, ed, *Language in the Legal Process*, Basingstoke, Palgrave Macmillan, 2002, 228–245; Dumas, "Reasonable Doubt about Reasonable Doubt," in Cotterill, ed, *Language in the Legal Process*, Basingstoke, Palgrave Macmillan, 2002, 246–259.

[36] See https://www.plainlanguage.gov/examples/brochures/jury-instructions (accessed November 15, 2018).

[37] Solan/Tiersma, "Introduction," in idem, eds, *The Oxford Handbook of Language and Law*, Oxford, Oxford University Press, 2012, 1.

theology, where it has contributed to a growing awareness of language as being key to theological thought.[38] Interestingly, this impact that linguistics has had on theology often goes uncommented. Many theologians have quite naturally taken up linguistic findings without giving this reception any explicit consideration. Today, for instance, we often speak quite naturally of sacramental theology in the terms of speech act theory without paying any tribute to the theory itself.[39] The same applies to my study. It often stands on linguistic grounds without giving any specific credit to linguistics. This is not meant as ignorance but is rather the result of the paradigmatic character of the linguistic turn. As it made us aware of the relevance of language for each and all human acts, we often forget to mention exactly that.

Shedding more light on the relation between canon law and language is an interdisciplinary enterprise located in the intersection of theology, canon law studies, legal studies, and linguistics. Fortunately, however, it can build upon some previous work done by scholars of canon law. Although canonical scholarship has not yet devoted much attention to the law and language debate and to linguistic scholarship in particular, this does not mean that language matters have played a minor role. The myriad dictionaries and glossaries on the language of canon law testify to this interest.[40] As the official language of canon law is still Latin, legal norms require skillful translation into the local vernaculars, supported by vocabularies and thesauri. There is also a good deal of literature on the interpretation of canonical norms,[41] and even some articles that touch upon

[38] E.g., Clark, *Language and Theology*, Phillipsburg, NJ, Presbyterian and Reformed Publishing, 1980; Lawrence, *Linguistics and Theology*, Metuchen, NJ, Scarecrow Press, 1980; Lindbeck, *The Nature of Doctrine*, Louisville, KY, Westminster John Knox Press, 1984; Vanhoozer, *The Drama of Doctrine*, Louisville, KY, Westminster John Knox Press, 2005.

For an example of a mid-twentieth century apologetic approach toward the language of theology, see Holmer, "Language and Theology," *The Harvard Theological Review* 58 (1965), 241–261; for an example of how to employ cognitive linguistics for ecumenism, see Rinderknecht, *Mapping the Differentiated Consensus of the Joint Declaration*, New York, Palgrave Macmillan, 2016; for developing an approach to a "linguistic theology" in the light of twentieth-century linguistic philosophy, see Tran, "Linguistic Theology," *Modern Theology* 33 (2017), 47–68.

[39] Exceptions include Appleyard, "How Does a Sacrament 'Cause by Signifying'?," *Science et Esprit* 23 (1971), 167–200; Martinich, "Sacraments and Speech Acts," part 1 and part 2, *The Heythrop Journal* 16 (1975), 289–303 and 405–417; Searle, "The Uses of Liturgical Language," *Liturgy* 4 (1985), 15–19; Chauvet, *Symbol and Sacrament*, Collegeville, MN, The Liturgical Press, 1995; Duffy, *How Language, Ritual and Sacraments Work*, Rome, Editrice Pontificia Università Gregoriana, 2005.

[40] E.g., on the old Code: Köstler, *Wörterbuch zum Codex Iuris Canonici*, Munich, Josef Kösel, 1927; on the current Code: Ochoa, ed, *Index Verborum ac Locutionum Codicis Iuris Canonici*, Rome, Libreria Editrice Vaticana, 1983; Chiappetta, *Dizionario del Nuovo Codice di Diritto Canonico*, Naples, Dehoniane, 1986; Zapp, *Codex Iuris Canonici*, Freiburg im Breisgau, Rombach, 1986; Corral Salvador et al., *Nuovo Dizionario di Diritto Canonico*, Milan, San Paolo, 1993; Werckmeister, *Petit Dictionnaire de Droit Canonique*, Paris, Cerf, 1993; Corral Salvador/Urteaga Embil, *Diccionario de Derecho Cánonico*, 2nd edn, Madrid, Tecnos Universidad Pontificia Comillas, 2000; Pulickal, *A Dictionary of Canon Law*, Manila, Logos, 2005.

[41] E.g., Pree, *Die evolutive Interpretation der Rechtsnorm im Kanonischen Recht*, Vienna, Springer, 1980; Orsy, "The Interpreter and His Art," *The Jurist* 40 (1980), 27–56; idem, "Models of Approaches to Canon Law and Their Impact on Interpretation," *The Jurist* 50 (1990), 83–101; Potz, "Ökumenische

aspects of canon law terminology, particularly by reflecting on the use of specific legal terms in the Code of Canon Law.[42] Klaus Mörsdorf, already mentioned for his work on the relevance of "word" and "sacrament" for the foundation of canon law, even published a book entitled *Die Rechtssprache des Codex Iuris Canonici* [*The Legal Language of the Code of Canon Law*][43] in 1937 in which he analyzed the legal terminology of the old law, the Code of Canon Law of 1917 (hereinafter abbreviated as CIC/1917). Canonists sometimes even lament the lack of a comparable study dealing with the terminology of the present Code of 1983.[44]

Interpretation," *Österreichisches Archiv für Kirchenrecht* 35 (1985), 62–82; Huels, "Interpreting Canon Law in Diverse Cultures," *The Jurist* 47 (1987), 249–293; idem, "Classifying Authentic Interpretations of Canon Law," *The Jurist* 72 (2012), 605–640; Castillo Lara, "Die authentische Auslegung des Kanonischen Rechtes im Rahmen der Tätigkeit der Päpstlichen Kommission für die authentische Interpretation des Ius Canonicum," *Österreichisches Archiv für Kirchenrecht* 37 (1987/88), 209–228; Sobánski, "Zu den Interpretationsregeln des kirchlichen Gesetzbuches," in Lüdicke et al., eds, *Iustus Iudex*, Essen, Wingen, 1990, 693–707; Brown, *Canon 17 CIC 1983 and the Hermeneutical Principles of Bernard Lonergan*, Rome, Editrice Pontifica Università Gregoriana, 1999; Gerosa, *Grundlagen und Paradigmen der Gesetzesauslegung in der Kirche*, Münster, LIT, 1999; Polvani, *Authentic Interpretation in Canon Law*, Rome, Editrice Pontifica Università Gregoriana, 1999; Kowal, *Understanding Canon 17 of the 1983 Code of Canon Law in Light of Contemporary Hermeneutics*, New York, Edwin Mellen Press, 2000; idem, "Some Remarks on Understanding the Concept of *Propria Verborum Significatio*," *Studia Canonica* 34 (2000), 489–504; Lederhilger, "Repetition oder Innovation?," *Archiv für katholisches Kirchenrecht* 172 (2003), 58–83; Schüller, "Auslegung von Gesetzen im Kirchenrecht," in Ohly et al., eds, *Theologia Iuris Canonici*, Berlin, Duncker & Humblot, 2017, 127–138.

42 E.g., Barion, "Über doppelsprachige Konkordate," *Deutsche Rechtswissenschaft* 5 (1940), 226–249; Griffin, "Introduction to the Jargon of Canon Law," *The Jurist* 44 (1984), 19–27; Erdő, "Expressiones obligationis et exhortationis in Codice Iuris Canonici," *Periodica de Re Morali Canonica Liturgica* 76 (1987), 3–27; Koury, "Necessity, Utility, Scarcity," *The Jurist* 49 (1989), 95–111; idem, "From Prohibited to Permitted," *Studia Canonica* 24 (1990), 147–183; idem, "The Limits of Collaboration," *Studia Canonica* 26 (1992), 415–436; Frank, "Die Sprache kirchlicher Ehegerichte und ihre Wahrnehmung durch Betroffene," in Puza/Weiß, eds, *Iustitia in caritate*, Frankfurt am Main, Peter Lang, 1997, 463–473; idem, "Ehenichtigkeitserklärung," in Weiß/Ihli, eds, *Flexibilitas Iuris Canonici*, Frankfurt am Main, Peter Lang, 2003, 501–514; Olschewski, "Der Begriff 'iusta causa' in der kirchlichen Rechtssprache," in Reinhardt, ed, *Theologia et Ius Canonicum*, Essen, Wingen, 1995, 235–257; Amann, "Gebot und Verbot in der Rechtssprache des CIC," in Geringer/Schmitz, eds, *Communio in Ecclesiae Mysterio*, St. Ottilien, EOS, 2001, 3–28; Weber, "Rechtssprachliche Anmerkungen zur Verwendung von christifidelis, fidelis, baptizatus und christianus im CIC/1917 und im CIC/1983," in Geringer/Schmitz, eds, *Communio in Ecclesiae Mysterio*, St. Ottilien, EOS, 2001, 653–667; Haering, "Lateinische Sprache und Kanonisches Recht," *Seminarium* 43 (2003), 237–256; Ohly, "Gravis necessitas," *Archiv für katholisches Kirchenrecht* 175 (2006), 473–485; idem, "Officium ecclesiasticum," *Archiv für katholisches Kirchenrecht* 177 (2008), 56–72; Peters, "The Ordination of Men Bereft of Speech and the Celebration of Sacraments in Sign Language," *Studia Canonica* 42 (2008), 331–345; Hahn, "Recht verstehen," in Schüller/Zumbült, eds, *Iustitia est constans et perpetua voluntas ius suum cuique tribuendi*, Essen, Wingen, 2014, 163–198; Zeller, "Die Terminologie der kirchlichen Gesetzbücher," in Ohly et al., eds, *Theologia Iuris Canonici*, Berlin, Duncker & Humblot, 2017, 139–166, with further references in fn. 133.

43 Mörsdorf, *Die Rechtssprache des Codex Iuris Canonici*, Paderborn, Ferdinand Schöningh, 1937; 2nd edn, Paderborn, Ferdinand Schöningh, 1967.

44 E.g., Wächter, "Die Rechtssprache," in Campenhausen et al., eds, *Lexikon für Kirchen- und Staatskirchenrecht*, vol. 3, Paderborn, Ferdinand Schöningh, 2004, 379; Zeller, "Die Terminologie der kirchlichen Gesetzbücher," in Ohly et al., eds, *Theologia Iuris Canonici*, Berlin, Duncker & Humblot, 2017, 139.

Besides these contributions helping readers to decipher the words used in canonical norms and to extract their meaning mostly for application purposes, linguistic issues have scarcely attracted canonists' attention. The *Handbuch des katholischen Kirchenrechts* [*Handbook of Catholic Canon Law*] in its recently published third edition[45] contains no general article on the language of canon law. However, the *Lexikon für Kirchen- und Staatskirchenrecht* [*Lexicon of Ecclesiastical Law and Church and State Relations*] devoted a short article to the matter.[46] The subject is therefore at hand, but it clearly needs some further effort to elaborate the field of canon law and language, as canon law scholarship has yet to profit from the findings of the law and language debate. I cannot think of a canonist who addresses canon law's urgent need to become the subject of more rigorous interdisciplinary scrutiny in a more amicable way than the great American canonist Ladislas Orsy, who already stated in 1980, "Canon law has been a sheltered science. The great intellectual movements of our times have hardly touched it; at times this has been for the better, at times for the worse. But such a state of things cannot last for long, nor should it."[47] So Orsy encourages his colleagues to learn from other disciplines and to engage in interdisciplinary endeavors. I am happy to accept his words as an invitation and encouragement to forge ahead in linguistic matters.

Scope of My Study

In composing my study, I have focused on the language of canon law as used in the western churches of the Roman Catholic Rite, thereby largely sidestepping the specific language of the eastern Catholic Churches. As I am more concerned with the language of the Code of Canon Law, I leave the Code of Canons of the Eastern Churches (hereinafter abbreviated as CCEO) aside. Both Codes are composed in Latin, so there are significant parallels in terminology. However, legal scholar Hubert Kaufhold showed that it might be worth taking a closer look at the eastern legal terminology in its own right.[48] There are terms, mostly of Greek origin, that only appear in the East, like *myron* (canon 692 CCEO), or terms like those used for clerical offices and the members of the hierarchy ("patriarch," "eparchial bishop"), which are common only in the East. It would be

[45] See Haering et al., eds, *Handbuch des katholischen Kirchenrechts*, 3rd edn, Regensburg, Friedrich Pustet, 2015.

[46] See Wächter, "Die Rechtssprache," in Campenhausen et al., eds, *Lexikon für Kirchen- und Staatskirchenrecht*, vol. 3, Paderborn, Ferdinand Schöningh, 2004, 379–381.

[47] Orsy, "The Interpreter and His Art," *The Jurist* 40 (1980), 52.

[48] See Kaufhold, "Zum ostkirchlichen Charakter der Rechtssprache des Codex Canonum Ecclesiarum Orientalium," in Güthoff/Haering, eds, *Ius quia iustum*, Berlin, Duncker & Humblot, 2015, 221–245.

worth considering a comparison. But as I mentioned earlier, my study is concerned not so much with terminology but with identifying the place which canon law in general should occupy in the law and language debate. As a canon law scholar from the West, the examples I draw from legal texts are frequently taken from the Latin law. However, they are usually also applicable to eastern canon law and language.

Receiving the findings of law and language scholarship for canon law first of all requires a perusal of key studies in this field. My method therefore consists mainly in "hunting and gathering" what other researchers have already discovered. This raises the perennial challenge for every scholar in the field of law and language, namely, to consider the multidisciplinary layers of the debate. But although I derived tremendous enjoyment from reading through the multifaceted contributions, this does not make me an expert in the diverse disciplines with which I found myself confronted. This dilemma is, I believe, probably unavoidable when dealing with matters of a multidisciplinary nature. So whenever I speak about insights into other disciplines in my study, there is always a good chance that my observations contain slight inaccuracies. Curiosity is simply not a reliable substitute for expertise. I am personally particularly fascinated by scholarship with a translation studies background which has dealt with law and language intensively, primarily as transnational entities such as the European Union confront translation studies with urgent questions. Still, my fascination is not an adequate surrogate for my lack of knowledge. As a theologian, I can see that the debates in translation studies are closely linked with debates in biblical exegesis. So translation and exegetical scholars could probably engage in a truly in-depth debate about some of the topics that I have touched upon rather lightheartedly. I am aware of this, but can do little to change the fact that I am a canonist and not a biblical scholar. The same applies to obvious parallels between translation issues and liturgical topics. Scholars of liturgy have engaged in a parallel debate to the one that is now being conducted about canon law, namely, the question of how to deal with Latin as the language of liturgy—and of canon law respectively. Strangely enough, there is hardly any scholarship that has dealt with the parallels between both theological disciplines; neither are there any studies that confront these two disciplines with the findings of translation studies. For my part, I would like to see a triangular debate between translation studies, liturgical studies, and canon law studies on this issue; alas, it does not yet exist, and I cannot compensate for it adequately in my study. My alluding to this deficiency is intended neither as a lament nor a critique. I prefer to understand it as charting the research landscape to discover where further study would be helpful. The task of identifying those missing pieces that help us to grasp the language of canon law somewhat better—also as a prerequisite for these further studies—requires a comparatist's eye. As I am not a linguist but a canonist, and am therefore always looking back and forth between the law of the church and the secular law which surrounds the church in modern societies, my view on the matter and my method of approaching it resemble the approaches of comparative legal scholars more than the approaches taken by linguists to law and language. While this might be less creative than engaging in linguistic studies themselves, it should nevertheless prove helpful in the quest to learn more about the language of the law and the language of canon law in particular.

2
The Function of Language in Law

Language is constitutive for the law. The law needs language to become real and take shape. With the help of language, the law usually takes on the form of a text that coherently groups signs—words mostly—that convey meaning. This meaning is a legal message, a means of communication which, following the thinking of the famous sociologist Niklas Luhmann, operates using the codification "legal"/"illegal." This binary code identifies communications as legal speech. They constitute a social system as a structure of "congruently generalised normative behavioural expectations."[1] Law thus derives from the generalization of behavioral expectations which can be identified by looking out for codes such as "legal"/"illegal" or "lawful"/"unlawful."

2.1 Purposes of the Law

As texts which identify a particular behavior as legal or illegal and formulate specific expectations with regard to legal behavior, legal texts fulfill specific purposes. They do not primarily follow an aesthetic ratio but have a specific aim that lies within the legal system. Legal scholar Karl Olivecrona noted, "The primary purpose of legal language is not to reflect reality but to shape reality."[2] Its aim is to shape reality according to the expectations of a social group regarding what constitutes legal and illegal behavior.

Creating Social Cohesion

It is the language of the law that makes a social reality first of all by turning that group into a legal community. In this vein, legal scholar Harold Berman regarded legal communication as a "process of making community" or of "communification."[3] Berman developed the idea of using the law and its

[1] Luhmann, *A Sociological Theory of Law*, London, Routledge, 2014, 77.
[2] Olivecrona, "Legal Language and Reality," in Newman, ed, *Essays in Jurisprudence in Honor of Roscoe Pound*, Indianapolis, IN, Bobbs-Merrill, 1962, 190.
[3] Berman, *Law and Language*, Cambridge, Cambridge University Press, 2013, 150.

The Language of Canon Law. Judith Hahn, Oxford University Press. © Oxford University Press 2023.
DOI: 10.1093/oso/9780197674246.003.0002

language as a tool to integrate communities during the Cold War when, as a legal scholar, he traveled between the United States and Russia to build academic bridges between scholars of both nations. He was motivated by the hope of establishing academic bonds which would serve as bridgeheads for the broader communification of both estranged nations. Words, Berman was convinced, could create cohesion. He stated,

> Among the words that create social cohesion are the ceremonial ones, such as the language used at inaugurations, weddings, anniversaries, and funerals. Equally important is the language of scholarship, economic cooperation, and political authority. But still another language can do this, the language of law, which has been strangely neglected by both writers on language and writers on law.[4]

Law, as Berman found, has always been regarded as an instrument of social cohesion due to the social functions that it fulfills. As such, it has always brought together foreign groups. However, it has rarely achieved this because it uses a similar language, strikes a similar tune, or represents similar linguistic patterns, as Berman observed when he wrote, "The social functions of law have in general been found in the authority of legal rules, the morality which law reflects, and the nature of legal institutions, but rarely in its linguistic form, that is, in its vocabulary, structure, and style."[5] Yet, as he noted, "It is the linguistic aspect that is common to all legal systems."[6] In his view, it is the fact that law is language which is primarily responsible for creating the social entities which we call legal communities, and likewise for building bridges between them.

Influencing Behavior

That law is communification via its directive function, directing the members of legal communities to fulfill legal expectations, has direct consequences for legal language. The main purpose of legal language, as Olivecrona observed, is to express a directive meaning. He wrote,

> The purpose of all legal enactments, judicial pronouncements, contracts, and other legal acts is to influence men's behavior and direct them in certain ways. The legal language must be viewed primarily as a means to this end. It is an

[4] Ibid., 151.
[5] Ibid., 151–152.
[6] Ibid., 152.

> instrument of social control and social intercourse. We may call it a *directive* language in contrast to a *reporting* language. It is advisable to lay stress on this distinction; for our inveterate habit of regarding language as primarily a means of describing facts easily leads to misinterpretations.[7]

The law therefore mostly employs a directive style of language, which, in any case, differs to a significant degree depending on the genre of legal texts. Legal philosopher H.L.A. Hart explained the extent to which directive language varies by differentiating between the way statutes and the way precedents communicate, noting, "One of them makes a maximal and the other a minimal use of general classifying words."[8] Hart clarified the difference by using the example of a father on his way to church, who tells his son in a general manner, "Every man and boy must take off his hat on entering a church."[9] Alternatively, the father could also make use of precedent logic by taking of his hat and telling his son, "Look: this is the right way to behave on such occasions."[10] However, Hart noted that communicating via example often leaves open more questions than remain after establishing a general rule. While examples are always indeterminate, general rules are more easily applicable to future situations of the same kind. General rules provide the addressee with "a verbal description which he can use to pick out what he must do in future and when he must do it. He has only to recognize instances of clear verbal terms, to 'subsume' particular facts under general classificatory heads and draw a simple syllogistic conclusion."[11] Having said this, it would be to miss Hart's point to assume in consequence that statute law is always well defined and precedents more difficult to grasp, as he himself made clear. He called this a "naïve contrast."[12] As it is always language that constitutes a legal text, be it a statute or a precedent, there is always uncertainty and the need for interpretation. I will not pursue this topic of language as an indeterminate and ambiguous medium any further here, but will return to it in chapter 4. At this point in my study, it is of importance merely to take note of the different ways legal texts convey their directive messages.

The directive language of the law is functional and designed to fulfill the purpose of influencing social reality. When it comes to norms, this is usually achieved by using language that commands, permits, prohibits, or entitles. Yet norms which fulfill these functions are not necessarily legal texts, as social or moral norms frequently also have a directive purpose. Again, it is only through

[7] Olivecrona, "Legal Language and Reality," in Newman, ed, *Essays in Jurisprudence in Honor of Roscoe Pound*, Indianapolis, IN, Bobbs-Merrill, 1962, 177.
[8] Hart, *The Concept of Law*, 3rd edn, Oxford, Oxford University Press, 2012, 124.
[9] Ibid.
[10] Ibid.
[11] Ibid., 125.
[12] Ibid., 126.

language that law may be identified *as law*. This, at least, is an idea shared by those legal theorists and sociologists of the law who follow Niklas Luhmann's previously mentioned approach of identifying law by recognizing codifications which work with the binary code "legal"/"illegal."[13] This legal code, expressed by the language of the law—be it explicitly or implicitly—is what differentiates between legal communications and directive speech as used by other subsystems in society. So it is language and language codes that make the law visible as law and enable us to understand communications as legally directive.

Exchanging Information

Nevertheless, the language of the law is not only a language that legally commands, permits, prohibits, and entitles. Besides texts which have a directive quality—Peter Tiersma called them "operative legal documents"[14]—as they serve as rules, such as laws and statutes, or apply these rules, as do court or administrative decisions, other legal texts have more of a descriptive quality, as they describe or discuss rules or decisions.[15] Legal language has a descriptive function when it comes to expert opinions, legal commentaries, or scholarly texts. And it has an informative purpose, which legal linguist Ingrid Simonnæs identified with regard to opinions of the court.[16] The dissenting opinion of a collegiate judge parting from the majority of the judges has no directive quality as does the decision of the majority, but serves an informative purpose, encouraging further debate on the matter and maybe even encouraging differing decisions in the future. Tiersma called these legal texts "expository documents."[17]

Concealed Purposes

Because legal language serves these different functions, it has to be formed according to the purpose of the legal communications in which it is used. Yet legal language may be confusing in this respect. Legal norms, for instance, are often phrased in a descriptive fashion even though they have a directive meaning, as legal scholar Ralf Poscher shows with regard to article 5, paragraph 3 of the

[13] E.g., Nobles/Schiff, "Legal Pluralism," in Freeman/Smith, eds, *Law and Language*, Oxford, Oxford University Press, 2013, 100–114.
[14] Tiersma, *Legal Language*, Chicago, IL, The University of Chicago Press, 1999, 139.
[15] See Sandrini, "Translation zwischen Kultur und Kommunikation," in idem, ed, *Übersetzen von Rechtstexten*, Tübingen, Narr, 1999, 20–21.
[16] See Simonnæs, "Fachkommunikation im Recht unter Berücksichtigung der Mehrfachadressierung," in Lerch, ed, *Recht vermitteln*, Berlin, Walter de Gruyter, 2005, 380–381.
[17] Tiersma, *Legal Language*, Chicago, IL, The University of Chicago Press, 1999, 139.

German Basic Law.[18] The text states, "Art and science, research and teaching are free" ("*Kunst und Wissenschaft, Forschung und Lehre sind frei*"). However, this sentence is not a descriptive statement indicating that art and scholarship are fortunate enough to enjoy freedom in Germany, but a norm, ordering that freedom *shall* rule where art and science are concerned. Interestingly, in the English translation of the German constitution published by the *Bundestag*, the German Federal Parliament, the same text reads, "Arts and sciences, research and teaching shall be free."[19] So the translator in the unofficial translation decided to express the directive meaning of the rule by inserting "shall," even though this auxiliary verb does not appear in the original German wording. Legal language can therefore be misleading. A descriptive text might actually have a directive meaning, particularly where statute law is concerned. This is in fact often the case in canon law, where many norms of the Code of Canon Law do not explicitly express their directive meaning. Canon 7 CIC/1983, for instance, states, "A law is established when it is promulgated." And canon 1056 CIC/1983 defines the indispensable properties of marriage in a purely descriptive fashion, outlining, "The essential properties of marriage are unity and indissolubility, which in Christian marriage obtain a special firmness by reason of the sacrament." These canons nevertheless carry a directive meaning. Canon 7 CIC/1983, for instance, expresses the ecclesiastical legislators' obligation to promulgate a law to bring it into being. And canon 1056 CIC/1983 serves as a basic norm for the following canons on grounds of nullity which render a marriage null and void in cases in which the spouses excluded their marriage from being an exclusive or an indissoluble union (see, for instance, canon 1099 CIC/1983). Appliers of the law who are charged with analyzing the possible invalidity of a marriage are thus directed to examine whether a contested marriage lacks essential properties which render it void. While it is evident for canonists that these canons intend to convey a directive message, this meaning is fairly well concealed behind a descriptive surface.

2.2 Law as Communication

If we conceive of the law as communication, as I have done in the previous section, it is nevertheless clear that we are in fact dealing with a specific form of conversing with others.[20] However, like all communication, the law is about

[18] See Poscher, "The Hermeneutics of Law," in Forster/Gjesdal, eds, *The Cambridge Companion to Hermeneutics*, Cambridge, Cambridge University Press, 2019, 327.

[19] Deutscher Bundestag, *Basic Law for the Federal Republic of Germany*, May 23, 1949, Berlin, Deutscher Bundestag, 2018, 16.

[20] E.g., Sandrini, "Translation zwischen Kultur und Kommunikation," in idem, ed, *Übersetzen von Rechtstexten*, Tübingen, Narr, 1999, 11–14; Simonnæs, "Fachkommunikation im Recht unter

conveying meaning from a sender to a receiver by using signs. These signs are manifold when it comes to the law: they range from Lady Justice's scales, through the robe of the judges and the ritual of arraignment, to all words spoken or texts written in legal contexts and for legal purposes.[21] These latter signs, linguistic signs, are of particular interest for my study.

Defined as an act of exchanging signs, communication—both written and oral—might be easily misunderstood. Many scholars, including those engaged in the law and language debate, are critical of the way that communication is often perceived merely as an act of signal transmission, in the sense used by information technology.[22] Conceiving of communication in this vein results in a mechanical understanding of the way meaning is transported between a sender and a receiver. Ladislas Orsy identified the same problem for canon law when stating that legal "communication is not mechanical. It is not like transmitting electronic signals from one station to another."[23] Dietrich Busse mocks this static understanding of communication with a different image, comparing it with a farmer who carries potatoes to a market.[24] He stresses that communication is not simply a matter of transferring a piece of information from a sender to a receiver. Unlike the potato example, the sender remains part of the message. And unlike potatoes, the sender can never be fully sure if the message remains the same when it is received by the receiver. Unlike potatoes, it is not irrelevant how a message is carried to the "market." The medium in which the message is conveyed is important for the message itself, whereas a sack, bag, or a basket might all do just as well when it comes to transporting potatoes. Addressing the question of how law might be properly understood as communication, Busse's image points at the three major aspects of communication: it alludes to the sender who issues a legal statement; to the receiver who takes on the message and tries to decode its meaning; and to the medium, the language or silence of the law, with which legal meaning is conveyed.

Berücksichtigung der Mehrfachadressierung," in Lerch, ed, *Recht vermitteln*, Berlin, Walter de Gruyter, 2005, 377–397; Shaer, "Toward a Cognitive Science of Legal Interpretation," in Freeman/Smith, eds, *Law and Language*, Oxford, Oxford University Press, 2013, 259–291.

[21] See Seibert, "Semiotik im Recht," in Felder/Vogel, eds, *Handbuch Sprache im Recht*, Berlin, Walter de Gruyter, 2017, 3–21.

[22] See Lerch, "Recht vermitteln," in idem, ed, *Recht vermitteln*, Berlin, Walter de Gruyter, 2005, XV–XVII; Busse, "Ist die Anwendung von Rechtstexten ein Fall von Kommunikation?," in Lerch, ed, *Recht vermitteln*, Berlin, Walter de Gruyter, 2005, 24–25.

[23] Orsy, "The Interpreter and His Art," *The Jurist* 40 (1980), 48.

[24] See Busse, "Ist die Anwendung von Rechtstexten ein Fall von Kommunikation?," in Lerch, ed, *Recht vermitteln*, Berlin, Walter de Gruyter, 2005, 24–25.

Sending Legal Messages

In defining law as communication, Ladislas Orsy found, "Law is communication. . . . Every law is an act of communication between the legislator and those who are subject to his power."[25] However, Orsy's definition, which perceives the law mainly as an act of communication between the legislators and the receivers of their commands, is a very narrow approach to legal communication as it fails to acknowledge that legal messages consist of more than just the legislators' ordinances to their legal subjects. It fails to see that communication has a mutual quality. And it also misses the fact already mentioned that informative speech such as speaking about the law might also be part of legal communication. This strict focus on the legislators, who are taken as the sole senders in legal communications, is quite typical for canon law—and also one of the difficulties it faces when it comes to interpreting the law. I will return to this issue of interpretation later in chapter 7. Nevertheless, at this point in my study it is necessary to identify the role the legislators play as senders when it comes to understanding law as communication. Undoubtedly, the legislators are key senders of legal messages. It is therefore a matter of heated debate in US legal theory between intentionalists and textualists whether communication between the legislator and the legal subjects is *the* most relevant communication of the law. This alludes to the question of whether law is mainly about the legislator and his intent, as intentionalism suggests, or rather about the legal text itself and the message that it conveys, as textualists claim. Textualists find it unhelpful to present the legislator as the main agent in legal communication. The message of the law is conveyed by the legal text itself, not by the legislator behind it. Indeed, as we may find, a primary focus on the legislator is in fact unrealistically narrow, as the message of the law is spread by many different senders: by judges, administrative officers, lawyers, and legal scholars.

This question of whom we perceive to be the main sender of legal messages also has to be discussed in the context of canon law. In canon law, there is a manifest tendency to rely on ecclesiastical legislators, primarily the pope and the bishops, as Orsy shows in his definition of legal communication. But it is debatable whether this focus is helpful and whether legal communication always involves the legislator, as Orsy suggests. While I am in no doubt that legislators are indeed agents of legal communication whenever acts of legislation are concerned, I wish to raise some doubts at this early point in my study about whether the legislators really do have the enduring relevance within legal communications which Orsy's approach suggests. I personally consider it to be one of the core problems of canon law theory that we often fail to see the independent

[25] Orsy, "The Interpreter and His Art," *The Jurist* 40 (1980), 48.

existence of the law apart from the legislator, and that as a consequence our focus is always on the legislator whenever legal issues are concerned. Some strands of secular legal theory might help us to overcome this problematic tendency, particularly those which help canonists to understand that legal communication is really about the law itself. The message of the law is passed on by many senders, namely, by all who attempt to convey a legal meaning to receivers.

Receiving Legal Meaning

As communication is a mutual exchange of signs, it depends on sender and receiver alike. And it only works when the receiver comprehends the signs used by the sender. So communication, and likewise legal communication, is dependent on some mutual understanding between the sender and receiver of a legal message. Lawrence Solan maintains,

> When I say something to you, I expect that you will understand it more or less as I would if you said it to me. Similarly, when you say something to me, I expect that you intended to express more or less what I understood you to have said. . . . When we communicate, all we have are intentions and some confidence that our language faculties are more or less the same.[26]

That communication thus depends on shared knowledge poses a major challenge for the law, as it is not certain that a legal message will indeed be received by somebody who interprets it in the way it was originally conceived. Just how necessary comprehension is for the law to be regarded as a form of communication is a topic that I will discuss in greater depth over the course of this book. At this point in my study it is worth noting that this challenge, namely, keeping messages comprehensible, is particularly connected with legal communications, insofar as they frequently addresses multiple receivers.[27] This problem does not apply to all legal texts and not to all of them in the same way, but it is a key issue for the law as it affects legal communications at their most fundamental level. Law, as law and literature scholar Peter Goodrich recognizes, usually speaks to three audiences: legal professionals, litigants, and the general public.[28] The decisions taken by courts, for instance, address the litigants, who are usually legal laypeople, and they likewise address the judges of the higher instance.[29] Composing

[26] Solan, *The Language of Statutes*, Chicago, IL, The University of Chicago Press, 2010, 111.

[27] See Simonnæs, "Fachkommunikation im Recht unter Berücksichtigung der Mehrfachadressierung," in Lerch, ed, *Recht vermitteln*, Berlin, Walter de Gruyter, 2005, 377–397.

[28] See Goodrich, "Rhetoric as Jurisprudence," *Oxford Journal of Legal Studies* 4 (1984), 117.

[29] See Simonnæs, "Fachkommunikation im Recht unter Berücksichtigung der Mehrfachadressierung," in Lerch, ed, *Recht vermitteln*, Berlin, Walter de Gruyter, 2005, 386.

decisions that are both directive to the litigants and instructive to the higher instances poses a significant challenge for judges. It is not hard to tell from the way many decisions are formulated that judges usually have the higher instance in mind when writing their arguments and tend to rely on the litigants' lawyers when it comes to communicating their decision to them. However, besides criticizing this tendency to prioritize certain receivers over others, the phenomenon as such clearly underlines the general problem, namely, that legal senders frequently have to face the enormous challenge of communicating their message to plural and very diverse receivers.

Making Legal Meaning

The observation that successful legal communication depends on a receiver receiving a legal message with some understanding also alludes to the important insight that the meaning of a legal text is not in the text itself. Harold Berman observed, "a word does not 'have' a meaning. Instead, it *transfers* a meaning; indeed, it *gives* a meaning where there was no meaning before."[30] So meaning is connected with the text to some degree, but does not lie within it. It is attached to the text by those who read it or hear it. Linguist David Frank explains, "meanings are in people's heads, and when a text is involved, the meaning attributed to that text is in the heads of as many people who encounter that text who share the same linguistic code."[31] Ladislas Orsy made a similar observation for canon law, stating,

> [T]he meanings that the words and sentences signify exist in the minds of living persons who perceive and understand everything in the context of their own universe. . . . And because in a healthy person, every single meaning is integrated with all the others in his mind, a message communicated to another is received in a different world, different mentality. By necessity it receives a different meaning. When a picture is transported from one room to another, because of the change in surroundings the picture itself presents a different image for those who are looking at it.[32]

Meaning, and likewise legal meaning, is utterly dependent on context, on the "universe," as Orsy puts it, on the culture that weaves webs of meaning around the receivers of a message. Legal messages are therefore more like pictures, the

[30] Berman, *Law and Language*, Cambridge, Cambridge University Press, 2013, 69.
[31] Frank, "Do We Translate the Original Author's Intended Meaning?," *Open Theology* 2 (2016), 654.
[32] Orsy, "The Interpreter and His Art," *The Jurist* 40 (1980), 48.

meaning of which changes whenever the surroundings change, and less like potatoes, which remain the same at one market or at another. Yet it is not only the singular perspective of the individual viewer of a picture or an individual receiver of a legal message that creates meaning, it is also the social context in which the creation of meaning takes place. David Frank expresses this idea by stating that meaning is always connected with communal ideas, that it "is."[33] This includes the premise that, as with all culture, legal meaning is open to change.

Communal Meaning

The complex contextuality of receiving a legal message has a twofold consequence for the question of how legal communication is possible. First, it renders communication, including legal communication, a fragile business; it is never possible to ensure that the meaning the senders connect with their original message is actually received in the same or a similar way by the receivers. As meaning depends heavily on communal cultural knowledge, it becomes incredibly difficult to transfer meaning across cultural borders. Because canon law is a global legal order, this poses a major challenge, which I will discuss more intensively in the course of this study. A second challenge is posed by the finding that law somehow seems to resist the fact that meaning is actually community property. In this vein, Dietrich Busse observes that law and its meaning is primarily an institutional phenomenon. He therefore questions whether the exchange of legal information can even be seen as an act of communication at all. While this might seem plausible at first sight, Busse challenges this understanding by stating that unlike terms in regular conversation, the meanings of legal terms are not particularly open to change and largely institutionally determined. While the meaning of most terms is community property and changes with the use of terms in communal practice, these changes are less admissible when it comes to the law or legal terms which fulfill a specific legal function.[34] Of course, legal terms also change their meaning. Yet legal institutions have a tight grip on the meaning of legal terms, widely immunizing them from the changes in meaning that most terms are subject to in their common use. Bearing this in mind, Busse notes that individuals do not usually understand "communication" as the exchange of signs predefined by an institutional framework which exerts strict control over the meaning of a term. It might still be possible to regard the law as communication in any case—depending on how one defines communication—but,

[33] Frank, "Do We Translate the Original Author's Intended Meaning?," *Open Theology* 2 (2016), 655.

[34] See Busse, "Ist die Anwendung von Rechtstexten ein Fall von Kommunikation?," in Lerch, ed, *Recht vermitteln*, Berlin, Walter de Gruyter, 2005, 48.

following Busse, it does not express what individuals usually understand as communication.[35] In this study, I will nevertheless speak of law as communication, because the exchange of legal information shares many qualities with other acts of communication, which can be explained best using a communication model. However, as Busse rightly reminds us, the impact of legal institutions on legal communication and on determining the meaning of legal texts is ubiquitous and must always be kept in mind.

The Media of the Law

In communication, the medium in which a message is conveyed is important for the message itself, as Busse contends. Hence, understanding law as communication alludes to the importance of the media of the law with which legal messages are carried to the legal markets. Legal scholar Kent Lerch dedicated one of his three impressive volumes on the language of the law to *Conveying Law* [*Recht vermitteln*],[36] thus indicating that law has to be imparted to the legal subjects. Law needs a medium; it is communicated through media, which convey a legal meaning to others. The primary medium through which the law is conveyed to a legal community is language. Then secondary media are used to convey the language of the law: written texts, oral statements, and, not least, digital media, a topic to which law and language scholars have devoted increasing attention in recent years.[37] Traditionally, law and language scholars refer either to the written texts of the law or to speech in legal contexts.[38] Written legal texts are found in statutes, rules, and regulations, as well as in contracts, agreements, and insurance policies. The law is written down in judicial decisions; legal ideas are noted in scholarly books and articles. Professional legal agents like lawyers orally express legal ideas in client consultations or when acting in court, for instance, when examining litigants and witnesses; judges also do this when hearing a case or in issuing jury instructions. Legal scholars speak about the law at legal conferences and in educational settings when giving lectures to law students.

[35] See ibid., 51.

[36] See Lerch, ed, *Recht verstehen*, Berlin, Walter de Gruyter, 2004; idem, ed, *Recht verhandeln*, Berlin, Walter de Gruyter, 2005; idem, ed, *Recht vermitteln*, Berlin, Walter de Gruyter, 2005.

[37] See Lerch, "Recht vermitteln," in idem, ed, *Recht vermitteln*, Berlin, Walter de Gruyter, 2005, XXIV–XXV; Vogel, "Rechtslinguistik," in Felder/Vogel, eds, *Handbuch Sprache im Recht*, Berlin, Walter de Gruyter, 2017, 221–223.

[38] See Bhatia, "Language of the Law," *Language Teaching* 20 (1987), 227–231; Hoffmann, "Mündlichkeit im Recht," in Felder/Vogel, eds, *Handbuch Sprache im Recht*, Berlin, Walter de Gruyter, 2017, 67–90; Deutsch, "Schriftlichkeit im Recht," in Felder/Vogel, eds, *Handbuch Sprache im Recht*, Berlin, Walter de Gruyter, 2017, 91–116.

The Silence of the Law

This study is first of all about how the law expresses legal meaning, for instance, in legal texts or speech. Yet, when it comes to law and language, it is not only of interest to investigate how the law deals with embodied, written, or oral expressions and utterances but also how it deals with the absence of such expressions, which make their presence felt in oral conversations as silence. Some might understand silence as the absence of language and communication, and for that reason perceive silence as an issue that a study on language need not address. Yet upon closer inspection it becomes evident that silence has a communicative meaning in itself, as legal scholar Janet Ainsworth argues, "Silence in communicative interaction, however, is not just the 'blank space' setting off the audible elements of spoken utterances. . . . Speech and silence mutually frame each other in discourse, with this reciprocal contextual framing giving both speech and silence their fullest meaning."[39] Communication, Ainsworth contends, therefore employs a pattern of utterances and silence. Within this pattern, silence may serve semantic, pragmatic, and socio-pragmatic functions. Scholars who are aware of these functions, for instance, see the need to indicate moments of noticeable silence when they transform oral speech into written texts, such as when compiling transcripts. As silence is not "nothing" in a communicative sense, it needs textual representation; in transcripts it is usually denoted by inserting dots between the utterances.

The communicative relevance of silence is particularly clear with regard to law enforcement and legal action, where silence has multiple roles to play.[40] As in most legal orders, canon law, for instance, knows regulations on confidentiality, obliging church officials to keep confidential sensitive matters they come across when exercising their office. This duty includes officials involved in ecclesiastical adjudication. Judges and tribunal personnel are obliged to keep confidential penal cases and that knowledge gained in civil cases the disclosure of which could be disadvantageous to the parties (see canon 1455 §1 CIC/1983). Furthermore, judges must always remain silent about their deliberations in collegiate tribunals (see canon 1455 §2 CIC/1983); breaking confidentiality may be justly punished (see canon 1457 CIC/1983). Yet the relevance of keeping silent is not limited to confidential issues. Silence in court hearings is another topic which has attracted the interest of forensic linguists. It may have a myriad of meanings, an issue legal

[39] Ainsworth, "Silence, Speech, and the Paradox of the Right to Remain Silent in American Police Interrogation," in Freeman/Smith, eds, *Law and Language*, Oxford, Oxford University Press, 2013, 374.

[40] See Kurzon, *Discourse of Silence*, Amsterdam, John Benjamins, 1998, particularly chapter 3 on "The Transitivization of Silence: Legal Discourse," 51–71.

scholar Stefan Krieger raised with regard to forensic communication.[41] Silence may express unwillingness or inability to contribute to fact-finding, it may be an expression of fright, anger, or ignorance, and in some cases it may even be an admission of guilt, as the Latin saying implies, "She or he who is silent seems to agree" ("*Qui tacet consentire videtur*"). Yet silence is also a right or a demand in forensic settings. In some contexts it is suggested or requested by law, for instance, when the law allows suspects or defendants to remain silent when faced with a charge, privileges witnesses not to testify under certain conditions, or excludes certain witnesses from being questioned. I will shed some more light on these diverse manifestations of silence in the context of ecclesiastical adjudication in chapter 8.

2.3 The Sacramentality of the Law

My previous considerations reveal that the language of the law is not entirely directive. However, legal discourse and legal language do revolve around texts and expressions with a directive function. This is what Karl Olivecrona meant when he described the language of the law as a language which purposed to create and shape reality. For it to do this, the law makes use of a performative language which brings about the legal facts that it describes. By using performative utterances the law creates the legal world, as linguist Maurizio Gotti explains,

> Language in the law is probably more performative than in any other field . . . Indeed, the mere statement of guilt or innocence pronounced by a judge makes the culprit guilty (or not guilty) of a crime, whether or not he actually committed it. Similarly, a court can declare legally "deceased" a person who has been missing for a long time, even if that person may have moved to another country or changed his identity and therefore is not, physically speaking, dead.[42]

The performative functioning of legal language is particularly evident in adjudication, which revolves around speech. Historian Gian Marco Vidor identifies courtroom speeches "[a]s a way of 'performing the law.'"[43] Performative speech, in any case, is similarly present in legal texts, such as statutes, administrative

[41] See Krieger, "A Time to Keep Silent and a Time to Speak," *Oregon Law Review* 80 (2001), 199–266.

[42] Gotti, "Text and Genre," in Solan/Tiersma, eds, *The Oxford Handbook of Language and Law*, Oxford, Oxford University Press, 2012, 57.

[43] Vidor, "Rhetorical Engineering of Emotions in the Courtroom," *Rechtsgeschichte—Legal History* 25 (2017), 286.

instructions, sentences, and contracts as textual genres packed with performative expressions.

The Language of Magic

The performative functioning of legal statements mirrors the way "word" and "sacrament" function in the church, as Klaus Mörsdorf noted. I provided a brief sketch of Mörsdorf's approach to "word" and "sacrament" as basic structural elements of the church and its law in the introduction. His idea of comparing the way in which the law and the sacraments function is shared by law and religion scholars such as Harold Berman. Berman contended, "We would compare such performative utterances in law with the sacraments of the church, which are called 'effective symbols' because they effectuate that which they symbolize."[44] In performing the designated rites and uttering the words intended to achieve the designated effect, the law—just like the sacraments—brings about what is symbolized in legal ritual. Berman therefore speaks of "a sacramental quality to much of the language of the law,"[45] which he traces back to the law's religious roots. He argues that the nexus between law and religion is still alive in the symbol practices of the law as well as in its language. Berman explains this by taking an example from judicial procedure, writing, "In English and American law the petitioner still 'prays' for relief, and the witness swears an oath. There is a liturgical quality in all judicial procedure."[46]

Berman's observations allude to the common root shared by legal and sacramental thought and by legal and religious ritual. This common root seems to lie in the idea that a thing comes into being by a word uttered or a ritual performed. "Magic" may be the more common category to describe this event. Many legal scholars embrace this outline by comparing law and magic with regard to its power to change the world through speech.[47] Olivecrona stated, "The legal language has its origin in the language of magic."[48] Jessie Allen describes

[44] Berman, *Law and Language*, Cambridge, Cambridge University Press, 2013, 83.
[45] Ibid.
[46] Ibid.
On the striking similarity between legal and religious language, see also Pyle, "Law, Ritual and Language," *American Legal Studies Association Forum* 8 (1984), 381–392.
[47] E.g., Gurvitch, "Magic and Law," *Social Research* 9 (1942), 104–122; Pyle, "Law, Ritual and Language," *American Legal Studies Association Forum* 8 (1984), 381; Allen, "A Theory of Adjudication," *Suffolk University Law Review* 41 (2008), 773–831; Corcos, ed, *Law and Magic*, Durham, NC, Carolina Academic Press, 2010; eadem, "Magical Images in Law," in Wagner/Cheng, eds, *Exploring Courtroom Discourse*, Farnham, Ashgate, 2011, 131–175; Neuwirth, "Law and Magic," *Thomas Jefferson Law Review* 37 (2014), 139–190; Alvarez-Nakagawa, "Law *as* Magic," *German Law Journal* 18 (2017), 1247–1275; De Sutter, "On the Magic of Law," *Law Text Culture* 21 (2017), 123–142.
[48] Olivecrona, "Legal Language and Reality," in Newman, ed, *Essays in Jurisprudence in Honor of Roscoe Pound*, Indianapolis, IN, Bobbs-Merrill, 1962, 190.

both law and magic as "performances to transform reality."[49] Christine Corcos compares lawyers' performances in court with the stage acting of magicians.[50] In performing the designated rites and uttering the words intended to achieve the designated effects, the law and those who apply it create and shape reality like magicians. Corcos also edited a compilation of essays on *Law and Magic* to which she invited legal scholars and magicians and, most ingeniously, legal scholars who are practicing hobby magicians to share their insights into the interrelationship between law and magic.[51] This connection between law and magic, as all agree, lies in its capacity to bring about new facts with the help of speech. Legal reality only comes into being through the language of the law and its rituals, as Olivecrona observes, "That which is held to be performed is the creation of a nonphysical relationship or property through the pronouncing of some words. Such doings fall under the category of magic."[52] Hence, the law performs its work not primarily with the help of those things which it finds in the physical world, but with the help of magical speech, which creates legal ties between the members of a legal community by subjugating them under the law. Legal magic summons legal realities into being, realities which have no empirical counterparts in the physical world. Alexis Alvarez-Nakagawa remarks, "[W]e can think of some modern legal practices as a secularized way of performing certain material effects through symbolical acts; rituals that work in the imaginary but have unmistakable consequences in the 'real' world."[53] In a similar vein, Berman explains the functioning of legal magic with regard to the functioning of conflict resolution through the intervention of law as a real but nonphysical process of bringing about real but nonphysical effects, "Some have found the process of resolving conflict by legal language to be magic, since the terms appear to have no empirical referents. This is because legal statements do not describe what exists; rather they *ascribe* rights and duties and thereby *create* relationships."[54] This magic is based purely on language, as Allen notes, comparing the language of the law with the functioning of spells, "The efficacy of both magic spells and judicial determinations partakes of the 'performative' force of language, so that when judges and sorcerers speak in the proper ritual contexts, the act of saying it does make it so."[55] The law uses spells in many contexts. The words of a registrar make a couple married partners and endow them with those duties and

[49] Allen, "A Theory of Adjudication," *Suffolk University Law Review* 41 (2008), 777.

[50] See Corcos, "Magical Images in Law," in Wagner/Cheng, eds, *Exploring Courtroom Discourse*, Farnham, Ashgate, 2011, 131–175.

[51] See Corcos, ed, *Law and Magic*, Durham, NC, Carolina Academic Press, 2010.

[52] Olivecrona, "Legal Language and Reality," in Newman, ed, *Essays in Jurisprudence in Honor of Roscoe Pound*, Indianapolis, IN, Bobbs-Merrill, 1962, 175.

[53] Alvarez-Nakagawa, "Law *as* Magic," *German Law Journal* 18 (2017), 1250.

[54] Berman, *Law and Language*, Cambridge, Cambridge University Press, 2013, 152.

[55] Allen, "A Theory of Adjudication," *Suffolk University Law Review* 41 (2008), 777.

rights attached to marital status in family law, inheritance law, and tax law. The judge declaring the guilt of a defendant turns the defendant into an offender. An authorized representative of the state transforms a citizen into a state official through words of installation and endows her or him with the authority attached to the office and with its particular obligations.

Ritual Speech

The proximity of law and magical ritual as social practices with the power to use speech to bring about new realities also has an impact on the language of the law itself. Legal language is for the most part ritual language, as Peter Tiersma observed.[56] This is all the more the case where legal rituals are directly concerned, for instance, with regard to the rituals that take place in adjudication. The ceremony of adjudication, though different in every legal culture, always has a ritual flavor and is accompanied by a corresponding ceremonial language, as Tiersma noted, "The ritualistic language and ceremonies of the courtroom have much in common with a religious service, and serve much the same purpose,"[57] namely, to show the distinctiveness of the occasion, to distinguish it from secular everyday life, and to demonstrate the power of the law and of those who execute it. Tiersma, as his words convey, compares law with religious ritual and its language with liturgical language, whereas the legal scholars cited in the previous section associated it with magical ritual and its language with magical spells. However, there might be reason to wonder whether there is truly an essential difference. While there is most certainly a difference between magic and religion from a theological point of view, this distinction is less important for a comparative argument between law and magic or religious ritual with regard to the power of language, as I want to argue. From the point of most humanities and social sciences, the distinction between religion and magic has been an object of criticism and debate over the last couple of decades. It was particularly the merit of the empirical sciences to emphasize that for an outside observer, the difference between religion and magic is hardly discernible. Sociologist George Homans already noted in 1941, "To an anthropologist from western civilization, a magical rite and a religious rite are equally devoid of definite, practical results, in the usual sense of the phrase."[58] Homans's negative approach, namely, of dismissing the distinction between religion and magic because both practices seem useless,

[56] See Tiersma, *Legal Language*, Chicago, IL, The University of Chicago Press, 1999, 100–104.
[57] Ibid., 101.
On the theatrical elements of adjunction and its staging of justice, e.g., Leiboff, "Theatricalizing Law," *Law and Literature* 30 (2018), 351–367.
[58] Homans, "Anxiety and Ritual," *American Anthropologist* 43 (1941), 165.

intersects with more constructive approaches dismissing the boundary between religion and magic due to their similar functioning. In this light, even Catholic theologians such as systematic theologian Robert Schreiter acknowledge, "Distinctions between theology, magic, and superstition may be valid in theology, but are questionable in anthropology."[59] Hence, when analyzing the language of the law by comparing it with ritual language, it is likewise feasible and helpful to allude to language as used in magic or liturgical services.

The parallel between the law and magical or religious ritual with regard to the language applied in both contexts accords with some parallels which are manifest in their styles. Both law and religion tend to rely on a "conservative or archaic language,"[60] as Tiersma found. They share a tendency to preserve language which is regarded as outdated in most other social contexts. Besides the convenience of abiding with traditional texts, Tiersma discovered a shared ideological reason for this in the "veneration of authoritative texts,"[61] which is strong in law and religion alike. There is also a critical parallel between the language of the law and the language of ritual, as both, in tendency, are difficult to understand, something which linguists Veda Charrow and Jo Ann Crandall and legal scholar Robert Charrow observed in a joint study.[62] They see a parallel in the fact that power as conveyed by religious ritual or the law might be overwhelming to many individuals precisely because they do not understand the language that creates the religious or legal effect. The legal or religious ritual might be impressive exactly because it remains mysterious. And it is for the lawyer-sage, the magician, or the priest to reveal the secrets to those who do not understand ritual language. I will discuss this intended incomprehension of the majority of a community's members and its critical implications at greater length in chapter 5.

Law as a Matter of Belief

However, to return to the performative functioning of ritual language, there is one more feature that law and magical or religious ritual share, namely, that all are reliant on belief in order to be effective. A legal reality is created by legal language only with the help of the faith of those involved, just as the emergence of a sacred reality from sacred rituals requires faith. It was Harold Berman who pointed out the law's dependence on belief. Berman stressed that the belief essential for the functioning of the law does not necessarily have to be a religious

59 Schreiter, *Constructing Local Theologies*, Maryknoll, NY, Orbis Books, 1985, 43.
60 Tiersma, *Legal Language*, Chicago, IL, The University of Chicago Press, 1999, 95.
61 Ibid., 96.
62 See Charrow/Crandall/Charrow, "Characteristics and Functions of Legal Language," in Kittredge/Lehrberger, eds, *Sublanguage*, Berlin, Walter de Gruyter, 1982, 181–182.

belief—even though, most interestingly, he took religious faith as supporting the people's belief in the law—but does have to be a belief in the law *itself*. This is how John Witte in his introduction to Berman's book *Law and Language* quotes Berman from memory,

> You have to believe in law at least. If you can't accept God, then just focus on the law that God has written on all of our hearts. Even children intuitively sense this law within us. Every child in the world will say, "That's my toy." That's property law. Every child will say, "But you promised me." That's contract law. Every child will say, "It's not my fault. He hit me first." That's tort law. Every child will say, too, "Daddy said I could." That's constitutional law. Law ultimately comes from our human nature, and our human nature is ultimately an image of God.[63]

This quote is interesting for several reasons, and above all for canonists, insofar as Berman—in referring to the law that God has written on all of our hearts—uses a biblical idea (see Deuteronomy 30:14; Romans 2:15), which has been quoted frequently throughout the history of Christian law to explain the divine origin of natural law. Berman thus reveals his thoughts as being deeply rooted in both natural law theory as well as a religious natural law theory, which maintains a typical link with Christian creation theology. Nevertheless, I will not discuss this issue any further in this study. There are two more assertions, in any case, that make his statement worthy of further consideration with regard to how law and language interact. First, Berman seems to support the idea that the law has natural origins, as he regards the law as a normativity that comes to us so naturally that even a child could invent it. This requires further critical discussion. Is law really something natural—or rather something cultural? Over the past few years, the *law as culture* debate has carried forward the argument that while the idea of law being grounded in the nature of humankind is not entirely unconvincing, the law as it presents itself concretely is more a result of culture than of nature.[64] I tend to think of the law as a cultural achievement, particularly as it is language that brings it about. Language is certainly always a cultural phenomenon.[65] This becomes clear if we return to Berman's example. A child claiming her or his toy

[63] Witte/Manzer, "Introduction," in Berman, *Law and Language*, Cambridge, Cambridge University Press, 2013, 6–7.

[64] For canon law, see Hahn, *Church Law in Modernity*, Cambridge, Cambridge University Press, 2019.

[65] E.g., Whorf, *Language, Thought, and Reality*, Cambridge, MA, The Technology Press of Massachusetts Institute of Technology, 1956; Geertz, "'From the Native's Point of View,'" *Bulletin of the American Academy of Arts and Sciences* 28 (1974), 26–45; Huels, "Interpreting Canon Law in Diverse Cultures," *The Jurist* 47 (1987), 249–293; Legrand, "Foreign Law," *Journal of Comparative Law* 6 (2011), 67–177; Engberg, "Word Meaning and the Problem of a Globalized Legal Order," in Solan/Tiersma, eds, *The Oxford Handbook of Language and Law*, Oxford, Oxford University Press, 2012, 175–186.

is already doing so in a context deeply imbued with the idea of property and property rights. A child who refers to one parent as the authority who permitted a certain action is doing so against the background of a hierarchical structure which identifies certain authorities as capable of authorizing a specific behavior. So I am not convinced that law flows directly from our nature. I rather tend to think that it is sourced in our culture. At the same time, I do not seek to challenge the idea that there is something in human nature that encourages human beings to interpret the world in legal terms and to bring about laws as cultural artifacts.

Legal Speech Acts

A second thought connected with Berman's conception of the origin of the law in language is the emergence of law from speech acts. Berman understands speech acts as making the law. In other words, by making a performative utterance, the person making a legal statement creates a legal reality. It was John Austin who first introduced the idea of performative utterances as those acts of speech "in which to say something is to do something"[66] to the twentieth-century debate on the functioning of language.[67] Austin makes clear that "performative" as a term derived from the verb "to perform" is always connected with action. Performing an act is "action," including cases in which it is speech that performs the act. Reflecting the performative effect of speech thus "indicates that the issuing of the utterance is the performing of an action,"[68] as Austin contends. As a result, he discerns that while statements might be true or untrue, it is impossible to subject performative speech to the categories of right and wrong.[69] Performative utterances are actions and therefore they are never true nor false, but rather felicitous or infelicitous.[70] If saying "I do" within a marriage ceremony does not result in a marriage, the act was not "untrue" but only unsuccessful, as Austin observes, thereby differentiating between those felicitous speech acts the intended effect of which comes into being, and infelicitous speech which goes awry. Austin also calls these failed acts "misfires." He explains, "When the utterance is a misfire, the procedure which we purport to invoke is disallowed or is botched: and our act (marrying, etc.) is void or without effect, etc. We speak of our act as a purported act, or perhaps an attempt—or we use such an expression as 'went through a

66 Austin, *How to Do Things with Words*, Oxford, Clarendon Press, 1962, 94.

67 For a prominent and recent contribution, see Taylor, *The Language Animal*, Cambridge, MA, The Belknap Press of Harvard University Press, 2016.

68 Austin, *How to Do Things with Words*, Oxford, Clarendon Press, 1962, 6.

69 See ibid., 6, 10–11.

70 See ibid., 14; idem, "Performative Utterances," in idem, *Philosophical Papers*, Oxford, Clarendon Press, 1979, 237–241, 247–251.

form of marriage' by contrast with 'married.'"[71] Canon law knows a similar distinct terminology to express successful and unsuccessful sacramental and legal acts, calling these acts "valid" and "invalid." I will return to the confusing canon law terminology of "nullity" or "annulment" connected with invalid marriages in chapter 4, section 4.2.

To distinguish between the ways in which speech takes action, Austin differentiates between locutionary, illocutionary, and perlocutionary speech. I already gave a brief outline of this differentiation in the introduction. He understands the act of uttering meaningful words as a locutionary act. Illocutionary acts are those speech acts like stating, commanding, thanking, or promising, which are conventionally defined and have a specific conventional effect. Performing the conventional act constitutes that which it denotes as it brings about a conventionally defined reality. Saying "thank you" is thanking another person. Saying "I promise" is making a promise. Austin posits with regard to the example of marriage, "[T]he performative 'I do' is a means to the end of marriage."[72] Perlocutions are distinguished from illocutions as they bring about immediate effects on hearers. Austin maintains, "Saying something will often, or even normally, produce certain consequential effects upon the feelings, thoughts, or actions of the audience, or of the speaker, or of other persons."[73] Perlocutionary speech is "what we bring about or achieve *by* saying something,"[74] like the guests' emotions witnessing a marriage ceremony or a person's fear in reaction to another individual's threat.

Classes of Illocutions

Speech act theory at its core revolves around performative speech, that is, around illocutions as acts in which saying a thing and doing it converge. They are of key importance for understanding the performative power of legal speech. Austin, for instance, refers to the jury rendering a verdict of guilt.[75] As I mentioned, one of his most-quoted examples refers to the act of marrying somebody by saying "I do (sc. take this woman to be my lawful wedded wife)"[76] and also to the act of bequeathing some valuables to an heir by writing in a will, "I give and bequeath my watch to my brother."[77] Austin even identified two types of speech

[71] Austin, *How to Do Things with Words*, Oxford, Clarendon Press, 1962, 16.
[72] Ibid., 129.
[73] Ibid., 101.
[74] Ibid., 108.
[75] See ibid., 42–43; idem, "Performative Utterances," in idem, *Philosophical Papers*, Oxford, Clarendon Press, 1979, 247.
[76] Austin, *How to Do Things with Words*, Oxford, Clarendon Press, 1962, 5.
[77] Ibid.

acts, verdictives and exercitives, typical for most legal acts.[78] Whenever judges, juries, arbitrators, or umpires render a verdict, they use verdictive speech, according to Austin. The exercise of powers, influence, or rights, as in ordering, advising, appointing, or voting, makes use of exercitive speech—"It is a decision that something is to be so, as distinct from a judgement that it is so,"[79] as Austin contends. Legal judgments are therefore mostly verdictives, according to him, while legislative and executive acts are frequently exercitives. He notices, however, that some judicial decisions, like decisions on legal costs, are exercitives and not verdictives.

Overall, his taxonomy of illocutionary speech did not prove overly convincing. It was philosopher John Searle who took up Austin's approach to illocutions to refine it and modify some of Austin's classifications. Speech act theorists today rather refer to Searle's taxonomy. He distinguishes illocutionary speech with regard to its "direction of fit."[80] Thus, he differentiates between illocutions which endeavor "to get the words . . . to match the world" and "others to get the world to match the words."[81] While some speech acts have a word-to-world direction as they use speech to describe, assert, or explain reality, others have a world-to-word direction as they form reality by using speech. Asking what humans may achieve with speech, Searle observes, "[T]here are a rather limited number of basic things we do with language: we tell people how things are, we try to get them to do things, we commit ourselves to doing things, we express our feelings and attitudes and we bring about changes through our utterances."[82] Correspondingly, Searle identifies five classes of illocutions: assertive, directive, commissive, expressive, and declarative speech acts. Assertive speech acts are those acts with a word-to-world fit, which are in use to assert how reality is. They oblige the speaker to speak the truth with regard to the proposition which he or she expresses. Typical assertives are expressions like "I state . . . ," "I report . . . ," "I claim . . . ," or "I admit . . ." Directives are acts with a world-to-word fit to achieve another person's action or inaction. Searle calls directives "attempts . . . by the speaker to get the hearer to do something."[83] Typical directive phrases are "I request . . . ," "I command . . . ," "I order . . . ," or "I advise . . ." Speech acts are called commissives when they express the speaker's commitment to a future action or inaction. Commissives follow a world-to-word direction. Typical examples are speech acts like "I swear . . . ," "I promise . . . ," "I offer . . . ," or "I guarantee . . ." Expressive speech expresses the speaker's feelings or attitudes. Typical examples

[78] See ibid., 152.
[79] Ibid., 154.
[80] Searle, "A Classification of Illocutionary Acts," *Language in Society* 5 (1976), 4.
[81] Ibid., 3.
[82] Ibid., 22–23.
[83] Ibid., 11.

are "Congratulations," "Thank you," "I am sorry," or "Hello!" Unlike the other types of illocutions classified by Searle, expressives do not have a direction of fit, as they attempt neither to say anything about the world nor to change the world. It is, in any case, the main purpose of declarative speech to transform reality by speaking. Declaratives are those "cases where, so to speak, 'saying makes it so,'"[84] as Searle notes. Declarations change the status or the condition of the object to which they refer. Searle explains, "A declaration is a speech act whose point is to create a new fact corresponding to the propositional content."[85] As declarations employ speech to create new facts, they come with a specific direction of fit. Searle suggests understanding directives as having both a word-to-world and a world-to-word fit. He explains this phenomenon inter alia with the example of a judge rendering a penal verdict.[86] The judge's action has a word-to-world fit insofar as she or he attempts to capture the reality of the case, thus rendering a guilty verdict only if the defendant has in fact committed the crime. But the judge's performative act of declaring a defendant guilty, as Searle observes, has its effect regardless of the defendant's guilt or innocence. By declaring guilt, the defendant *becomes* guilty in the eyes of the law. This corresponds to the world-to-word fit of declaratives. Searle notes,

> [S]uccessful performance guarantees that the propositional content corresponds to the world: if I successfully perform the act of appointing you chairman, then you are chairman; if I successfully perform the act of nominating you as candidate, then you are a candidate; if I successfully perform the act of declaring a state of war, then war is on; if I successfully perform the act of marrying you, then you are married.[87]

Legal Illocutions

In drawing on the performative power of speech, the law makes use of various kinds of speech acts. Linguist Risto Hiltunen analyzed "The Grammar and Structure of Legal Texts" to find that legal texts and in particular legislation are full of speech act expressions, like verbs signaling illocutionary action.[88] In light of the sheer quantity of speech act phenomena in legal language, it comes as little surprise that many of the standard examples for speech acts as mentioned by

[84] Ibid., 13.
[85] Searle, "How Performatives Work," *Linguistics and Philosophy* 12 (1989), 549.
[86] See Searle, "A Classification of Illocutionary Acts," *Language in Society* 5 (1976), 15.
[87] Ibid., 13.
[88] See Hiltunen, "The Grammar and Structure of Legal Texts," in Solan/Tiersma, eds, *The Oxford Handbook of Language and Law*, Oxford, Oxford University Press, 2012, 49.

speech act theorists are taken from the law, as I have already mentioned. The law relies on assertive speech whenever the parties or witnesses in a case state, claim, describe, hypothesize, or swear what the truth is in a case. A court giving a verdict makes an assertive statement about the facts in the case. Many verdicts also relate to justice and the social order and assert how they contribute to reconciling justice and restoring the social order. In a similar vein, we may discover directive elements in verdicts, as they not only concentrate on the present case and its consequences but also aim at achieving a different future, for instance, by directing an offender to change his or her behavior or by directing others to abstain from similar offenses. When verdicts refer to theories of criminal justice, like social rehabilitation and general prevention, they usually apply elements of directive speech. Directives are probably the main category of speech acts that many scholars connect with the law, as one may identify not only single acts of legal speech as directive but also the law as such as directive speech. In this respect, John Searle differentiates between the law's formation as the result of a declarative act and its intent, which is directive.[89] In a similar way, linguist Dennis Kurzon understands entire statutes to be speech acts "with the illocutionary force of enacting."[90] Legal scholar and philosopher Andrei Marmor's remark that the law tells us what to do or what not to do points in the same direction.[91] On the other hand, Marmor is careful to avoid the term "directive" for the law in general, probably to avoid confusion with single acts of directive legal speech. Other authors share similar concerns. Legal scholar and philosopher Paul Amselek and legal linguist Ross Charnock emphasize that not all legal rules are directives. This classification applies to obligations, but regularly not to constitutive rules or to those rules that convey power, rights, or permissions.[92] However, one may understand all of these rules as directive in a broader sense, as they aim to achieve a certain action, even though they do not command it. Marmor's solution is to avoid the term "directive" for the law itself. He prefers to speak of the law as "imperative." There is an "imperative mood" behind most legal statements, irrespective of whether concrete legal utterances are grammatical imperatives or phrased in a different mood. They serve as imperatives as "their function is to motivate conduct,"[93] as Marmor maintains, explaining, "Laws grant rights of various kinds, impose obligations, grant various agents, private and public, powers to introduce normative changes in the law, and so on

89 See Searle, "A Classification of Illocutionary Acts," *Language in Society* 5 (1976), 22.

90 Kurzon, *It Is Hereby Performed*, Amsterdam, John Benjamins, 1986, 5.

91 See Marmor, "Truth in Law," in Freeman/Smith, eds, *Law and Language*, Oxford, Oxford University Press, 2013, 45.

92 See Amselek, "Philosophy of Law and the Theory of Speech Acts," *Ratio Juris* 1 (1988), 192–193; Charnock, "Overruling as a Speech Act," *Journal of Pragmatics* 41 (2009), 402.

93 Marmor, "Truth in Law," in Freeman/Smith, eds, *Law and Language*, Oxford, Oxford University Press, 2013, 46.

and so forth. The unifying element, however, is conduct guidance. In one way or another, legal norms and legal decisions purport to guide conduct."[94] Exceptions apply, as Marmor admits. However, he understands the general direction of the law as being imperative, even in those cases in which the law does not order a specific action or inaction, but allows, grants, and enables a specific action or inaction. I follow Marmor's understanding of the law and find his hesitance to apply the term "directive" to the law itself favorable, as this helps to differentiate between the imperative direction of the law and single acts of legal speech with a directive illocutionary effect, such as legal commands, jury instructions, citations, and appeals.[95] These acts, as Marmor explains, directly "purport to motivate conduct on part of the hearer."[96] He calls these directives "exhortatives" to avoid the narrowness implied by the term "directive"; however, I will not follow him in this respect, as I want to show precisely that these legal "exhortatives" are "directives" in the sense of speech act theory. While legal norms are not entirely directive, the law does revolve around speech acts with a directive function due to its imperative thrust. Common legal commands which permit, order, or prohibit are directive speech. Whenever the law speaks of "may," "shall," or "shall not," this terminological choice suggests directive acts.[97] More often, however, the legal wording hides the directive function of norms. Paul Amselek observes that modern legal norms frequently use indicative speech instead of the imperative mood.[98] In section 2.1 of this chapter I already mentioned Ralf Poscher's example of article 5, paragraph 3 of the German Basic Law using the indicative to express the directive that art, science, research, and teaching shall be free.[99] Similarly, linguists Nicholas Allott and Benjamin Shaer have recently established that penal laws seldom use directive formulations, either directly or indirectly. Allott and Shaer therefore suggest analyzing penal statutes as "effective speech" instead of looking out for their directive elements, as they are "clearly behaviour-guiding in that they set up new norms or social facts that guide subsequent behaviour."[100] Nevertheless, this terminological refinement, as I want to argue, does not change the fact that many legal norms have a directive function, even though they use an indicative mood to express it. Amselek rightly rejects arguments which demand the imperative mood in norms to express a directive

[94] Ibid.

[95] See Danet, "Language in the Legal Process," *Law & Society Review* 14 (1980), 458.

[96] Marmor, "Truth in Law," in Freeman/Smith, eds, *Law and Language*, Oxford, Oxford University Press, 2013, 47.

[97] See Kurzon, *It Is Hereby Performed*, Amsterdam, John Benjamins, 1986, 15–16; Hiltunen, "The Grammar and Structure of Legal Texts," in Solan/Tiersma, eds, *The Oxford Handbook of Language and Law*, Oxford, Oxford University Press, 2012, 50.

[98] See Amselek, "Philosophy of Law and the Theory of Speech Acts," *Ratio Juris* 1 (1988), 191.

[99] See Poscher, "The Hermeneutics of Law," in Forster/Gjesdal, eds, *The Cambridge Companion to Hermeneutics*, Cambridge, Cambridge University Press, 2019, 327.

[100] Allott/Shaer, "The Illocutionary Force of Laws," *Inquiry* 61 (2018), 366.

meaning as openly "absurd."[101] I agree with him and want to suggest speaking of legal speech acts as directive in all cases in which they have a directive purpose, regardless of their grammatical mood. I find this a consistent approach for my study, insofar as I propose a broader approach to understanding speech anyway. If we understand as legal speech all those words, gestures, and moments of silence which communicate a legal message, we might as well understand as legal directives all those words, gestures, and non-actions with which the law aspires to direct a person's action or inaction.

The law is also highly reliant on commissives, which play a key role whenever individuals or legal persons commit themselves to a future action or inaction: the witness who swears to tell the truth in a case; the employer who offers a contract to a job applicant; the company who guarantees perfect service or the prompt delivery of a good; a happy couple who get engaged and promise marriage to each other. I have to mention, though, that I do not principally regard legal oaths, contracts, or marriages as commissive speech. These acts may contain commissive elements but are rather declarative acts at their core, declaring a reality to exist and by doing so bringing it to life. Commitments which precede these acts and commit the speaker to perform a certain act in the future or to refrain from performing a certain act in the future are commissive acts.

There is certainly less expressive speech in legal language compared with the other categories of illocutionary speech. This is surprising at first sight, as legal practice is undoubtedly full of expressions of feelings or attitudes.[102] Legal scholar Denis Brion, for instance, observes that rituals of adjudication intersperse dispassionate rational phases with fairly emotional interludes.[103] By way of an example, sociologist Brenda Danet points at the tradition of the judge allowing the defendant to add something after the hearing of evidence as an opportunity to express emotions such as remorse or complaint about unfair treatment.[104] However, the law itself is hesitant when it comes to attributing feelings and their expressions a legal function. This explains why there is not much expressive speech to be found in legal language itself. Nevertheless, legal scholar Ho Hock Lai has emphasized that expressive speech can be found in some types of guilty verdicts. Every verdict of guilt is primarily declarative, as it changes the defendant's status from accused to convict. Having said this, some adjudication traditions also use verdicts to express the social unworthiness of the deed, as Ho

[101] Amselek, "Philosophy of Law and the Theory of Speech Acts," *Ratio Juris* 1 (1988), 191.

[102] E.g., Posner, "Law and the Emotions," *The Georgetown Law Journal* 89 (2001), 1977–2012; Abrams/Keren, "Who's Afraid of Law and the Emotions?," *Minnesota Law Review* 94 (2010), 1997–2074; Bandes/Blumenthal, "Emotion and the Law," *Annual Review of Law and Social Science* 8 (2012), 161–181; Grossi, "Understanding Law and Emotion," *Emotion Review* 7 (2015), 55–60.

[103] See Brion, "The Ritual of the Judicial Opinion," in Lindgren/Knaak, eds, *Ritual and Semiotics*, New York, Peter Lang, 1997, 13–14.

[104] See Danet, "Language in the Legal Process," *Law & Society Review* 14 (1980), 459.

finds, "A guilty verdict does more than declare or assert an ascription of a legal character to the facts; it also communicates the negative attitude that is expressed in that ascription."[105] Ho is careful not to confuse the jurors' or judge's expressive speech with their personal moral judgments, as moral judging is not a legal category. He therefore clarifies that the expressive dimension of sentencing must be part of the verdict itself to rate as legal speech. He discerns this to be the case whenever one may detect "an attitude of criticism or blame for the act that is, at the same time, declared and asserted in the verdict."[106]

Declarations are the last category of speech acts, according to Searle's taxonomy. They have a major relevance for the law. All legal speech acts that bring about something new and change a reality are declarative speech acts. Many of the examples alluding to the performative nature of the law as mentioned in my study so far are declarations: the judge's declaring the guilt of a defendant or the registrar's declaring a couple to be spouses. These acts share their declarative nature with legal acts such as charges, judicial confessions, pleas of guilty or not guilty, lawyers' objections, the creation of a corporation, a university's appointment of a professor, a manager's dismissal of an employee, and with sales contracts.[107]

Status Function Declarations

In his social ontology *Making the Social World*, Searle identifies declarations as those speech acts which underlie not just most of our legal realities but in fact all institutional facts. He holds them responsible for creating "status functions," those functions imposed on individuals or objects which enable them to transcend their natural functioning to act according to a collectively recognized status. Searle explains,

> [A] piece of private property, the president of the United States, a twenty-dollar bill, and a professor in a university are all people or objects that are able to perform certain functions in virtue of the fact that they have a collectively recognized status that enables them to perform those functions in a way they could not do without the collective recognition of the status.[108]

[105] Ho, "What Does a Verdict Do?," *International Commentary on Evidence* 4 (2006), 22.
[106] Ibid.
[107] See Danet, "Language in the Legal Process," *Law & Society Review* 14 (1980), 460; Searle, *Making the Social World*, Oxford, Oxford University Press, 2010, 97–100.
[108] Searle, *Making the Social World*, Oxford, Oxford University Press, 2010, 7.

According to Searle, it is the merit of declarations to achieve those status transformations which attribute individuals or objects with status functions. It is "the power of the Declaration," as he finds, which gives rise to "an institutional reality, a reality of governments, universities, marriages, private property, money, and all the rest of it."[109] He holds, "We create private property, money, government, marriage, and a thousand other phenomena by representing them as existing."[110] This power of declaratives to use speech to create an institutional reality according to the declaration is what makes declarative acts most interesting for my study.

Searle develops a twofold taxonomy of declarative speech as those acts which constitute linguistic institutional facts and those which constitute extra-linguistic institutional facts. He observes,

> [O]nly a very tiny number of changes can be brought about in the world solely by saying that one is making those changes by that very utterance. For nonsupernaturally endowed human beings, these fall into two classes: the creation of purely linguistic institutional facts . . . and extra-linguistic institutional facts.[111]

Searle speaks of linguistic institutional facts to denote those effects of declarative speech which rely on the power of language as an institution only. He mentions the example of a promise, which is a linguistic institutional fact, as the binding force of the promise comes into being merely through speech. Saying "I promise" brings about the obligation to fulfill the promise. Extra-linguistic institutional facts, on the contrary, require extra-linguistic institutions to attribute speech with declarative power. Searle gives the example of a command, which is effective only if an extra-linguistic institution—like the parent-child relationship, a working relationship, or a military rank—attributes the speaker's command with declarative effectiveness. Searle also mentions the example of marriage, as the registrar's power to declare a couple married does not derive from speech only but requires the effective frame of extra-linguistic institutions, such as a state's marriage law and administrative regulations based on which a certain person assumes the registrar's office.

[109] Ibid., 16.
[110] Ibid., 86.
[111] Searle, "How Performatives Work," *Linguistics and Philosophy* 12 (1989), 554–555.

Deontic Powers

These institutions automatically hold "deontic powers," Searle's term for requirements, responsibilities, obligations, duties, rights, and authorizations. He maintains, "all institutional facts by definition carry a deontology, however limited or weak it may be."[112] He goes on to explain the reason for this by stating, "We have a capacity to create a reality by representing it as existing. The only reality that we can so create is a reality of deontology. It is a reality that confers rights, responsibilities, and so on."[113] So whenever declarative speech brings an institution into being, it also creates deontic powers like requirements, responsibilities, obligations, duties, rights, or authorizations. For Searle, this finding is of core relevance for his social ontology, as he reckons "these rights, responsibilities, and so on are the glue that holds human society together."[114] Deontic powers have this essential social function as they do not merely apply to key institutional facts of human society, such as property, the presidency, or money, but apply to every declarative speech act. Searle explains this everyday deontology of declarations by giving the example of buying some friends a beer in the pub. He narrates,

> Let us suppose in a pub that I get up from the table and go to the bar and order three beers. I then carry the beers back to the table and set them down. I say, "This one is Sally's; this one is Marianne's; and this one is mine." . . . By making these utterances, I have in fact created new rights. Indeed, they were more than statements; they were deontic commitments of a very special kind. I created a reality according to which, for example, Sally has certain rights that Marianne does not have and Marianne has rights that Sally does not have. This would come out in the fact that if Marianne tried to drink Sally's beer, Sally would have a legitimate complaint.[115]

In this context, Searle also illuminates that declarative speech does not necessarily come with words. He writes, "Indeed I need not say anything. Just pushing the beer in the direction of their new owners can be a speech act."[116] This observation is particularly relevant with regard to my study, as legal communications function not only based on words but also based on gestures serving as speech. Facial expressions, body movements, postures, and other nonverbal elements of communication are part of the performative repertoire of the law. Legal scholar Bernard Hibbitts dedicated an article to "The Embodiment of Law in Gesture,"

112 Searle, *Making the Social World*, Oxford, Oxford University Press, 2010, 24.
113 Ibid., 89.
114 Ibid.
115 Ibid., 88–89.
116 Ibid., 89.

focusing on the role that gestures play as legal expressions. He emphasizes that legal speech is not about verbal expressions alone but also relies on the physical performance of those involved. He mentions, for instance, "raising one's right hand close to the body to signify the taking of an oath"[117] and the joining of the spouses' hands as the gesture with which a marriage was contracted according to Roman law and in medieval times.[118] Hibbitts admits that literate modernity has curbed the richness of the legal gestures of the past to some extent, so that the law has become more of a textual reality than a physically performed one.[119] What he fails to note when proposing this is that writing might also often rate as a legal gesture. In most modern legal cultures, signing is one essential action of numerous legal transactions. Signing is most certainly one of the most common gestures in legal practice with a constitutive effect for many legal realities. Contracts, wills, and confessions—many legal acts of literate modernity require a signature, some acts require a signature to come into being, and others exist prior to signing but require a signature for confirmation and documentation. However, Hibbitts is certainly right to observe that literate modernity has focused on words so that performative gestures are seldom far from verbal action, uttered or written. Hence, legal speech frequently employs both verbal and gestural elements to constitute speech acts.

Early speech act theory was fairly absorbed with words. Speech act theorists mostly focused on verbal expressions, detecting declaratives in expressions like "I declare . . . ," "I pronounce . . . ," "I install you as . . . ," "I baptize you . . . ," and "You are dismissed." Some much-cited examples of declaratives are those sentences Searle quotes repeatedly in his studies, like " 'I resign', 'You're fired', 'I excommunicate you', 'I christen this ship, the battleship Missouri', 'I appoint you chairman', and 'War is hereby declared.' "[120] However, his more recent works, like *Making the Social World*, while still showing a great fascination for verbal declarations, are more sensitive to the fact that human speech is not entirely about words and also about nonverbal acts of communication. But in identifying declarative speech, it is still helpful to look out for verbal expressions like "I declare," "I order," and so forth. Yet sometimes, declarative utterances are less explicit. In legal language, as John Austin discerns, the indicators are often tinier, as certain words like "hereby" might serve as markers of performative legal speech.[121] Dennis Kurzon takes up this observation as a riposte to legal scholar David Mellinkoff's prominent critique of legal language. Mellinkoff had criticized legal language precisely because it uses whimsical words like "hereby," as he found

[117] Hibbitts, "Making Motions," *Journal of Contemporary Legal Issues* 6 (1995), 53.
[118] See ibid., 58.
[119] See ibid., 72.
[120] Searle, "A Classification of Illocutionary Acts," *Language in Society* 5 (1976), 13.
[121] See Austin, *How to Do Things with Words*, Oxford, Clarendon Press, 1962, 57–58, 61.

those expressions vague, lacking any particular utility in legal communication, and unnecessarily pompous. I will return to his criticism in chapter 5. Kurzon, on the contrary, detects a distinct merit to terms like "hereby" as they help to identify speech clearly as declarative speech. He notes, "Mellinkoff . . . may be right when he says that *hereby* gives the flavour of the law but it is certainly not vague, as he maintains; it is a marker of a performative and more specifically a legal performative."[122]

Sacramental Speech

Studying how the law relies on performative and particularly declarative language to bring about legal realities and how it frequently uses archaic, mystical, and liturgical language to do so raises the evident question about points of intersection between law and religion. With regard to the Catholic debates, one such intersection is exceptionally manifest in the phenomenon of the Catholic sacraments. The sacraments are performative actions which pivotally operate with declarative speech. As such they are obviously religious symbols which bring about a religious reality by signifying it. However, they can also serve as legal signs, as some sacraments also signify a legal reality and by alluding to it bring it about. Baptism is a good example of this performative double function of the sacraments. As a religious ritual, baptism effectuates grace. As a legal act, it effectuates church membership. Hence, the law and the sacraments have much in common, something which becomes evident when explaining how they function in terms of speech act theory. I want to illuminate this by referring to the Catholic law of sacraments. The law of the sacraments is a field in which the performative functioning of the law and the legal character of religious acts are intertwined with the most remarkable results, including for the law and language debate. One case example which I find most instructive combines both perspectives. It is a case from the law of baptism, to which the Congregation for the Doctrine of the Faith responded in 2008.[123] The congregation was confronted with a baptismal practice that had taken root in Australian parishes, where the pastors performing baptism had used an alternative baptismal formula to avoid the masculine sound of the classical Trinitarian formula, "I baptize you in the

[122] Kurzon, *It Is Hereby Performed*, Amsterdam, John Benjamins, 1986, 7.

[123] See Congregation for the Doctrine of the Faith, "Responses to Questions Proposed on the Validity of Baptism Conferred with the Formulas 'I baptize you in the name of the Creator, and of the Redeemer, and of the Sanctifier' and 'I baptize you in the name of the Creator, and of the Liberator, and of the Sustainer,'" February 1, 2008, https://www.vatican.va/roman_curia/congregations/cfaith/documents/rc_con_cfaith_doc_20080201_validity-baptism_en.html.

For further reading on this case and on a more recent 2020 case, see Hahn, "Invalid Baptismal Formulas," *Ecclesiastical Law Journal* 23 (2021), 19–33.

name of the Father, and of the Son, and of the Holy Spirit." Instead, they had used the formulas "I baptize you in the name of the Creator, and of the Redeemer, and of the Sanctifier" and "I baptize you in the name of the Creator, and of the Liberator, and of the Sustainer." The congregation had to answer to the question if a baptismal ritual in which those two formulas were used could be regarded as a valid baptism. Speech act theory could likewise ask whether the illocution "I baptize you" in combination with the altered Trinitarian formula did indeed effectuate what it was supposed to, namely, a successful act of baptism. The congregation answered this question in the negative. While it did not provide any reason why it had decided in this way, an explanation might lie in the Council of Trent's teaching on the sacraments. According to Tridentine doctrine, a sacrament is only considered to have been administered validly if the right matter and the right formula are used.[124] In cases in which the formula is altered, thus deviating from the exact wording prescribed, the whole procedure is suspected of being invalid, thereby giving rise to the presumption that the illocutionary speech act has failed to achieve its purpose.

sMost intriguingly, this case, which was decided by the Congregation for the Doctrine of the Faith, is very similar to one of John Austin's famous examples of illocutionary speech acts which go awry. Austin referred to the baptism of a ship several times to explain illocutionary acts. A person chosen to perform the act, frequently a celebrity, smashes a bottle of champagne against the stem of a ship while uttering a naming sentence like "I name this ship the Queen Elizabeth."[125] This describes a successful ship-naming ceremony. Austin then used the same example to show how illocutionary acts can fail, stating,

> Suppose, for example, I see a vessel on the stocks, walk up and smash the bottle hung at the stem, proclaim 'I name this ship the *Mr. Stalin*' and for good measure kick away the chocks: but the trouble is, I was not the person chosen to name it (whether or not—an additional complication—*Mr. Stalin* was the destined name . . .). We can all agree . . . that the ship was not thereby named.[126]

The act was unsuccessful—"void," as Austin called it—insofar as the ship was not successfully named by the action performed, because the person performing it was not the person chosen to perform it, thus acting without the necessary "capacity," as Austin called it—"power" or "authority" would be a typical canonical term to express the same thought. This is one reason why illocutionary acts may

[124] See Council of Trent, "Decree *Ad consummationem* on the Sacraments," seventh session, March 3, 1547, in Mansi et al., eds, *Sacrorum Conciliorum Nova et Amplissima Collectio*, vol. 33, Paris, Hubert Welter, 1902, 48–60.

[125] Austin, *How to Do Things with Words*, Oxford, Oxford University Press, 1962, 5.

[126] Ibid., 23.

fail; not choosing the right procedure could be another one, Austin contended. A successful illocutionary act, he stated, required the following, "There must exist an accepted conventional procedure having a certain conventional effect, the procedure to include the uttering of certain words by certain persons in certain circumstances."[127]

Ex Opere Operato

For a theologian like me, it is utterly fascinating to read this dense description of all that it takes to perform illocutionary acts successfully, as it fully evokes Trent's doctrine on the sacraments. The Council of Trent, in teaching how the sacraments function, formulated the doctrine of *ex opere operato*, understanding the sacraments as efficacious only in those cases in which they are administered correctly, irrespective of the individual godliness of the person administering them.[128] It is sufficient, the council taught, if the ministers act with the intention of doing that which the church does.[129] In a similar vein, the receiver of a sacrament, in order to receive it validly, needs no personal faith but only a readiness to acquiesce to whatever the church connects with the sacrament. So the personal requirements for the valid administration of sacraments are very basic. As such, they serve as "certain circumstances" which Austin cited as one condition for performing illocutionary acts successfully. All eyes then are on the correct administration of the sacraments, the "procedure," as Austin called it. The ritual needs to be flawless, as in Austin's example of a ship's baptism. The receiver must be capable of receiving the sacrament. The minister must be competent to administer the sacrament and authorized to perform the act; Austin, in this vein, referred to "certain persons." In administering the sacrament, the minister must use the right matter and the right formula—"certain words." Take away one of those conditions and the validity of the sacrament is in question, just as the declarative act of a ship's baptism goes awry.

[127] Ibid., 26.

[128] See Council of Trent, "Decree *Ad consummationem* on the Sacraments," seventh session, March 3, 1547, canon 8, in Mansi et al., eds, *Sacrorum Conciliorum Nova et Amplissima Collectio*, vol. 33, Paris, Hubert Welter, 1902, 52–53.

[129] See ibid., canon 11, in Mansi et al., eds, *Sacrorum Conciliorum Nova et Amplissima Collectio*, vol. 33, Paris, Hubert Welter, 1902, 53.

True Communication

The core moment of the sacramental ritual culminates in the uttering of the correct formula, or in a declarative speech act, in Austin's terms. We can identify the importance of that speech act for the effectiveness of sacramental acts by relating to a twentieth-century canon law debate, namely, how relevant it is that the words of a sacramental formula are actually vocalized. Canonist Edward Peters dedicated an article to the related question of whether and under which conditions the church may ordain deaf-mute priest candidates that could celebrate the sacraments in sign language only.[130] The church did not in fact ordain deaf men until the 1970s due to doubts over whether they could administer the sacraments validly without vocalizing the sacramental formulas. Peters collected a number of canon law interpretations which, even in the twentieth century, still considered the ordination of deaf-mute men as forbidden by divine law, because only those capable of uttering the formulas vocally and audibly could administer the sacraments validly.[131] So for a long time it was a cause of disagreement whether a sacramental formula gestured in sign language only would meet the Tridentine requirements on valid sacraments. While there was never any doubt that a formula that was both vocalized and signed met the requirements, some canonists were doubtful whether sign language alone could be interpreted as the "utterance" of words required by sacramental and liturgical law. Peters himself, after weighing up both sides of the debate, concluded that what doctrine and law required was "the direct *expression* or *communication* of the form, not its 'orality.' "[132] Consequently, he found sign language did in fact meet the Tridentine requirement on sacramental form. Ecclesiastical practice nowadays accords with this view. Since the 1970s, it has been possible for deaf-mute men to be ordained. Today, their ministry is appreciated as being exceptionally valuable for deaf-mute communities. This development is noteworthy for several reasons. It shows that the church in the twentieth century adopted a broadened concept of language in which "utterance" is not restricted to oral communication like speech but includes forms of visual communication such as that performed by sign language. However, it also shows the relevance of direct, immediate, and presentist speech for many declarative acts. In many cases, only a live expression is accepted as effective for the successful performance of sacramental rituals, in the same way as it is often merely a particular utterance or signature at a certain time and in a specific context which is capable of performing "legal magic." Hence, law and religion likewise struggle to define which forms of speech fulfill the conditions

[130] See Peters, "The Ordination of Men Bereft of Speech and the Celebration of Sacraments in Sign Language," *Studia Canonica* 42 (2008), 331–345.
[131] See ibid., 334.
[132] Ibid., 343.

of successful sacramental speech. We can also discover a similar tension in the Catholic debates on administering sacraments online, which were specifically vivid during the COVID-19 pandemic. Admittedly, Catholic doctrine is rather traditional and therefore still struggles to accept online sacraments. However, there are at least some voices which seem open to the idea of administering some sacraments, such as the sacrament of penance, remotely—over the phone or online—while they generally dismiss the idea of administering them via email or text message.[133] This illustrates that there is a tendency to accept declarative speech as constitutive of sacramental effects in liturgical settings merely when it is live speech which simultaneously brings about its intended effect.[134] Legal scholar and theologian Matthew Cavedon connects this observation with the finding that both law and religion share a tendency to insist on the physical presence of religious or legal subjects, discerning, "Litigation and liturgy have much in common. Both demand rapt attention. And both recognize that that cannot be achieved without engaging the body."[135] He applies his observation to typical liturgies of law and religion, namely, adjudication and worship, noting, "Courts and the Catholic Church still expect you to show up. Both aim to hold high attention. And both understand that this depends on fleshier aspects of who, when, where, and with whom we are."[136] Hence, Cavedon connects presentist characteristics of legal and religious liturgies with control over the congregation's attention by taking some kind of physical hold of them. We can, in any case, also understand his argument in relation to language issues. In sacramental rituals which culminate in the uttering of a declarative formula, such as the Eucharistic transubstantiation or the judge's guilty verdict which transforms an accused into a convict, the correct utterance is of paramount importance. The ministers in charge must therefore take the utmost care to utter the words correctly and ensure that there is a congregation present which perceives and receives these words and their result. Consequently, direct and often also synchronic communication is key to both the Catholic sacraments and legal declarations, which we can call the "sacraments of the law." Of course, this does not exclude the possibility that our understanding of what is direct and synchronic communication

[133] E.g., Congregation for the Doctrine of the Faith, "Note on the Validity and Liceity of Administering the Sacrament of Penance via Phone," 25 November 1989, *Archiv für katholisches Kirchenrecht* 158 (1989), 484.

[134] Dennis Kurzon, in any case, alluded to the peculiarity of declarations with a pending effect, such as wills, which do not effectuate the intended action of bequeathing a certain thing on a certain person *in* declaring it, but postpone their effect, as a will becomes effective only after the testator's death. Hence it does not bring about the new reality instantaneously, as do most other declarations, but constitutes it now to take effect in the future; see Kurzon, *It Is Hereby Performed*, Amsterdam, John Benjamins, 1986, 42.

[135] See Cavedon, "Physical Presence for Court and the Catholic Church," October 2, 2020, https://canopyforum.org/2020/10/02/attention-physical-presence-for-court-and-the-catholic-church.

[136] Ibid.

can change. Just as the church could learn that words expressed in sign language are true utterances, traditional institutions at present have the chance to learn that words exchanged through videoconferencing can be a real conversation. We may expect that our understanding of what is appropriate performative language is in a constant process of development and is also currently subject to change due to what many of us have learned about online communication during the COVID-19 pandemic.

3
Idiosyncrasies of Legal Language

The law and language debate has inspired many authors to take a closer look at the particular characteristics of legal language. These characteristics differ profoundly depending on the source language consulted to shape a legal language and on the legal tradition in which a legal terminology has developed. The "sound" of the law is, for instance, significantly different in legal texts created by a common or a civil law tradition. Nevertheless, I would like to set aside these differences for a moment and ask if there are any commonalities in grammar and style that most legal languages share.

3.1 The Grammar of the Law

There seem to be at least some features which may be found in all or most of the legal languages worldwide. On the whole, most legal languages rely heavily on nouns and nominalizations rather than on verbs or verbal constructs.[1] Legal linguist Heikki Mattila suspects this prevalence of nouns is grounded in the idea that nouns appear to be more objective than other word classes.[2] One consequence is certainly that it makes legal language more difficult to understand, as Veda and Robert Charrow explained in their empirical study on the comprehensibility of jury instructions. The authors alluded to a finding from linguistic theory, namely, that nouns and nominalizations are more difficult to comprehend than verbs because "verbs and verb phrases are more basic than certain classes of nouns," insofar as "anything that makes a verb less verb-like and more noun-like creates abstraction."[3] A second reason why a heavily nominal style is more difficult to understand might lie in the fact that nouns are often used in the place of subordinate clauses, thus condensing the content of a clause into one or just a few words.

[1] E.g., Tiersma, *Legal Language*, Chicago, IL, The University of Chicago Press, 1999, 77–79.

[2] See Mattila, "Legal Vocabulary," in Solan/Tiersma, eds, *The Oxford Handbook of Language and Law*, Oxford, Oxford University Press, 2012, 32.

[3] Charrow/Charrow, "Making Legal Language Understandable," *Columbia Law Review* 79 (1979), 1321.

The Language of Canon Law. Judith Hahn, Oxford University Press. © Oxford University Press 2023.
DOI: 10.1093/oso/9780197674246.003.0003

Gender Issues

In languages in which nouns are marked according to grammatical gender, such as Latin, French, or German, legal language is dominated by the use of the generic masculine, something which has been criticized by feminist legal scholars and linguists alike.[4] The same is true for the language of canon law. Neither the authentic Latin text of the Code nor its translations bother much with gender equality when it comes to language. While this is irritating in many respects, it does occasionally have its funny side, as the gender use in ecclesiastical marriage law shows. The first norm of marriage law, canon 1055 CIC/1983, is eager to state that marriage according to Catholic doctrine is a covenant between a man and a woman, only to continue referencing the spouses in the generic masculine as *baptizati* and *catholici* (see canons 1055 §§1 and 2, 1059, 1061 §1 CIC/1983), as baptized and Catholic subjects who are, according to their respective generic endings, grammatically male. A similar example is mentioned by Heike Simon and Gisela Funk-Baker with regard to German criminal law, which criminalizes pimping by threatening with a prison sentence any grammatically male person who exploits "his" *Ehegatten oder Lebenspartner* (generic male spouse or partner) in prostitution (see section 181a, subsection 3 of the German Criminal Code).[5] Simon and Funk-Baker call this an oddity. However, these slightly comical examples do not conceal the fundamental problem connected with male dominance in many legal languages, which is the linguistic marginalization of women. Depriving society's female half of the chance to identify with the law, as Simon and Funk-Baker state, is a major problem which has not been solved at all satisfactorily in any of the languages concerned.

Passive Constructions

Most legal languages are equally infamous for making excessive use of the passive voice—canon law is no exception in this respect. German style fancies the passive anyway, so the difference between everyday language and legal language might not be so obvious in this particular case. However, interestingly, there is also a tendency to use the passive voice in legal speech in language cultures which do not usually tend to use the passive. English style typically prefers the

[4] E.g., Grabrucker, "Sprache als Herausforderung an die Rechtsgleichheit," in Fritsch-Oppermann, ed, *Die Rechtssprache*, Loccum, Evangelische Akademie, 1998, 68–79; Tiersma, *Legal Language*, Chicago, IL, The University of Chicago Press, 1999, 73–74; Simon/Funk-Baker, *Einführung in das deutsche Recht und die deutsche Rechtssprache*, 5th edn, Munich, C.H. Beck, 2013, 32–33.

[5] See Simon/Funk-Baker, *Einführung in das deutsche Recht und die deutsche Rechtssprache*, 5th edn, Munich, C.H. Beck, 2013, 32.

active voice rather than the passive, which is nevertheless still found disproportionately often in legal English. The passive voice has more of an abstract, impersonal sound to it than the active voice, which must always name a subject, an active agent, in a sentence. The truncated passive, on the contrary, allows speakers and writers to obscure the agent.[6] The use of the passive voice therefore frequently has the effect on the hearers or readers of sounding purely imperative without specifying the source of a command, thereby avoiding giving it a face, so to speak. The passive, to some extent, recalls the authoritative sound of the authoritarian state. For this reason, it sometimes strikes a discordant note in the ears of modern legal subjects, as legal scholar and novelist Heinz Müller-Dietz observed.[7] As the church has a monarchical structure and applies an absolutist style of governance, it might be less surprising to find this sound in canon law, too. This authoritative sound is often expressed by the use of the passive voice in canonical texts. A typical example is ecclesiastical penal law. The regular structure of ecclesiastical penal norms consists of a "Qui . . . puniatur" ("Who . . . is to be punished") construction confronting wrongdoers with a faceless threat of suffering penalties for transgressing ecclesiastical laws. It is a latent irony though, that this tune no longer impresses many Catholics, particularly in the churches of the West, a phenomenon due to canon law's rapid loss of effectiveness in modernity. Hence, the language of canon law cultivates an authoritarian tune which nevertheless often fails to have its desired effect of coercing ecclesiastical legal subjects into abiding by the law. While this is interesting to note from a sociological point of view, I will not follow up on this train of thought in this study.[8]

Challenging Syntax

All over the globe, the syntax of legal sentences is usually "distinctly idiosyncratic in terms of both the structure and arrangement of the principal sentence elements,"[9] notes Risto Hiltunen. Common law legal texts contain remarkably long and complex sentences, often with more than one main clause and several subordinate clauses; they contain longer sentences than are usually found in other kinds of prose, and are often more complex.[10] Maurizio Gotti explains the peculiarity of common law's "remarkable sentence length" as "required by the

[6] See Tiersma, *Legal Language*, Chicago, IL, The University of Chicago Press, 1999, 74–79.

[7] See Müller-Dietz, "Rechtssprache," in Fritsch-Oppermann, ed, *Die Rechtssprache*, Loccum, Evangelische Akademie, 1998, 26.

[8] On this issue, see Hahn, *Foundations of a Sociology of Canon Law*, Cham, Springer Nature, 2022.

[9] Hiltunen, "The Grammar and Structure of Legal Texts," in Solan/Tiersma, eds, *The Oxford Handbook of Language and Law*, Oxford, Oxford University Press, 2012, 41.

[10] See ibid., 41–43; Gotti, "Text and Genre," in Solan/Tiersma, eds, *The Oxford Handbook of Language and Law*, Oxford, Oxford University Press, 2012, 53–54.

great number of details to be inserted and the requirement that specifications should be precise and clear."[11] However, it is not sentence length as such which makes a legal sentence challenging to understand, but a mix of contentual, terminological, and grammatical complexity, as Charrow and Charrow observed.[12] These elements can be found in many common law texts. Gail Stygall, who linguistically analyzed US immigration forms, found them extremely complex in comparison with the sentence structure used in English conversation. Whereas 74 percent of sentences spoken in English conversation consisted of one clause only, as Stygall found, a mere 28 percent of the sentences used in the application form I-485 were single-clause sentences. 25 percent were two-clause sentences, compared to 22 percent in conversation, and 25 percent three-clause sentences, compared to only 4 percent in conversation. 22 percent of the sentences used in the form consisted of *four* clauses (!)—whereas four-clause sentences basically *never* appear in English conversation.[13] Stygall concluded, "On clause embedding alone, the I-485 presents a much higher level of difficulty, even for the native-English-speaking, highly proficient and educated reader."[14] The difficulty is increased, she found, by embedded clauses, containing exceptions or conditions. Many Anglo-American statutes are similarly difficult to digest due to their enormous sentence length, particularly for untrained readers from a civil law background. I attempted to read the British Equality Act 2010[15] a couple of months ago—and failed. To explain my problem, I will just mention the title of the act here:

> An Act to make provision to require Ministers of the Crown and others when making strategic decisions about the exercise of their functions to have regard to the desirability of reducing socio-economic inequalities; to reform and harmonise equality law and restate the greater part of the enactments relating to discrimination and harassment related to certain personal characteristics; to enable certain employers to be required to publish information about the differences in pay between male and female employees; to prohibit victimisation in certain circumstances; to require the exercise of certain functions to be with regard to the need to eliminate discrimination and other prohibited conduct; to enable duties to be imposed in relation to the exercise of public

[11] Gotti, "Text and Genre," in Solan/Tiersma, eds, *The Oxford Handbook of Language and Law*, Oxford, Oxford University Press, 2012, 58–59.

[12] See Charrow/Charrow, "Making Legal Language Understandable," *Columbia Law Review* 79 (1979), 1320.

[13] See Stygall, "Textual Barriers to United States Immigration," in Cotterill, ed, *Language in the Legal Process*, Basingstoke, Palgrave Macmillan, 2002, 44.

[14] Ibid., 45.

[15] See Parliament of the United Kingdom, "Equality Act 2010," April 8, 2010, *2010 Chapter 15*; for further examples, see Williams, "Legal English and Plain Language," *ESP Across Cultures* 1 (2004), 113–114.

> procurement functions; to increase equality of opportunity; to amend the law relating to rights and responsibilities in family relationships; and for connected purposes.

That was just the title. I will try again to read the whole document on a day when I am more focused; the arrangement of the text, especially the paragraphing, is so complex that I will need all of my concentration to work through it. Maybe someone more used to the composition of Anglo-American statute law would not agree, but as a reader who is used to civil law I find it extremely difficult to cope with the common law style of composing statutes. Mercifully, there seems to have been a tendency over the last couple of years to shorten common law statute sentences and to make them less complex, as Hiltunen observes,[16] so there is still hope for me.

Sentences found in civil law texts are usually less long and less complex. Gotti describes their characteristic as follows, "Civil law sentences are shorter with a less strict use of paragraphing; this makes the understanding of the sentence easier, but renders the reconstruction of the relationship between the various sentences more complex."[17] When it comes to the length and complexity of legal sentences, the difference between common law and civil law is at least slightly surprising, because English—as the main language of common law—usually sticks to shorter and less complex sentences compared to some civil law languages such as German. While German prose is infamous for its horribly long and complex sentences, English prose is less so. So it is somewhat unexpected to find examples of the exact opposite when it comes to legal texts. Gotti illuminates this phenomenon, when writing:

> [I]n the civil law system the judiciary is entrusted with the task of construing, interpreting, and applying the general principles outlined in the civil code to specific real-life situations; this requirement therefore privileges stylistic choices such as generality and simplicity of expression. The common law system, instead, is based on the principle of precedence, by means of which the decisions taken by one judge become binding on all subsequent similar cases; this system therefore regards certainty of expression as the most valued quality in legal drafting.[18]

16 See Hiltunen, "The Grammar and Structure of Legal Texts," in Solan/Tiersma, eds, *The Oxford Handbook of Language and Law*, Oxford, Oxford University Press, 2012, 50.

17 Gotti, "Text and Genre," in Solan/Tiersma, eds, *The Oxford Handbook of Language and Law*, Oxford, Oxford University Press, 2012, 59.

18 Ibid., 58.

However, it is impossible to generalize this point. While sentences in German statute law are usually clearly arranged, German judges rarely win any prizes for uncluttered speech. And exceptions also apply for European legislation. It is hard to think of any texts from a civil law tradition which are composed more poorly than some European directives. Even individuals with a general legal training often find their content hard to understand. As a sample, I can suggest reading European Council Directive 2000/78/EC for establishing a general framework for equal treatment in employment and occupation.[19] It leaves a vivid impression of how complicated it is to work through European documents and why European legislation is often received unfavorably even by those European citizens who support a strong Union.

Canon law presents itself today mostly as typical civil law. The sentences used in ecclesiastical legal texts are not always easy to understand, as many of them contain relative clauses and so-called "whiz deletions," the deletion of an introductory phrase such as "which is" for subordinate clauses. However, the norms are usually short—there are merely slightly more than a dozen norms in the Code of Canon Law which contain more than 60 words; in comparison, the title of the British Equality Act 2010 contains 140 words. One of the longest norms in the Code is 85-word canon 377 §3 CIC/1983, which describes the complex procedure of the pontifical legate who has to make a list of three suitable candidates for a vacant episcopal see to prepare the papal appointment of a new diocesan bishop by involving agents such as the local metropolitan and suffragan bishops of the region, members of the local college of consultors and cathedral chapters, and the Apostolic See. Here it is principally the multiple agents which require previous consultation which make the text slightly lengthy. Another example taken from the Code may illustrate that the principle "the longer the better" is not true in all cases, particularly when it comes to legal norms. The legal complex of the Code in which the legislator is by far the wordiest is in canons 528 and 529 CIC/1983. These two canons, each subdivided into two paragraphs, together contain 278 words—and virtually no justiciable content. In short, they use inspiring and uplifting prose to describe the duties and qualities of a good pastor, who has to take care of all and everything within the boundaries of his parish. The abundant list of pastoral duties, ranging from more concrete obligations such as giving the Sunday homily to rather abstract obligations such as the striving to know his parish members, is more of a poem than a legal text. As a piece of devotional literature for zealous pastors one would expect this kind of genre more in a pastoral

[19] Council of the European Union, "Council Directive 2000/78/EC Establishing a General Framework for Equal Treatment in Employment and Occupation," November 27, 2000, *Official Journal* L 303, vol. 43, December 2, 2000, 16–22.

companion than in ecclesiastical statute law. Many words, as one can derive from this example, often serve to make legal texts longer rather than better.

Expressing Commands

As legal rules are key for the law and its language, law and language scholars have paid considerable attention to the way norms are phrased, particularly to the way in which the legislators verbalize legal commands. For canon law, some scholars have contributed to shedding more light on the language of canonical norms. Canonist Péter Erdő scrutinized the canonical obligation terminology as found in the authentic Latin text of the Code,[20] and canonist Thomas Amann devoted a study to analyzing the Latin terminology of obligations and prohibitions in ecclesiastical law.[21] First of all, they found that Canon Law Latin uses a wide range of terminology to express permission. Erdő, who collected all the different ways of permitting used in the present Code of Canon Law, detected permissions in verbs such as *permittere*, *posse*, *competit*, *spectat*, *non prohibetur*, *valere*, and *licet*; in noun and verbal constructions such as *fas est*, *ius est*, *ius habet*, *ius gaudet*, *facultatem habere*, and *postestatem habere*; connected with nouns such as *facultas*, *libertas*, and *licentia*; and in adjectival and verbal constructions such as *liber est*, *habilis est*, *capax est*, and *licite est*.[22] Amann then meticulously described the ways in which the legislator expresses duties and prohibitions. He observed that the legislator mostly uses the present tense and rarely the future tense to verbalize obligations and prohibitions. Exceptions in the future tense are found in canons 354, 401 §1, 690 §1, 1233, 1281 §3, 1455 §3, 1479, 1550 §1, 1565 §2, 1610 §1, 1651, 1703 §2, and 1706 CIC/1983. Commands are usually expressed with certain verbs (for instance, *obligari*, *teneri*, *debere*, *requirere*, *exigere*, *oportet*), with verbs in the subjunctive mood or as gerundives, or with nouns (such as *obligatio*, *onus*, *officium*), sometimes in the possessive genitive case.[23] Canon law often uses the subjunctive mood in a jussive sense to articulate obligations or in a prohibitive sense to express prohibitions. Examples can be found in canons 209 §2, 227, 233, 245 §1, 246, 254 §1, 275 §2, 276 §2, 279 §1, 282 §1, 287 §1, 328, 339, 383 §3, 384, 385, 386 §2, 387, 528, 529, and 532 CIC/1983.[24] Gerundives are used in canons 280, 1105 §2, 1111 §2, 1117, 1148 §2,

[20] See Erdő, "Expressiones obligationis et exhortationis in Codice Iuris Canonici," *Periodica de Re Morali Canonica Liturgica* 76 (1987), 3–27.

[21] See Amann, "Gebot und Verbot in der Rechtssprache des CIC," in Geringer/Schmitz, eds, *Communio in Ecclesiae Mysterio*, St. Ottilien, EOS, 2001, 3–28.

[22] See Erdő, "Expressiones obligationis et exhortationis in Codice Iuris Canonici," *Periodica de Re Morali Canonica Liturgica* 76 (1987), 11–16.

[23] See Amann, "Gebot und Verbot in der Rechtssprache des CIC," in Geringer/Schmitz, eds, *Communio in Ecclesiae Mysterio*, St. Ottilien, EOS, 2001, 7–27.

[24] See ibid., 10 fn. 47.

1158 §1, 1524 §3, and 1737 §2 CIC/1983. Amann named canons 182 §1, 377 §3, 449 §1, 457, 458, 473 §2, 493, 500 §1, 503, 533 §3, 567 §2, 576, 631 §1, 686 §2, 690 §1, 755 §§1–2, 757, 775 §2, 788 §3, 790 §1, 802 §1, 804 §1, 831 §2, 872, 892, 914, 767 §4, 1064, 1126, 1264, 1272, 1276 §1, 1277, 1296, 1297, 1428 §3, 1445 §3, 1553, and 1610 §2 CIC/1983 as examples for the use of a possessive genitive case.[25] It is interesting to note that the legislator barely uses the imperative to express a command.[26] There are a few examples of the imperative's use in the Code though: in canons 262, 637, 639 §4, 1564, and 1603 §2 CIC/1983. The Code therefore makes use of a wide range of terminological and grammatical choices to voice obligations and prohibitions in Latin. Their meanings are usually clear and may be transferred into the vernacular languages of the local churches without losing too much of a canon's original meaning. There is, however, one challenge which arises from those canons which use the subjunctive mood in a jussive or prohibitive sense respectively to express obligations and prohibitions. The use of the jussive presents difficulties, as Amann contended, because with regard to its meaning it is never obvious whether it constitutes a strict obligation or prohibition or rather a piece of advice, encouragement, or discouragement to do something or refrain from doing it.[27] A similar problem applies in other legal languages. In the English law and language community, there is a similar debate over whether the auxiliary verb "shall" is the best way of articulating a legal obligation and the use of "shall not" the optimal way of uttering a legal prohibition, as neither seem to disclose the obligatory nature of legal commands explicitly enough.[28] Legal scholar Catrin Fflur Huws reports with regard to legislation in the Welsh language that the National Assembly for Wales decided to use "must" for all legal obligations instead of "shall," which appears typically in British legislation elsewhere, to emphasize the obligatory nature of legal commands.[29] For the same reason Thomas Amann criticized the ecclesiastical legislator for not using clear expressions like *debere* or *necesse est* more often, to explicitly show whenever the law signifies strict obligations or prohibitions.[30]

For canon law, this problem of differentiating linguistically between strict legal rules and social or moral norms is exacerbated whenever translations of the law are concerned. Many languages including English do not have a jussive mood. Others, such as German, do, but then face the same challenge as the Latin

[25] See ibid., 9 fn. 36–38.

[26] See ibid., 8.

[27] See ibid., 10; on the same problem in the old Code, see Mörsdorf, *Die Rechtssprache des Codex Juris Canonici*, 2nd edn, Paderborn, Ferdinand Schöningh, 1967, 32.

[28] See Tiersma, *Legal Language*, Chicago, IL, The University of Chicago Press, 1999, 105–106.

[29] See Fflur Huws, "(Language + Law)2 = ?," in Freeman/Smith, eds, *Law and Language*, Oxford, Oxford University Press, 2013, 409.

[30] See Amann, "Gebot und Verbot in der Rechtssprache des CIC," in Geringer/Schmitz, eds, *Communio in Ecclesiae Mysterio*, St. Ottilien, EOS, 2001, 11.

text of the Code, namely, of leaving open whether the expression is meant to articulate strict obligation or prohibition or a softer encouragement or discouragement. The German canonists who translated the 1983 Code into German therefore engaged in intense discussion about how to deal with the Latin jussive in German.[31] With regard to obligations they decided against a literal translation of the jussive, and reviewed the alternative possibility of using auxiliary verb constructions, including either *sollen* ("shall") or *hat/haben zu* ("has/have to") and *ist/sind zu* ("is/are to") or *muss/müssen* ("must"), and mostly decided for the two middle options. They voted against "shall" as it sounds too soft, but also against "must," as the legislator usually expresses "must" with the Latin term *debere* in the authentic text. With regard to prohibitions they mostly translated the prohibitive mood with *darf nicht* ("may not").

3.2 The Terminology of the Law

With regard to terminology, legal texts consist of terms mostly taken from the local vernacular language supplemented by specific terms introduced for legal use only. I should already mention at this point in my study that the situation is slightly different for canon law when it comes to the use of vernacular languages, insofar as the official language of canon law is still the Latin language, which can hardly be called a "vernacular" anymore these days. Official legal texts of canon law are composed in Latin and use Latin terminology. However, for adjudication and administration as well as for canon law scholarship, the vernacular languages of the various local churches come into play. Canon law therefore always operates with a double terminology: the terms as found in the Latin texts and their translations in the respective languages of the local churches. This is somewhat unique compared with most other legal languages. Yet similarly to other legal languages, it is also the case for canon law that both the Latin and the vernacular texts exhibit a mix of common terminology and specific legal terminology. So there are always different categories of terms that are used in legal language. The majority of terms are taken from common language, terms which are used in legal contexts with the same or similar meanings to those attributed to them in their common use. Besides, the language of the law contains specific legal terms. These terms are either technical terms, which only exist in legal language, or terms which appear in legal and common language alike but carry a distinct meaning in legal language. I will provide an overview and examples of these categories in the following section.

[31] See Aymans, "Aus dem Vorwort zur ersten Auflage," in *Codex des Kanonischen Rechts*, 7th edn, Kevelaer, Butzon & Bercker, 2012, III.

Common Terms as Legal Terms

When the law speaks of "darkness," "velocity," or "windows," Dietrich Busse observes, it does so by referring to the meaning that is attributed to these terms by common language. Busse calls these terms "factual terms" in contrast to "legal terms," which describe specific legal facts.[32] However, legal terms also frequently coincide with terms used in common language. That the language of the law broadly overlaps with common language is by no way coincidental, as Busse shows with regard to the history of the German language. He identifies two historical movements which bear responsibility for this.[33] Busse finds the first wave of translating Law Latin into German in the eighteenth century to have been influential on the formation of standard German during that time. So German legal language and German standard language emerged not only during the same period in history, their development was also mutually influential. Later, a second wave of translation continued the Germanization of legal language during the processes of codification which yielded the penal code (*Reichsstrafgesetzbuch*) and the civil code (*Bürgerliches Gesetzbuch*). Relics of Law Latin were widely replaced with German terminology, thereby using standard German to create new German legal terms.

When it comes to the meaning of terms which exist in both languages, vernacular and legal language, it is, however, deceptive, as Busse warns his readers, to expect the same meaning to exist in common and legal language. This assumption would fail to account for the fact that the law is only interested in a specific segment of reality and views the social only through the lens of the law. So the meaning of a term is often slightly different in legal terminology than it is in everyday language. As a result, the meanings of terms in legal language, as intuitive as they may seem at first, might differ from everyday language so that making sense of them requires an awareness of the legal context in which they are used. Jo Ann Crandall and Veda and Robert Charrow mention the example of "fresh fish," which in common language is usually understood as describing fish which has been caught recently. In legal language, "fresh fish" does not refer to the date on which the fish has been caught or killed, but to the fish never having been frozen;[34] these different meanings likewise apply to the German term *Frischfisch*. To receive the message correctly, one first of all needs to know that common and legal language differ with regard to the meaning of "freshness" regarding fish, and, second, one needs to be aware of whether the term is used with a common

[32] See Busse, "Rechtssprache als Problem der Bedeutungsbeschreibung," *Sprache und Literatur* 29 (1998), 35.

[33] See ibid., 44–45.

[34] See Charrow/Crandall/Charrow, "Characteristics and Functions of Legal Language," in Kittredge/Lehrberger, eds, *Sublanguage*, Berlin, Walter de Gruyter, 1982, 179.

or a legal meaning in a particular situation. This is challenging, not only for sushi lovers.

"Lending" and "Loaning"

It was legal scholar Ulfried Neumann who used the example of a clichéed neighborly transaction concerning some eggs to demonstrate that terms cannot always simply be transferred from everyday use to the law and back into the German vernacular.[35] If somebody approaches his or her neighbor to get some eggs to bake a cake, German people in everyday language would call this "borrowing" some eggs and "lending" them to a neighbor, respectively. This does not concord with the legal language which regards "lending" as an agreement in which the lender of a thing permits the borrower to use the item at no charge (see section 598 of the German Civil Code), whereas the borrower is obliged to return the thing at the end of the period of time specified (see section 604, paragraph 1 of the German Civil Code). However, the terminology of "lending" is commonly used for helping out with this and that, including helping out with some eggs, even though nobody really expects the same eggs back after a period of time has elapsed. So "borrowing" and "lending" in everyday language are broad terms describing the act of helping somebody out with something, connected with the expectation of receiving either the same or an *equivalent* item in return after a while. However, the second meaning obviously does not concord with German legal language. In legal language, giving somebody some eggs with the expectation of getting back some *different* eggs after a period of time has elapsed is not "lending" (*leihen*) but "loaning" (*ein Darlehen geben*), an expression which nobody would ever use in everyday German for "lending" some eggs to a neighbor. Neumann stressed that this obvious difference between common and legal language does not mean that common language is less precise or sloppy in dealing with words.[36] In fact, both languages simply follow different rules. It would be ridiculous to ask a neighbor for a "loan" of three eggs, whereas it would simply be wrong to consider the giving of the eggs as "lending" in a legal context. Both languages follow their own rules, and terms have to make sense according to those rules and in each language system. This has to be kept in mind whenever common and legal language use concur—something which happens constantly. These differences are interesting to note and reveal a great deal about the necessary yet fragile relationship between the legal reality and the social reality of

[35] See Neumann, "Juristische Fachsprache und Umgangssprache," in Grewendorf, ed, *Rechtskultur als Sprachkultur*, Frankfurt am Main, Suhrkamp, 1992, 110.
[36] See ibid., 110–111.

everyday life. In this sense, Lawrence Solan and Peter Tiersma once noted that it is possible to learn much about a legal order by studying the language it uses. In any case, they contended, it is possible to learn most about it by comparing the language used within the legal system with the everyday language used in the same society or community.[37]

"Possession" and "Property"

Noting the differences or identifying the border between common and legal language is in any case challenging, to say the least. Harold Berman mentioned that many terms with a specific legal meaning even "disguise" the fact that they have been appropriated by the law by retaining their closeness to terms used in everyday language. This is even the case with those terms, Berman observed, which were derived by ancient or medieval lawyers or canon lawyers from colloquial Latin with the express intention of using them as legal terms. Berman explained his insight by referencing the term "property," which was initially taken from Latin legal terminology for legal use, but then also became widespread in common language, "Thus 'property' (from the Latin *proprietas*) still has the connotation of 'one's own,' and may be found outside the law, as we speak of the 'properties' of chemicals or the 'propriety' of a course of conduct."[38] So "property" today is used as a term in legal and common language alike, albeit not necessarily with the same meaning, as European languages show.[39] German legal language differentiates precisely between things we own (*Eigentum*), for which we can claim legal ownership, and things we possess (*Besitz*), if we actually have them. So possessing a thing—like a rental car—does not necessarily imply ownership in a legal sense. This is particularly evident with stolen goods. A thief takes possession of somebody else's property. By stealing goods, he or she becomes their possessor but not their owner.

This differentiation is not uniquely German. In a recent contribution, Bénédicte Savoy, the art historian famous for her work on art looting during colonialism and who is actively involved in the current debates on art restitution, showed that the legal dualism of "property" and "possession" from Roman law became widespread in most European codifications.[40] It is found, for instance, in French (*possession* and *propriété*) and Italian (*possessione* and *proprietà*) law. Not

[37] See Solan/Tiersma, "Introduction," in idem, eds, *The Oxford Handbook of Language and Law*, Oxford, Oxford University Press, 2012, 4.

[38] Berman, *Law and Language*, Cambridge, Cambridge University Press, 2013, 88.

[39] E.g., Busse, "Rechtssprache als Problem der Bedeutungsbeschreibung," *Sprache und Literatur* 29 (1998), 24.

[40] See Savoy, "Property and Possession," September 18, 2018, https://voelkerrechtsblog.org/property-and-possession.

surprisingly, this differentiation was also adopted for shaping 1917 canonical property law.[41] For Savoy and her work, the distinction is of major importance as it allows her to explain the current situation in which European museums possess indigenous works of art, while this possession does not exclude that somebody else, such as the successors of colonialized peoples, can be understood as the rightful legal owners of this art. In the legal and political debates about art restitution, distinguishing between "possession" and "property" can therefore be a central step to identifying the corresponding rights of possessors and proprietors. It could even serve as a political tool for establishing models for how to deal with foreign art works in European museums. Savoy notes, "Museums . . . are arenas for the oscillation between property and possession. They have even become (among other things) architectural and institutional temples of these legal classifications."[42] I will not deepen this contemporary debate here; nevertheless, it is interesting to note from a law and language point of view how legal concepts and terminology can help to refine positions and claims in legal debates. Yet in order to underline my point about terms that differ in meaning when used in legal and common terminology, I want to restrict myself to analyzing "possession" and "property" in this respect alone. While the terminological differentiation between "possession" and "property" is clear with regard to European legal languages, Savoy also shows that the corresponding everyday languages do not necessarily follow the legal logic. She writes,

> In the daily to and fro between languages we quickly realise that there are difficulties in distinguishing between property and possession across borders, never mind the common Roman root. In everyday parlance, a German big landowner is a Großgrund*besitzer* (from the Latin possessio), while his French equivalent is a grand *propriétaire* (from the Latin proprietas). An Englishman's cultural *property* is a German's Kultur*besitz*; conversely, the French *propriété* intellectuelle (or the British intellectual *property*) is in German geistiges *Eigentum*. Crossing borders, it seems, confuses legal categories and even turns them into exact opposites.[43]

It seems obvious, as Savoy contends, that "the [legal] distinction has not seeped into collective consciousness and consequently into the respective everyday languages."[44] The common languages largely make no difference between the

[41] See Mörsdorf, *Die Rechtssprache des Codex Juris Canonici*, 2nd edn, Paderborn, Ferdinand Schöningh, 1967, 261–264.
[42] Savoy, "Property and Possession," September 18, 2018, https://voelkerrechtsblog.org/property-and-possession.
[43] Ibid.
[44] Ibid.

categories and tend to use "property" or "possession" interchangeably for basically any form of ownership.

Changing Meaning

So whenever the law employs terms taken from common language this does not necessarily mean that those terms have exactly the same meaning when used by the law as they do when used by speakers of the common language. The problem becomes even more difficult because the meaning of terms may change over time when used by the law. "Death" might be one example of this. When speaking about the performative quality of legal language in chapter 2, section 2.3, I already mentioned the example of courts declaring the "death" of missing persons. Hence, the attribute "dead" in a legal sense is sometimes attributed to people who are physically alive and would not be called "dead" in common language. This is a meaning that the law has developed. "Dead" initially meant "physically dead" in the realm of the law too, but the term was broadened to include the phenomenon of "legal death." So the meaning of the term in legal language changed according to its legal use, whereas it did not do likewise in common language.

Another example that Dietrich Busse mentioned is taken from German civil law judicature, which in deciding compensation cases developed the practice of interpreting the brokenness of an acquired object to be "maliciously concealed" when the seller has failed to pay due attention to the functionality of the sold object.[45] This of course is not what would be classified as "maliciousness" in a regular conversation or what was initially meant with "maliciousness" in the law. "Maliciousness" initially meant an inner stance, the fraudulent intent of a seller, but today it is no longer reduced to that meaning in legal terminology, due to the judges' decision to treat gross carelessness as a form of maliciousness to decide those civil cases accordingly.[46] According to the civil courts, even a friendly person up to no wrong might act "maliciously" if he or she when selling an object fails to pay due attention to the functionality of that object. Interestingly, one can make similar observations with regard to the use of the term "maliciousness" in canon law. In several norms, the Code of Canon Law refers to *dolus*, which could be translated as "malice," "deceit," or "willful intent," to describe conditions which cause a defect in a contract. The English translation of canon 125 §2 CIC/1983

[45] See Busse, "Rechtssprache als Problem der Bedeutungsbeschreibung," *Sprache und Literatur* 29 (1998), 32; idem, "Ist die Anwendung von Rechtstexten ein Fall von Kommunikation?," in Lerch, ed, *Recht vermitteln*, Berlin, Walter de Gruyter, 2005, 48.

[46] E.g., Bundesgerichtshof, January 29, 1975, file number VIII ZR 101/73, https:// research.wolterskluwer-online.de/document/c260be7a-eaf0-4a5a-b65f-5710f8ed7795 (accessed September 4, 2022).

reads, "An act placed out of grave fear, unjustly inflicted, or out of malice is valid unless the law provides otherwise." And canon 1098 CIC/1983 notes, "A person contracts invalidly who enters into a marriage deceived by malice, perpetrated to obtain consent, concerning some quality of the other partner which by its very nature can gravely disturb the partnership of conjugal life." These canons suggest that "maliciousness" under certain circumstances affects the validity of the contract. However, the interpreters of these norms hasten to say that *dolus* not only means an act carried out with fraudulent intent but rather *each* act of deception intended to cause the other party to contract.[47] An act of deceit performed with the best of intentions, motivated maybe by the intention to do some good to the other, is an act of "malice" according to canon law if it causes the other partner to contract under those false pretensions. As with the German civil judges, this shows that the term "maliciousness" in canon law has developed over the course of its legal use to embrace a broader meaning than it did initially and, thus, now diverges to some extent from the meaning of the term in common language. So terms develop a life of their own, be it in common or in legal language. The same term might thus even develop independently in common and legal language, until its meaning is so distinct in each field that it defies understanding in the other. Busse revealed how terms change when used by the law by using a step-by-step example from German criminal law, namely the term *Gewalt* ("violence"), the legal meaning of which has changed over the past hundred years of German criminal law history.[48] Initially "violence" meant an offender's use of physical force while committing a crime. The term then changed its meaning as it began to relate more to the cause-and-effect relationship between violence and the deed and to focus on the effect of violence on the victim. The meaning then broadened again when, predominantly in the 1970s—with regard to the protest movement and its blockades and sit-down strikes—judges began to interpret nonphysical acts of coercion as acts of "violence." Busse remarked that it was paradoxical that the judges labeled peaceful ("nonviolent") sit-down strikes as "violence," something which the strikers found hard to accept. Busse was actually particularly critical as he saw the courts not only changing the meaning of legal terms over time—which is a normal process—but also regarded their revised definitions as attempts to influence the public mind explicitly and to change the public view on violence.[49] Most interestingly, his critique, which he put forward in 1991, was obviously shared by the German Federal Constitutional Court, which put an end to interpreting "violence" in the way mentioned only a few years later in 1995. The

[47] E.g., Lüdicke, "Canon 1098," in idem, ed, *Münsterischer Kommentar zum Codex Iuris Canonici* (suppl. sheets 41, July 2006), 13 no. 4.

[48] See Busse, "Juristische Fachsprache und öffentlicher Sprachgebrauch," in Liedtke et al., eds, *Begriffe besetzen*, Opladen, Westdeutscher Verlag, 1991, 164–175.

[49] See ibid., 183.

court ruled that subsuming nonphysical acts of coercion like sit-down strikes under the term "violence" (as used in section 240 of the German Criminal Code) was unconstitutional, as this interpretation violated the constitutional prohibition of interpreting analogically in penal law (see article 103, paragraph 2 of the German Basic Law).[50] This example of "violence" as interpreted by the German courts is interesting as it allows us to study two aspects of the way the law changes the meaning of terms employed by legal language. It first of all shows that "violence" as a legal term has developed its own independent existence, distancing itself from the common use of the term. Yet it also reveals that this occurrence is never fully detached from historical events and social development. This sheds some light on the phenomenon that legal and common language constantly interact to some degree, and necessarily have to do so, as the law deals with contemporary events. However, this does not guarantee that legal and common terminology develop in parallel, remain connected, or overlap. Nevertheless, the preceding example also demonstrates that higher courts, and above all constitutional courts, often prevent the distance between legal and common language from becoming too great. The interference of the German Federal Constitutional Court in the lower courts' interpretation of "violence" is therefore not only an example of the court acting to protect the constitution but also an example of its control over the development of legal language.

Technical Terminology

Every legal order knows terms which are specifically legal, technical terms of the law which only make sense in a legal context as distinct legal terminology. Some of these terms make sense in all or several legal orders—most individuals who speak Legalese, for instance, understand the meaning of "injunction suit"—while others belong to a particular legal order and its language. These terms are understood merely by experts in this specific order. "Promoter of justice" and "defender of the bond" are terms from canon law language which are unfamiliar to anyone without some knowledge of canon law. Both describe offices in canonical adjudication. In each diocese, the bishop appoints a canonist as a promoter of justice (see canon 1435 CIC/1983) whose duty it is "to provide for the public good" (canon 1430 CIC/1983) in contentious cases which can endanger the public good and in penal cases which naturally affect the public good. In these cases where the public good is at stake, it is the duty of the promoter of justice to initiate the procedure by presenting a *libellus* to the judge (see canons 1501–1504,

[50] See Bundesverfassungsgericht, January 10, 1995, file number 1 BvR 718/89, 1 BvR 719/89, 1 BvR 722/89, 1 BvR 723/89 ("Sitzblockaden II"), *Entscheidungen des Bundesverfassungsgerichts* 92, 1.

1721 CIC/1983). Defenders of the bond—who are also canonists appointed by the bishop (see canon 1435 CIC/1983)—have a specific function in ecclesiastical nullity cases regarding marriage or ordination. Their duty is to argue in favor of the validity of the contested marriage or ordination in the procedure, "to propose and explain everything which reasonably can be brought forth against nullity or dissolution" (canon 1432 CIC/1983). While these offices have some parallels with offices in other legal systems—the "promoter of justice" resembles in some way the function of public prosecution—it is nevertheless obvious that it is only possible to understand the technical terms "promoter of justice" or "defender of the bond" if one is familiar with the specific canonical terminology.

Adding to these terms which defy common comprehension, there are terms which used to be widespread in several legal orders but have become part of the specialist terminology of one specific order. The term "moral certitude," which I want to mention by way of example, used to describe the common standard of proof not only in canon law but also in Anglo-American legal procedures. It is basically identical with the legal standard of proof "beyond a reasonable doubt," as common in Anglo-American criminal procedures.[51] Today, however, the term itself is widely unknown in the secular orders, while it is still a familiar term in canon law language.

One particular challenge is posed by legal terms that are used in a technical sense in several legal languages, but which do not carry the same meaning in each. For instance, the term "murder" is used differently in US and German law. What is called first-degree and second-degree "murder" in the United States is treated differently when it comes to German terminology. Only first-degree murder is called "murder" (*Mord*), whereas second-degree murder is never called "murder" in German legal language but always "manslaughter" (*Totschlag*) to clearly distinguish it from first-degree murder. However, people on the street tend not to pick up that difference.[52] The unlawful killing of a person is called "murder" by many individuals without any further distinction. This sometimes has the consequence that people complain about the comparably low penalties for "murder" in manslaughter cases. In canon law, this problem is avoided by speaking of "committing a homicide" instead of applying "murder" terminology. Canon 1397 §1 CIC/1983 addresses a person "[*q*]*ui homicidium patrat*" and in doing so includes all degrees of murder in the term "homicide."

[51] See Hahn, "Moral Certitude," *Oxford Journal of Law and Religion* 8 (2019), 300–325.

[52] See Busse, "Rechtssprache als Problem der Bedeutungsbeschreibung," *Sprache und Literatur* 29 (1998), 37.

3.3 Legal Terms, Foreign Words

Besides terms that already exist in legal language and adjust their meaning according to the requirements of legal communication, there is also the need to adopt new terms for legal language to express new phenomena with which the law finds itself confronted. There are several approaches to coining new legal terms. Heikki Mattila named three ways of creating legal terms: by enriching a word from everyday language with a specific legal meaning—I have already presented some examples of that approach—by borrowing a legal expression from a foreign language, or by creating neologisms.[53]

Borrowed Terms

It is relatively easy to tell that some legal expressions have been borrowed from foreign languages. Prominent examples include relics from Law Latin and Law French in the English legal languages. Before the Norman Conquest, vernacular Anglo-Saxon law and Latin canon law were dominant in England. After the Normans had arrived, French exerted an ever-greater influence on the law. While communication between professional lawyers and their clients was usually in English, French became the language of the royal and legal courts. Latin remained the language of many statutes and written law, even though written law also saw the increased use of French over time. Composing texts in French had become common practice by about 1300.[54] Norman French nevertheless borrowed many Latin terms too, as revealed by the many legal terms used in Law French with evident Latin roots.[55] This remains visible today, as Harold Berman pointed out, stating, "Most of the vocabulary of English and American law stems from Latin roots, brought into English from Roman law and canon law, in most cases via Norman French."[56] Law French established itself as the standard usage and served as the main language of the law until the seventeenth century, when English stepped up to become the language of common law.[57] But English legal

[53] See Mattila, "Legal Vocabulary," in Solan/Tiersma, eds, *The Oxford Handbook of Language and Law*, Oxford, Oxford University Press, 2012, 33; idem, *Comparative Legal Linguistics*, 2nd edn, London, Routledge, 2016, 145–151.

[54] See Tiersma, "A History of the Languages of Law," in idem/Solan, eds, *The Oxford Handbook of Language and Law*, Oxford, Oxford University Press, 2012, 21.

On the whole historical process, see idem, *Legal Language*, Chicago, IL, The University of Chicago Press, 1999, 19–34.

[55] See Mellinkoff, *The Language of the Law*, Boston, MA, Little, Brown and Company, 1963, 71–72.

[56] Berman, *Law and Language*, Cambridge, Cambridge University Press, 2013, 88; see also Solan/Tiersma, "Introduction," in idem, eds, *The Oxford Handbook of Language and Law*, Oxford, Oxford University Press, 2012, 4.

[57] See Tiersma, *Legal Language*, Chicago, IL, The University of Chicago Press, 1999, 35–47.

texts composed in later years also preserved a great deal of French terminology. Peter Tiersma once noted with regard to the enduring presence of Law French in modern legal English,

> Words relating to courts and trials are almost entirely of French origin: *action, appeal, attorney, bailiff, bar, claim, complaint, counsel*, and *court* are but a few examples. Just about every area of the common law is full of French terminology, as attested by words for basic legal categories like *agreement, assault, easement, estate, felony, lease, license, misdemeanour, mortgage, property, slander, tort* and *trespass*. French word order (noun + adjective) is apparent in terms like *attorney general, condition precedent, letters patent*, and *notary public*.[58]

So the impact of French on the legal language of common law countries today is broadly visible in terms ranging from *acquis communautaire* to *voir dire*.

In most civil law cultures today it is above all the impact of Latin that is still visible—Heikki Mattila was foremost in devoting himself to the in-depth study of the Law Latin legacy in modern European legal languages.[59] The presence of Latin terms in many legal terminologies of civil law countries is regularly owed to their common root in the medieval reception of the *Corpus Iuris Civilis*, as Tiersma noted,

> Civil law countries . . . all share, to a greater or lesser extent, a common legal heritage that began in Rome, was systematized in Byzantium, was re-discovered and elaborated in northern Italy, and then spread throughout much of Europe. They also share some core legal concepts, as well as the language needed to refer to those concepts. That language is, for the most part, heavily influenced by the Latin terminology of the *Corpus Iuris*.[60]

This influence of Law Latin on civil law was opposed in the eighteenth- and nineteenth-century codifications, which attempted to reshape law into vernacular languages. The French *Code Civil* of 1804 was composed in French. It became highly influential not only throughout Europe but also in many colonized countries during the age of colonization. The Prussian General State Laws (*Allgemeines Landrecht*) of 1794 made use of the German language, guided by

On the history and characteristics of Legal English, see Mattila, *Comparative Legal Linguistics*, 2nd edn, London, Routledge, 2016, 305–351.

58 Tiersma, "A History of the Languages of Law," in idem/Solan, eds, *The Oxford Handbook of Language and Law*, Oxford, Oxford University Press, 2012, 21.

59 See Mattila, *Comparative Legal Linguistics*, 2nd edn, London, Routledge, 2016, 161–201.

60 Tiersma, "A History of the Languages of Law," in idem/Solan, eds, *The Oxford Handbook of Language and Law*, Oxford, Oxford University Press, 2012, 15.

the idea of establishing a code which the Prussian citizens could understand without having to rely on legal experts.[61] In any case, this attempt at making law more understandable by using vernacular languages was not overly successful. Legal scholar Max Baumann observed that the codifications with their emphasis on written law had, to all intents and purposes, produced a "class of legal illiterates."[62] Hence, the codifications did not fully achieve their purpose of increasing comprehension, but they were successful in giving rise to the vernacular languages as modern languages of civil law. They prepared the ground for what is today, as Tiersma called it, "[t]he triumph of the vernacular," noting, "Today, each civil law country has developed its own variety of legal language. Despite the great importance of Latin and French, modern legal languages are simply varieties of the national languages in question."[63] Modern legal languages are therefore mostly distinct terminologies in a vernacular, sprinkled with relics of Law Latin and Law French, particularly when it comes to the technical terms of the law. These relics, as Harold Berman contended, resist the theory often promoted by nineteenth-century scholars that the language of modern law constitutes a specialized version of folk language; as he maintained, "Such an assumption rests on an entirely artificial conception of folk language, based on the romantic nationalism of the nineteenth century."[64] The debates on Latin versus folk language were fashionable in the nineteenth century, but misleading in several respects, according to Berman, because they missed the impact of Latin on the modern languages of the law, and also because the antagonism "Latin versus folk language" misinterprets the status of Latin in premodern societies. Latin, as Berman highlighted, was in fact an integral part of everyday medieval language, as "it was the language of worship, the language of scholarship, and the language of international relations, as well as the language of much of the law."[65] However, Berman's remark also draws attention to the fact that Latin was not the medieval language of the street but always a specialist jargon. It was a specialist language even in the Middle Ages, used by priests, scholars, and politicians. Law Latin was likewise a specialist language: the Legalese used by legal experts. In German, the term for "Legalese" is still *Juristenlatein*, "Lawyers' Latin." This term indicates that the language of the law still contains many Latin expressions, which the vernacular codifications were unable to erase. Many Latin phrases can still be found in German Legalese, mostly relics of ancient Roman law which survived the time of the codifications. These terms are used either openly, when

[61] See ibid., 17.

[62] Original quote, "Klasse der juristischen Analphabeten," Baumann, "Weg vom Text," in Lerch, ed, *Recht vermitteln*, Berlin, Walter de Gruyter, 2005, 12.

[63] Tiersma, "A History of the Languages of Law," in idem/Solan, eds, *The Oxford Handbook of Language and Law*, Oxford, Oxford University Press, 2012, 19.

[64] Berman, *Law and Language*, Cambridge, Cambridge University Press, 2013, 88–89.

[65] Ibid., 89.

speaking of *aberratio ictus*, *actus contrarius*, or *ultima ratio*, or their Latin origin is concealed, as with terms that were integrated into the vernacular language, like *Kodex* ("code"), *Delikt* ("delict"), or *Fakt* ("fact"). Yet calling Legalese "Lawyers' Latin" is not merely a qualification referring to its heavy use of Latin terms. It also signals the incomprehensibility of legal jargon to ordinary people. Legalese is a specialist jargon, beyond the understanding of most individuals, as is the Latin language.

Canon Law Latin

Undoubtedly, no legal language deserves the name "Lawyers' Latin" more than canon law, as Latin remains its principal language. Church Latin, which as Liturgical Latin was once part of the everyday language of the liturgy, still holds its ground in the official documents of the Roman papal church and particularly in its legal texts. Canon Law Latin is a specific tradition which developed from medieval Law Latin.[66] It never made use of classical Latin, as canonist Rudolf Köstler noted, but adopted the Law Latin of the late Roman Empire and the ancient Roman codifications and developed its specific style through the Middle Ages and the modern era.[67] Even today, the language of canon law echoes the Law Latin of medieval times, albeit in a modern—namely, codified—shape. Whereas the Canon Law Latin of the *Corpus Iuris Canonici* was the language of classical medieval case law, modern Canon Law Latin, as it appears in the twentieth century's codifications of 1917, 1983, and 1990, is used to form statute law, which is reflected in its language and style. The old Canon Law Latin, Köstler recalled, was heavily loaded with complex syntax, pompous phrases, and wordy explanations, whereas new Canon Law Latin tends to be clear, simple, and concise, at least when one compares it with the Canon Law Latin of the *Corpus Iuris Canonici*.

As the language of papal legislation, Canon Law Latin is the language of much of ecclesiastical statute law. The authentic text of the *Code of Canon Law* is the Latin text alone.[68] Under the Code of 1917 this claim was supported by the legislator actively suppressing translations of the Code into vernacular languages to avoid spoiling the original text.[69] Yet after 1983, diverse bishops' conferences and

[66] On the history of Canon Law Latin, see Mattila, *Comparative Legal Linguistics*, 2nd edn, London, Routledge, 2016, 170–173.

[67] See Köstler, *Wörterbuch zum Codex Iuris Canonici*, Munich, Josef Kösel, 1927, 9.

[68] See Secretariat of State, "Norms *Necessitas ipsa* on the Translation of the Code of Canon Law," January 28, 1983, no. 1, *Communicationes* 15 (1983), 41.

[69] The official Vatican edition of the 1917 Code contained the express prohibition to reprint or translate the Code, put in front of the preface. It read, "Nemini liceat, sine venia Sanctae Sedis hunc Codicem denuo imprimere aut in aliam linguam vertere."

canon law societies all over the globe issued translations of the new Code so that its text is now available in most of the common global languages. This step was motivated by the wish to increase public comprehension of the law. However, the translations only serve as working aids, as the Latin text remains the authentic text of the Code.

Similarly, most noncodified papal laws are also promulgated in Latin, although Italian, as the everyday language of the Roman Curia, is also gaining in importance, not merely for administration but also for legislation. This development reflects a certain trend in church. Similarly to the way the liturgical reform of the twentieth century promoted the vernacular for liturgical use, there are pressures on the legislator today to successively replace Law Latin with the vernacular languages of the local churches. This will eventually lead to an increase in the use of modern vernacular languages for global legislation, too. This development is somewhat anticipated in ecclesiastical adjudication where Latin is already declining in importance. According to the law of the old Code, all trial records except the records of interrogation had to be written in Latin (see canon 1642 §2 CIC/1917). As the new Code no longer provides any regulations on official court languages, ecclesiastical tribunals today use the local languages and also record the trials in the local vernacular. This only causes a problem when Roman appeal courts become involved. The Code states that the acts have to be translated into a language known to the Roman tribunal, "with due precautions taken that the translation is a faithful one" (canon 1474 §2 CIC/1983). In any case, the language chosen to communicate with a Roman tribunal no longer has to be Latin, in contrast to the old Code (see canon 1644 §2 CIC/1917). The Apostolic Constitution *Pastor Bonus* on the Roman Curia regulated accordingly, "Apart from the official Latin language, it is acceptable to approach the Roman Curia in any of the languages widely known today."[70] However, when papal tribunals publish their decisions, they still do so in Latin. The *Decisiones seu sententiae selectae*, decisions made by the Roman Rota, are published in Latin only. While these decisions do not have the function of precedents, they nevertheless claim a leading function for ecclesiastical adjudication in those cases in which the law is silent on a matter (see canon 19 CIC/1983). For ecclesiastical judges they are therefore of some value. Thus, ecclesiastical judges require a solid knowledge of Latin to receive the Rota decisions.

[70] John Paul II, "Apostolic Constitution *Pastor bonus* on the Roman Curia," June 28, 1988, article 16, *Acta Apostolicae Sedis* 80 (1988), 863.

Language Training

Until the twentieth century, Latin was not only the language of canon law itself but also the main language of canon law scholarship.[71] Scholarly publications from the early twentieth century were often published in Latin. Lectures held in the course of canon law formation at the time made regular use of Latin. In contrast, recent scholarship is usually published in the vernacular languages. The only Latin article on present canon law language that I came across when preparing this book was Péter Erdő's 1987 work "Expressiones obligationis et exhortationis in Codice Iuris Canonici,"[72] which I mentioned in chapter 3, section 3.1. Nowadays, there are very few canonical scholars who give their lectures in Latin. While Latin texts still play a major role as subjects of theological and canonical research and teaching, the Latin language is hardly used anymore as a medium of theological and canonical study and instruction.

The general decline of Latin as the language of theological training in the twentieth century can be observed most interestingly by studying the fate of the Apostolic Constitution *Veterum sapientia* on the Promotion of the Study of Latin, promulgated by John XXIII in 1962 to increase the use of Latin in theological teaching.[73] The document, obviously reacting to the declining importance of Latin in theological formation, advised all lecturers of theology to teach the main theological disciplines in Latin and to use Latin textbooks for instruction. The constitution even ordered the gradual replacement of any lecturers who could not manage to adjust to teaching in Latin. Canonist Bertram Griffin laconically remarked, "A few professors tried this for about a week and then gave up."[74] The Catholic universities and theological faculties never made any efforts to enforce the law or replace those who did not adhere to it. So *Veterum sapientia* became one example of a papal law that was not received by the legal subjects, as it was ignored by nearly all theological scholars and had next to no effect on theological training. The same rings true for canon law scholarship. Although one hears time and again of individual canonists who tortured their students by holding their lectures in Latin until the 1970s, the regular use of Latin in lectures and seminars must have stopped around the same time or a little later when theological scholarship dispensed with Latin for the most part.

Despite the finding that Latin plays an ever-diminishing practical role in canon law, particularly in adjudication and education, it still plays a major role

71 See Haering, "Lateinische Sprache und Kanonisches Recht," *Seminarium* 43 (2003), 241–242.

72 Erdő, "Expressiones obligationis et exhortationis in Codice Iuris Canonici," *Periodica de Re Morali Canonica Liturgica* 76 (1987), 3–27.

73 John XXIII, "Apostolic Constitution *Veterum sapientia* on the Promotion of the Study of Latin," February 22, 1962, *Acta Apostolicae Sedis* 54 (1962), 129–135.

74 Griffin, "Introduction to the Jargon of Canon Law," *The Jurist* 44 (1984), 25.

in legislation, as mentioned above. Consequently, the norms of canon law studies still inculcate prospective canonists with the need to become good Latinists. In the Congregation for Catholic Education's recently published Norms of Application for the Correct Implementation of the Apostolic Constitution *Veritatis gaudium* on Ecclesiastical Universities and Faculties it says, "A suitable knowledge of the Latin language is required for the faculties of the sacred sciences, so that the students can understand and use the sources of these sciences as well as the documents of the church."[75] In faculties of theology, Latin is treated as an auxiliary discipline in the first cycle of theological studies.[76] In faculties of canon law, Latin is an obligatory discipline in the first and second cycles of study,[77] the first cycle addressing students without a theological degree, the second cycle pertaining to students aspiring to a licentiate of canon law. In the third cycle, the doctorate program, "canonical Latin" is an obligatory discipline.[78] The same regulations can be found in the Congregation for Catholic Education's 2002 Decree *Novo codice* revising the order of studies in the faculties and departments of canon law.[79] The decree states that most of the students of canon law no longer possess a sufficient knowledge of Latin when they take up their studies. Nevertheless, by the end of the second cycle students "must know Latin in such a way as to be able to understand thoroughly the Code of Canon Law and the Code of Canons of the Eastern Churches, as well as the other canonical documents; this obligation also applies to the third cycle, so that they may be able to interpret correctly the sources of the law."[80]

Canon Law Jargon

Cultivating Latin as the language of ecclesiastical law in canon law formation has also inspired many to develop their own Latinized jargon when using the vernacular languages, as done in adjudication. This explains how many Latin terms and expressions have found their way into the local vernacular canon law languages. This fashion is hardly new. In his 1927 dictionary on the old Code, Rudolf Köstler criticized a contemporary trend of his time, namely, the Germanization of Latin

75 Congregation for Catholic Education, "Norms of Application for the Correct Implementation of the Apostolic Constitution *Veritatis gaudium*," December 27, 2017, article 26 §3, https://www.vatican.va/content/francesco/en/apost_constitutions/documents/papa-francesco_costituzione-ap_20171208_veritatis-gaudium.html.

76 See ibid., article 55 paragraph 1 letter c.

77 See ibid., article 61 paragraph 1 letter d and paragraph 2 letter d.

78 See ibid., article 61 paragraph 3 letter a.

79 See Congregation for Catholic Education, "Decree *Novo codice* Revising the Order of Studies in the Faculties and Departments of Canon Law," September 2, 2002, paragraph 2, no. 1 letter d, no. 2 letter d, and no. 3 letter a, *Acta Apostolicae Sedis* 95 (2003), 284.

80 Paragraph 3 no. 3, *Acta Apostolicae Sedis* 95 (2003), 284.

terms, thereby creating rather ridiculous expressions, even though appropriate vernacular alternatives were at hand.[81] Köstler gave the example of German canon lawyers speaking of *sich eine excommunicatio inkurrieren* ("incurring an excommunication") instead of using the common German expression *sich eine Exkommunikation zuziehen*. While "incur" as a derivation from the Latin *incurrere* is a common term in the English language, the Germanized equivalent *inkurrieren* is rather uncommon. It is a term invented by canon lawyers to draw Canon Law Latin into the German language. Köstler made it quite clear what he thought of this. He called this practice "nonsense" and "fully superfluous." Despite his critique, German canon lawyers today still like to refer to the "*iudex a quo*" instead of speaking of "the previous instance," and refer to the "*iudex ad quem*" when meaning "the next instance." They name the case a "*causa*" and the respondent the "*pars conventa*." Similarly, English canon lawyers often refer to the statement of claim as "*libellus*"—German canonists on the contrary rather call it "*Klageschrift*"—or refer to the marital "*vinculum*"—which, at least in most German texts, is called "*Eheband*". So there are obviously different fashions that determine which Latin terms are adopted and integrated into canon law vernacular, often depending most probably on the listening habits of the respective languages. That English canon law terminology easily took on "*libellus*" might be owed to the fact that "libel" is used in legal English anyway (yet, strangely enough, often with a different meaning altogether, as in "slander and libel"). Other adoptions are more of a mystery. Maybe they just represent random trends and habits in the local canon law cultures. Nevertheless, this observation concords with what Heikki Mattila observed in his comparative studies on the adoption of foreign languages in specific legal systems. Mattila found that Latin expressions picked up by civil law traditions and Latin terms received by common law traditions are not necessarily the same.[82] Each strand of legal tradition seems to have its own reception processes for deriving legal terminology out of Latin sources. The very different meanings of "equity" in common law and in civil law may serve as one example. The term "equity" as used in common law denotes a specific body of rules derived from courts of equity. In civil law contexts, in contrast, the term denotes a principle of fairness utilized in legal application. It attempts to ease hardship deriving from the law in a specific situation where a rule fails to respond adequately to a particular case. Canon law is clearly civil law in this respect. It cultivates a whole theory of canonical equity which compels appliers of the law to avoid inflicting undue hardship on legal subjects when they find a law in force but unjust in addressing a specific situation. In

[81] See Köstler, *Wörterbuch zum Codex Iuris Canonici*, Munich, Josef Kösel, 1927, 5.
[82] See Mattila, "Legal Vocabulary," in Solan/Tiersma, eds, *The Oxford Handbook of Language and Law*, Oxford, Oxford University Press, 2012, 35 fn. 9.

these cases, ecclesiastical administration and adjudication are authorized to mitigate the legal effects or even to avoid applying a law at all to ease the conflict between law and justice. This finding that canonical equity has a side to it which the term does not have in other legal languages concords with the observation that Canon Law Latin often uses Latin terms with a distinct meaning unparalleled in other legal traditions. The term "solicitation" can serve as a further example. As I mentioned in the introduction, in secular legal English it refers to suggesting or requesting that another person commit a crime. In canon law, however, the term denotes a specific crime, the crime of a priest "who in confession, or on the occasion or under the pretext of confession, solicits a penitent to commit a sin against the sixth commandment of the Decalogue" (canon 1385 CIC/1983). "*Crimen sollicitationis*" is the specialist term for this specific sexual offense, which has no parallel in secular criminal law.

Neologisms

Most legal terminologies contain a good number of compound words or compound phrases, a phenomenon which Mattila explains by pointing out their merit of adding a new facet to an existing legal concept. He finds this strategy "the easiest way to coin a term to express a new legal concept."[83] Instead of inventing brand-new terms and explaining their distinct meaning by comparing them to concepts that already exist, new conceptual terminologies are constituted by grouping new features around established terms. Critical voices object that this increases the obscurity and inelegance of Legalese. Others simply find this strategy pragmatic. Most interestingly, in any case, compound words or compound phrases rarely occur in canon law. Its Latin usually references ancient Roman legal expressions. Overall, in contrast to other legal systems, canon law is rather reluctant to develop neologisms or new terminology. Keeping Mattila's explanation in mind, this might be because canon law terminology is developing less rapidly than the terminology of secular law. As the legislator seldom introduces new legal concepts, there is little need to create new legal terms. One can also rephrase this finding in a more critical light to stress the ecclesiastical legislator's apparent reluctance to embrace new legal concepts and terms even in cases where this seems urgently advisable. The most recent reform of ecclesiastical penal law, for instance, has sparked criticism for the fact that the reformed canon on the sexual abuse of minors and other canons on clerical sex crimes still speak of sexual delicts as "offenses against the sixth commandment of the Decalogue"—as I just mentioned with regard to the crime of solicitation.

[83] Ibid., 32.

This expression has long been criticized for being both opaque and misleading. The wording is obscure insofar as it fails to use a clear terminology to describe the punishable offense. Furthermore, the phrase "offense against the sixth commandment of the Decalogue" is confusing, as the offense which appears in the sixth commandment of the Decalogue is in fact adultery, whereas the church uses the term for any kind of clerical breach of celibacy, including—without any terminological distinction—consensual sex between adult partners, sexual assault, rape, and the sexual abuse of minors. Many critical voices have therefore advised the legislator to revise this expression and, whenever sex crimes are concerned, to replace it with terminology more common in secular penal law such as speaking of offenses against sexual integrity or against the sexual self-determination of individuals. In the end, however, recent legislation was evidently unwilling to revise the traditional language referring to sex offenses and to embrace a language of individual autonomy unprecedented in canon law terminology. Instead of establishing terms such as "sexual integrity" and "self-determination" into canon law language, the law continues to refer to "offenses against the sixth commandment of the Decalogue."

Most interestingly, in any case, the church tends to embrace changes of law and language when they are forced upon it from the outside. I want to elucidate this by referencing how the Vatican City State operates as a member state of the European Union. With regard to the present European situation, Heikki Mattila identified the European Union as "the most important 'factory' of legal and administrative neologisms in Western Europe."[84] It mostly creates new terms in English or French, the leading working languages of the Union, and then translates them into the languages of the other member states. The Vatican City State is a member state. It therefore has to implement European directives. The Vatican regulations, which answer to European directives, as does for instance the Vatican anti-money laundering legislation,[85] therefore receives the one or the other neologism from European production via Italian legal terminology, like "*cambio valuta*" ("currency changing"), "*gestione di portafogli titoli*" ("portfolio management"), or "*titoli al portatore*" ("liquid securities"). But these are rather random effects which do not have a huge impact on Canon Law Latin in general, particularly as these modern Vatican City State regulations are usually published in Italian rather than in Latin. The terminology used to regulate these matters is therefore usually taken from modern Italian and Italian legal

[84] Ibid., 36; see also idem, *Comparative Legal Linguistics*, 2nd edn, London, Routledge, 2016, 152–159; Sosoni, "Language and Translation in EU Competition Law," in Marino et al., eds, *Language and Law*, Cham, Springer Nature Switzerland, 2018, 179–205.

[85] E.g., Francis, "Apostolic Letter issued Motu proprio *La Promozione* for the Prevention and Countering of Money Laundering, the Financing of Terrorism and the Proliferation of Weapons of Mass Destruction," August 8, 2013, *Acta Apostolicae Sedis* 105 (2013), 811–813.

terminology which—via European law—penetrates into the Roman Curia's Italian, without influencing Canon Law Latin to any greater degree.

3.4 Indeterminate Terms

A typical phenomenon of civil law languages is the intentional use of indeterminate terms in statute law. German legal language even provides the technical term "indeterminate legal term" ("*unbestimmter Rechtsbegriff*") in its legal theory to describe a term used in statute law, the content of which is not determined by legal language. Its meaning is therefore open to development through adjudication and administration. Indeterminacy in statutes can be found in factual terms and legal terms alike. A law regulating "noise" employs a factual term which leaves open to interpretation what constitutes "noise" in a specific situation. A law using a legal term like "public interest" likewise takes up a term where the meaning is vague and needs specification. Hence, indeterminate terms require interpretation by the appliers of the law to derive their meaning in a specific case. They serve as instruments of flexibility in legal application. Using indeterminate terms in statute law allows the appliers to relate the law to different situations and to make use of stable and steady legal norms even though reality is in a constant state of flux. At the same time, this practice also has a critical dimension as it leaves considerable leeway of interpretation to the appliers of the law. A large margin of interpretation collides with legal certainty and the rule of law, because these principles demand a maximum of determinateness of the law to confront the legal subjects with clear expectations and reliable legal prospects. So there is a fine line every legislator must walk when making use of the concept of indeterminate terms to allow the legal order to react flexibly to the changing realities of everyday life without toppling into arbitrariness. Employing indeterminate terms creates a breathing, living law. And yet, the excessive employment of indeterminate terms supports arbitrary decisions and infringes upon legal certainty and the rule of law.

"Grave Necessity"

This is obviously a serious problem in canon law, as the law of the church is somewhat infamous for excessively employing indeterminate terms, as several examples show. Canonist Christoph Ohly dedicated an article to the widespread use of the term "*gravis necessitas*" throughout the Code, enabling the applier of the law to decide whether or not a situation of fact fulfills the requirement of a "grave necessity." Ohly is critical of the lack of certainty that comes with the term, as canon law also should always be clear and certain, yet it lacks this quality when employing indeterminate terms to an excessive degree.[86] Adding to the indeterminacy of "*gravis necessitas*" is the problem that the term "necessity" itself is ambiguous. It may mean "need" as in a spiritual or material need, but it also frequently means "affliction," "hardship," or even "emergency." So "*necessitas*" sometimes describes a subjective state of neediness pertaining to a particular individual, whereas in other contexts it describes an objective state of individual or collective deprivation, or a pressing urgent challenge that has to be addressed. That the terminological ambiguity of "*necessitas*" adds to the indeterminacy of "grave necessity" was proven just recently when the German bishops quarreled over its precise meaning. Their conflict revolved around whether a non-Catholic spouse in an interchurch marriage could be interpreted as being in the state of *gravis necessitas* as prescribed in the norm on intercommunion, canon 844 §4 CIC/1983. If spiritual need evolving in an interchurch marriage with regard to the couple's shared sacramental practice may be regarded as constituting a situation of grave necessity, a Catholic minister according to the canonical norm on intercommunion is authorized to administer the Eucharist to the non-Catholic. If not, this practice is usually illegal. In February 2018, in a majority vote, the German Bishops' Conference decided to ease the situation for interchurch couples in the German church. They approved a so-called "Aid to Orientation"[87] permitting Catholic ministers to assist interchurch couples in working out a suitable solution for their common sacramental practice, thus inter alia enabling them to receive communion together in a Catholic Mass. However, not all bishops agreed with this initiative, causing a heated controversy between the members of the bishops' conference which has not yet been fully resolved. At present, some bishops follow the aid in their dioceses, others do not. Their controversy, as mentioned, was sparked precisely by the question of how to interpret "*gravis necessitas*" in canon 844 §4 CIC/1983. It revolves around the uncertainty of whether it is convincing to interpret the situation of a non-Catholic spouse in an interchurch marriage or of the interchurch couple as "grave need," and if so, whether this need is more of a singular or a general nature for the respective couple pertaining to individual situations or to their constant and common religious practice. Depending on how one answers these questions, from a legal point of view it is either rather difficult to justify a regular administration of Catholic sacraments to non-Catholics in interfaith marriages or fully justified. This in mind, it is evident that a norm which yields contradictory interpretations thanks to the use of indeterminate terms undermines legal certainty. As this

[86] See Ohly, "Gravis necessitas," *Archiv für katholisches Kirchenrecht* 175 (2006), 473–475.

[87] German Bishops, Aid to Orientation, Walking with Christ—Tracing Unity, February 20, 2018, https://www.dbk.de/fileadmin/redaktion/diverse_downloads/dossiers_2018/Walking-with-Christ_Tracing_Unity_Arbeits%C3%BCbersetzung-der-Orientierungshilfe_ENG.pdf.

example has proven in the meantime, Ohly's earlier critique of "*gravis necessitas*" did touch a nerve. He recommended changing the terminology to spell out what is meant in the specific contexts.[88] He proposed using "*desiderium*" ("desire" or "request") instead of "*necessitas*" to describe individual need, using "*casus necessitates*" whenever an emergency is meant, and keeping "*necessitas*" only to describe objective deprivation. This would in fact be an advisable change to remove one unnecessary uncertainty from the law of the church.

"Just Cause"

Another example of an indeterminate term used throughout the Code of Canon Law is "just cause," an expression to which canon lawyer Jürgen Olschewski contributed an article.[89] The expression is not exclusive to canon law, but taken from ancient Roman law, where "*iusta causa*" meant either an adequate reason for legal action or inaction or a legitimate reason excusing somebody from following the law in a specific case. It is precisely this last mentioned meaning which we can rediscover in the current canons of the Code on dispensation as "the relaxation of a merely ecclesiastical law in a particular case" (canon 85 CIC/1983) which can be granted by ecclesiastical authorities when "a just and reasonable cause" (canon 90 §1 CIC/1983) demands it. However, "just cause" as an indeterminate term can evidently have diverse meanings, thus causing uncertainty whenever the expression is used. In the old Code, "just cause" appeared in 109 canons; in the new Code it still appears in 60 canons.[90] This reduced use is still critical, as the expression leaves the appliers of the law considerable discretion to decide which cases provide an adequate reason for legal action or a legitimate reason for refraining from enforcing the law. However, the term does leave no room for arbitrariness, Olschewski hastens to say, as every decision based on its interpretation always has to be reasonable. He therefore praises the term for allowing a more flexible and pastoral application of the law to specific cases. Nevertheless, it is also manifest, as has been shown, that indeterminate terms do not contribute to legal certainty. As a result, I am more doubtful than Olschewski that the abundant employment of indeterminate terms and phrases is of benefit to canon law. It might benefit the appliers of the law, who enjoy a rather broad margin of interpretation

88 See Ohly, "Gravis necessitas," *Archiv für katholisches Kirchenrecht* 175 (2006), 484.

89 See Olschewski, "Der Begriff 'iusta causa' in der kirchlichen Rechtssprache," in Reinhardt, ed, *Theologia et Ius Canonicum*, Essen, Wingen, 1995, 235–257.

90 For an overview over the canons, see Olschewski, "Der Begriff 'iusta causa' in der kirchlichen Rechtssprache," in Reinhardt, ed, *Theologia et Ius Canonicum*, Essen, Wingen, 1995, 237 fn. 20 and 238 fn. 24.

when interpreting the norms, but it undermines legal certainty and the rule of law and in doing so eventually even undermines the character of canon law as law. In any case, both examples mentioned, "grave necessity" and "just cause," show that indeterminate terms, be it for good or for bad, are currently part of the linguistic reality of canon law.

4
Comprehension Difficulties

The specific character of legal language, which I sketched out in the previous chapter, poses challenges for listeners and readers of legal texts on several levels. Dietrich Busse lists five requirements for making sense of legal language: expertise, a feel for intertextuality, normativity, functionality, and the institutional character of legal terms.[1] As law is a complex system, it is possible to understand the language of the law only with the help of legal knowledge. This knowledge has to include a sensitivity for the intertextuality of the law, as the language of the law becomes understandable only when taking into account the diverse genres which contribute to its meaning. To discover the meaning of a legal term, for instance, it might be necessary to consult a statute, the adjudication on the statute, and commentary literature. Understanding the normativity of legal language not only includes knowing the specific way to express normative ideas but also identifying the hierarchy of normativities which constitute legal meaning; to discover the meaning of a legal term, it is, for instance, important to know whose interpretation counts and whose is of lesser importance. This also makes it necessary to have a sense of the institutional impact on legal language. An interpretation of a term given by a higher court has a greater impact than the interpretation given by a local court, for instance. It is likewise important to consider the function that a text or a term fulfills in a specific legal context. Busse observes the strategic use of terms in legal language;[2] they are used with a specific aim of achieving a certain meaning and this meaning, again, wants to serve a particular function. I have talked a fair bit about the assertive, directive, commissive, expressive, and declarative function of legal speech in chapter 2, section 2.3. So those who desire to understand legal terms must possess a sense of these different functions.

Busse's list of the requirements necessary to understand Legalese shows how demanding it is to decipher the language of the law. Just as it is possible to collect together some characteristics of legal language, as I have done in the previous chapter, it is likewise possible to classify key difficulties of comprehension connected with the language of the law and legal terminology. The previous chapter already indicated some challenges connected with the grammar, style,

[1] See Busse, "Rechtssprache als Problem der Bedeutungsbeschreibung," *Sprache und Literatur* 29 (1998), 40–43.
[2] See ibid., 43.

The Language of Canon Law. Judith Hahn, Oxford University Press. © Oxford University Press 2023.
DOI: 10.1093/oso/9780197674246.003.0004

and terminology of the law. I have already noted, for instance, that the excessive use of nouns and nominalizations as opposed to verbs or whole subordinate clauses makes sentences harder to understand. Long and complex sentences—connecting several main clauses with several subordinate clauses—can easily provoke misunderstandings. These grammatical features therefore make it more difficult to make sense of legal texts. In the following section, I will dig somewhat deeper into the difficulties connected with comprehending legal language by addressing selected problems which are particularly relevant, as I find, when it comes to grasping canon law: the lexical and syntactic ambiguity of legal texts, so-called "transfer problems" emerging in communications between legal experts and legal laypeople, and confusing genre mixes where legal texts mingle with nonlegal texts. While I could have chosen to address other problems, I have decided to restrict my study to these three challenges to legal comprehension, as I regard them to be the three key pitfalls in understanding the language of canon law.

4.1 Ambiguity of the Law

The term "ambiguity" is widely used to describe any lack of clarity or indeterminacy in meaning. Ambiguity is a major problem for the law, as it is a requirement of the law to be certain and unambiguous. This prerequisite equally binds canon law.[3] But it is actually not met by the legislator to any great extent. Klaus Mörsdorf once called the terminology of the former 1917 Code a "*Schmerzenskind*"[4] of the Code—an interesting choice of terminology in itself, as it is difficult to translate this term into other languages. A literal translation into English would be "child of pain," but it is unclear whether the term describes a crybaby who is in pain herself or himself, or the pain that a difficult child causes to his or her parents. So it is hard to know whether Mörsdorf imagined canon law language as a screamingly painful composition in itself or more as a pain for its legal subjects. Both interpretations are probably valid to some extent. And Mörsdorf's verdict on the old Code still holds true today. The language of the current 1983 Code does not differ to any great degree with regard to clarity, unambiguity, and comprehensibility;

[3] E.g., Mörsdorf, *Die Rechtssprache des Codex Juris Canonici*, 2nd edn, Paderborn, Ferdinand Schöningh, 1967, 34; Olschewski, "Der Begriff 'iusta causa' in der kirchlichen Rechtssprache," in Reinhardt, ed, *Theologia et Ius Canonicum*, Essen, Wingen, 1995, 235; Wächter, "Die Rechtssprache," in Campenhausen et al., eds, *Lexikon für Kirchen- und Staatskirchenrecht*, vol. 3, Paderborn, Ferdinand Schöningh, 2004, 379; Ohly, "Gravis necessitas," *Archiv für katholisches Kirchenrecht* 175 (2006), 473–475; Zumbült, "Ordnen," in Meyer/Wichard, eds, *Sprachen der Kirche*, Munich, dkv, 2018, 181–190.

[4] Mörsdorf, *Die Rechtssprache des Codex Juris Canonici*, 2nd edn, Paderborn, Ferdinand Schöningh, 1967, 34.

during the reform of the law, the reformers even deleted many definitions from the legal text to thin out the law. Hence, the 1983 Code retained many ambiguous terms, indeterminate language, and opaque concepts that are open to misunderstandings, as I will show in the following section.

Nevertheless, speaking of "ambiguity" from a linguistic point of view renders it necessary first to clarify what the term actually means, as linguist Sanford Schane notes, alluding to the irony that "ambiguity" also has several meanings. While it is commonly applied to any lack of clarity, its linguistic use is more precise. Ambiguity as referred to by linguists stands either for lexical ambiguity or for structural ambiguity, also called "syntactic ambiguity."[5] Both types can be found in secular and in canon law.

Lexical Ambiguity

Lexical ambiguity applies to terms with more than one meaning, like "bank"—one of Schane's examples—which could mean either a riverbank or a financial institution. Ambiguous terms are very common in canon law. Rudolf Köstler mentioned in his dictionary on the old Code the example of "*consensus*," which could mean either an agreement between different parties, such as a contract, the voluntary decision itself, or the act of expressing one's will;[6] his analysis is still applicable to the use of the term in the current Code. Another example of an ambiguous term present throughout the Code is "*ecclesia*," as Köstler likewise noted for the old Code. It stands for the church either as a theological entity or as a legal institution (in the sense of the Roman church or the particular churches), but it also refers to churches as buildings designed for liturgical actions.[7] Interestingly, "church" in the first two meanings appears in the Latin text of the Code starting with a capital letter ("*Ecclesia*"), whereas the lowercase ("*ecclesia*") serves as a sign that the building is meant. This difference, which Köstler observed for the old Code, is also repeated in the new one. A similar ambiguity occurs when canon law uses the noun "*obligation*" to express liabilities. While the meaning of "obligation" in a legal text seems clear at first sight, it is not unequivocal when used in canonical norms, as those norms sometimes also refer to the church members' religious or moral obligations, as Thomas Amann rightly remarked.[8] Canon 872 CIC/1983, for example, sets out the responsibilities of a sponsor whose task it is

[5] See Schane, "Ambiguity and Misunderstanding in the Law," *Thomas Jefferson Law Review* 25 (2002), 171–172; idem, *Language and the Law*, London, Continuum, 2006, 12–13.

[6] See Köstler, *Wörterbuch zum Codex Iuris Canonici*, Munich, Josef Kösel, 1927, 5 fn. 2.

[7] See ibid., 12.

[8] See Amann, "Gebot und Verbot in der Rechtssprache des CIC," in Geringer/Schmitz, eds, *Communio in Ecclesiae Mysterio*, St. Ottilien, EOS, 2001, 12–13.

to assist "the baptized person to lead a Christian life in keeping with baptism and to fulfil faithfully the obligations inherent in it." The obligations mentioned in this norm are not only legal obligations, but refer to the whole gamut of religious, moral, and legal obligations that address Catholics. Amann likewise mentioned the ambiguity of the term "*officium*" in the Code, which either means "duty" in a wider sense (see canons 209 §2, 211, 212 §3, 223 §1, 225 §2, 232, 233 §1, 394 §2, 747 §1, 781, 794 §1, 822 §2 CIC/1983) or serves as the technical term for "ecclesiastical office."[9]

"Fideles" as Legal Subjects

The examples mentioned show that lexical ambiguity in canon law is not restricted to terms of minor relevance for the church but also applies to terms which have a key meaning within the ecclesiastical order, like "church," "obligation," or "office." The problem of terminological ambiguity therefore penetrates deep into the heart of canon law, as illustrated by one further example, the terms "*fidelis*" ("faithful") and "*christifidelis*" ("Christian faithful"). Both terms are used widely throughout the Code, as they reference the subjects of canon law addressed by the commands of the law. While the overwhelming majority of the norms in the Code mentioning "*fidelis*" and "*christifidelis*" refer to members of the Catholic Church only, as can be detected from their context, they sometimes also seem to refer to *all* Christians. So there is an obvious ambiguity in the meaning of both terms, as they sometimes merely address Catholics, and sometimes include all baptized individuals. Canonist Margit Weber devoted a study to the ambiguity problem facing these central canonical terms.[10] She noted that the terms predominantly refer solely to Catholics. One specific problem is found in canon 1417 §1 CIC/1983, though, which authorizes "*cuilibet fideli*"—the English translation reads "any member of the faithful"—to transfer contentious or penal cases to the tribunals of the Apostolic See. With regard to this canon, it is not entirely clear whether only members of the Catholic Church have the right to approach the Apostolic See with their legal cases or if all the baptized are authorized to bring their cases to the Roman tribunals. The second option seems plausible to most canonists, as another canon of ecclesiastical procedural law, canon 1476 CIC/1983, entitles *anyone*, "whether baptized or not," to bring an

[9] See ibid., 13; for an overview of the terminology of ecclesiastical offices, see Ohly, "Officium ecclesiasticum," *Archiv für katholisches Kirchenrecht* 177 (2008), 56–72; for the old Code, see Mörsdorf, *Die Rechtssprache des Codex Juris Canonici*, 2nd edn, Paderborn, Ferdinand Schöningh, 1967, 183–184.

[10] See Weber, "Rechtssprachliche Anmerkungen zur Verwendung von christifidelis, fidelis, baptizatus und christianus im CIC/1917 und im CIC/1983," in Geringer/Schmitz, eds, *Communio in Ecclesiae Mysterio*, St. Ottilien, EOS, 2001, 653–667.

action to an ecclesiastical tribunal. In this light it is implausible to assume that the legislator would have wanted to restrict the right stated in canon 1417 §1 to Catholics alone. As canon 1417 §1 CIC/1983 probably wants to include non-Catholic Christians in the term "*fideles*," the term receives a manifest ambiguity, regularly meaning "Catholics," but also "Christians" in this mentioned norm. Weber subsequently goes on to discuss whether it would be advisable for the sake of lexical clarity to understand the terms "*fidelis*" and "*christifidelis*" as being restricted to the Catholic faithful, taking canon 1417 §1 CIC/1983 as one of the legislator's mishaps in drafting the norms. She suggests a terminological adjustment, using "*fideles*" and "*christifideles*" strictly for Catholics, as done in nearly all other canons of the Code, and "*baptizati*" whenever all baptized are meant. She consequently makes a suggestion that abides by the traditional use of the terms "*fidelis*" and "*christifidelis*" and frees them from their ambiguity by employing a different term, "*baptizatus*," for the rare moments in which the law relates to all Christians, regardless of their denomination.

However, this suggestion, as pragmatic as it may be, falls short in addressing the theoretical pitfalls behind the ambiguity. Lurking behind the ambiguity of "*fidelis*" and "*christifidelis*" is the significant problem that current canon law in some cases has yet to straighten out its terminology in accordance with modern ecclesiology. This observation alludes to the conflict from which the ambiguity emerged, namely, the fact that while the church's ecclesiology changed with the Second Vatican Council, the terminology of the law remained largely unaltered throughout the major legal reform of 1983. Until the Second Vatican Council and under the old 1917 law, all baptized were regarded as members of the Catholic Church (see canon 87 CIC/1917) and were consequently seen as subjects of canon law (see canon 12 CIC/1917).[11] As all baptized were in principle regarded as Catholics, the terms "*fideles*" and "*christifideles*" were plausibly applied to all Christians who were regarded as either voluntary or involuntary Catholics. The Second Vatican Council changed this ecclesiological idea. It accepted the other churches and Christian communities as separate ecclesial entities and consequently stopped regarding their members as Catholics.[12] Those formerly regarded as heretic "faithful" now became non-Catholic Christians, baptized members of the Church of Christ, which unites all churches and ecclesial communities but is not identical with the Catholic Church. When the new Code was drafted before 1983, this ecclesiological change carried with it a major legal consequence. Baptized non-Catholics were no longer regular subjects of canon law (see canons 11, 96 CIC/1983). Whenever the law now refers to its subjects, it

[11] See Mörsdorf, *Die Rechtssprache des Codex Juris Canonici*, 2nd edn, Paderborn, Ferdinand Schöningh, 1967, 129–130.

[12] See Second Vatican Council, "Dogmatic Constitution *Lumen gentium* on the Church," no. 15, *Acta Apostolicae* Sedis 57 (1965), 19–20.

frequently restricts itself to those baptized whom the Second Vatican Council understood were members of the Catholic Church. However and most surprisingly, this major doctrinal and legal change had no terminological consequences with regard to the use of the terms "*fidelis*" and "*christifidelis*" in the new Code. These terms meant "member of the Catholic Church" in the old Code, and the new Code continues to use the terms with this meaning even though the membership conditions of being Catholic were changed completely. So the terms mean the same, "Catholics," even though the group of individuals to whom they apply today is different. Hence, one could argue, as Weber does, that the ambiguity of the terms within the law is relatively easy to resolve by eliminating the inaccuracy in canon 1417 §1 CIC/1983. From the point of linguistic pragmatics, in any case, one can doubt if this clarifies the issue convincingly. This is at least doubtful if we consider ecclesiology as the evident context of legal speech relating to "*fideles*" and "*christifideles.*" If all baptized are members of the Church of Christ and are called to a life of faith in Christ, as the Second Vatican Council taught, it is rather implausible to argue that the terms "faithful" or "Christian faithful" when used in legal language mean Catholics only. Nobody with any sensitivity for what "*fidelis*" and "*christifidelis*" implies ecclesiologically could argue that both terms should apply solely to members of the Catholic Church where legal terminology is concerned. To keep the terminology of the old Code without noticing the major ecclesiological shift behind it is to prefer terminological tradition over ecclesiology which, in any case, serves as a context of legal speech and thus as a source of legal meaning. Surely, cultivating the traditional language of the old Code emphasizes the roots of canon law thought and language. Yet cultivating terminological tradition is not an end in itself. It becomes a problem when it obstructs contemporary understanding.[13] My proposition is consequently not to remove the present ambiguity of "*fideles*" and "*christifideles*" in the Code by reserving both terms for Catholics and using "*baptizati*" whenever all baptized are meant. This does not in fact solve the ambiguity issue, as a constant uncertainty derives from the ecclesiological context of legal speech. However, neither do I want to suggest the obvious alternative of using "*fidelis*" and "*christifidelis*" for all baptized individuals. Instead, I recommend avoiding terms such as "*fidelis*" and "*christifidelis*" to describe the legal subjects of canon law altogether. Being "faithful," according to our common understanding of the expression, describes the inner stance of a person toward a matter of belief. The law, in any case, is not about the individual's inner stance but mostly about the legal subjects' outward conduct. As a result, canon law does not restrict its binding force to those who believe but addresses individuals merely as members of the Catholic

[13] See Wächter, "Die Rechtssprache," in Campenhausen et al., eds, *Lexikon für Kirchen- und Staatskirchenrecht*, vol. 3, Paderborn, Ferdinand Schöningh, 2004, 380.

Church or, in some cases, as members of other churches. As being a legal subject of canon law is based on church membership and not on belief, it seems wise to stick with terms which relate to external attributes of the legal subjects rather than to their inner stance. I therefore favor using "Catholics" when Catholics only are meant, and "all baptized" or "all Christians," respectively, whenever the law includes all Christians regardless of their denomination.

Syntactic Ambiguity

The church, as has been shown, has a major difficulty with lexical ambiguity that reaches deep into its theological core. Compared to this, its trouble with structural ambiguity is less grave, but this also plays a role nevertheless. Structural or syntactic ambiguity refers to a lack of clarity that results from an ambiguous sentence structure such as a given word order. The structuring of sentences gives rise to grammatical relationships, yet some of them have more than one possible relation. Sanford Schane mentions the example sentence "John asked Bill to leave on Wednesday."[14] The phrase "on Wednesday" could refer either to the day John chose to ask, or to the day on which he wants Bill to leave. So there is structural ambiguity in the sentence regarding the affiliation of "on Wednesday."

One of the most prominent and tragic examples of syntactic ambiguity is connected with the sentencing of British diplomat and Easter Rising leader Roger Casement for his attempt to mobilize German military support for the 1916 Irish fight for independence.[15] Casement was tried by British courts and convicted for high treason, for which he received the death penalty based on the English Treason Act of 1351, a statute that is still in force in the United Kingdom today. The text of the statute allows for an ambiguous reading due to its structure. The act determines as treason "if a Man do levy War against our Lord the King in his Realm, or be adherent to the King's Enemies in his Realm, giving to them Aid and Comfort in the Realm, or elsewhere, and thereof be probably attainted of open Deed by the People of their Condition."[16] However, the original text of 1351 was written in Law French. It reads, "*si home leve leve de guerre contre nostre dit Seigneur le Roi en son Roialme, ou soit aherdant as enemys nostre nostre Seigneur le Roi & le Roialme, donant a eux eid ou confort en son Roialme, ou per aillours,*

[14] Schane, *Language and the Law*, London, Continuum, 2006, 16.

[15] See King's Bench Division and Court of Criminal Appeal, "The King v. Casement," 1 K.B. 98, 1917, http://uniset.ca/other/cs5/19171KB98.html (accessed December 16, 2018).

[16] Parliament of England, "Declaration what Offences shall be adjudged Treason," 1351, 25 Edw 3 St 5 c 2, https://www.legislation.gov.uk/aep/Edw3Stat5/25/2/section/II (accessed December 16, 2018).

& ceo provablement soit atteint de overt faite per gentz de lour condicion."[17] In contrast to the English version, the original French contained no punctuation. The punctuation, though, is of key relevance for the meaning of the section in question. If one inserts a comma between "in the realm" and "or elsewhere," as done by the translators of the statute, the text states that everybody who supports the king's enemies is guilty of treason, notwithstanding whether this support is given from inside or outside British territory. Without a comma, as in the original Norman French version, one may read the text in a different sense, so that treason is committed by an offender who supports the king's enemies—wherever they be, in the realm or elsewhere—but only when they are *within* British territory themselves. Thus, an ambiguous text was interpreted by the insertion of a comma to have a broad meaning, whereas the nonpunctuated text rather opts for a restricted reading. As Casement was outside Britain when he attempted to support the Irish independence movement, it was the comma inserted into the English translation of the French statute that sealed his fate. After being sentenced to death, he purportedly noted he had been "hanged on a comma."

Compared to the Casement case, the syntactic ambiguities of canon law have no such existential consequences, but they also present some challenges to understanding canonical norms, as can be shown with regard to canon 119 no. 1 CIC/1983. Relating to elections in ecclesiastical organizations, the rule declares a candidate elected after receiving the absolute majority of votes. The canon then goes on to order the proceedings if no absolute majority is reached in the first ballot, stating that "after two indecisive ballots, a vote is to be taken on the two candidates who have obtained the greater number of votes or, if there are several, on the two senior in age; after the third ballot, if a tie remains, the one who is senior in age is considered elected." The canon is therefore clear about the quorum to decide the second ballot: a candidate needs an absolute majority of votes. Yet it is less clear when it comes to the third ballot, as it is unclear if it again requires an absolute majority or if a relative majority suffices in this case. The structure of the text allows both readings. The mention of "absolute majority" in the part on the first ballot does include the second ballot without explicit mention, as revealed by the phrasing "two indecisive ballots" in the text. Yet it is unclear if it also includes the third ballot. It does not, as the Pontifical Council for Legislative Texts stated when interpreting the canon thus erasing the syntactic ambiguity from the norm by the way of authentic interpretation.[18] The canon itself, however, is not clear.

[17] Https://www.languageandlaw.org/TEXTS/STATS/TREASON.HTM (accessed December 16, 2018).

[18] See Pontifical Council for Legislative Texts, "Responsum ad propositum dubium," June 28, 1990, *Acta Apostolicae Sedis* 82 (1990), 845.

4.2 Transfer Problems

As Legalese is a specialist language, its comprehension requires specialist knowledge and methodical proficiency. Those lacking in legal knowledge or methodical training struggle to understand it. This happens frequently. Indeed, legal lays often misunderstand the language of the law. There are two main reasons which make it difficult to comprehend legal terminology. First, individuals without any legal training naturally have difficulty understanding specific legal terms. They have no access to the exclusive repertoire of legal language. Second, and often more misleading, is that even those legal terms which are taken from common language tend to be misunderstood or misused, as they receive a new or different meaning when they become legal terms. Failed communication between speakers and listeners with and without a legal background respectively are often due to "transfer problems," as Dietrich Busse called them, as sender and receiver attribute a different meaning to a term.[19] These problems are seldom deeply conflictive, but hinder legal communication from time to time. Busse even noticed an increase in misunderstandings between proficient speakers of legal language and legal laypeople, as legal language tends to become more specific gradually and over time, thus successively losing touch with common terminology.[20] Even terms which initially had the same meaning in legal and common language tend to develop a specified legal meaning over time, so that they become harder to understand for nonspeakers of Legalese.

"Annulment" Terminology

The same applies to the church and its law. Many of its legal terms are difficult to understand and tend to be misunderstood. I will explain this by using an example which has in fact a huge impact on the way individuals perceive ecclesiastical adjudication, namely, the "nullity" terminology of the ecclesiastical nullity cases, and primarily the marriage nullity procedures. Above all, speaking of an "annulment" of a marriage is confusing to many hearers. What the word legally means and what the nullity procedures do is to examine whether a marriage was entered validly at the time when it was contracted. In those cases in which certain reasons hindered the partners from contracting validly, the marriage is found to have been missing essential elements right from the time of its commencement and is thus regarded as never having enjoyed validity from its very beginning.

[19] See Busse, "Juristische Fachsprache und öffentlicher Sprachgebrauch," in Liedtke et al., eds, *Begriffe besetzen*, Opladen, Westdeutscher Verlag, 1991, 161.
[20] See Busse, "Rechtssprache als Problem der Bedeutungsbeschreibung," *Sprache und Literatur* 29 (1998), 45.

After examining this in a legal procedure and proving that essential elements of the marriage were indeed missing at the time of the contract, ecclesiastical tribunals issue a declaration that a marriage is found to be invalid. This does not constitute a divorce, as according to ecclesiastical doctrine there has never been a marriage which could be divorced. For the same reason annulment is not a "dissolution" either. It is the recognition that a marriage, even though the marriage formalities were executed, never came into being in the first place. However, when hearing the word "annulment" most listeners naturally think of divorce. Some also imagine something slightly different. They understand "annulment" as the church's active legal separation of two married partners, which, in contrast to divorce, renders their married life null and void. Whereas "divorce" implies that there was a marriage which no longer exists and which does not change anything about the history of the couple, "annulment" seems to imply to many individuals affected that everything, including their shared past, is actively erased by the church. Many individuals therefore suspect the church of making an ontological judgment about their past, telling them that the shared history with the now estranged partner never existed. Reacting to this finding, in 1983 the Canon Law Society of America entrusted a committee with examining whether the term "annulment" needed replacing because it had led to misunderstandings among many Catholics.[21] After more than two years of study (1984–1986), the committee indeed suggested the term "annulment" be erased and replaced with a more nuanced terminology in marriage issues, as it found the nullity terminology to be ambiguous and insensitive. The committee summed up the people's understanding of "annulment" as follows, "The question frequently heard is not 'What is a church annulment?' but, rather, 'How can you say my marriage never existed?' People hear such terms as 'annulment' or 'null and void' and they hear the Church saying there never was a marriage."[22] In the British Isles, practical theologian Timothy Buckley, on behalf of the Bishops' Conference of England and Wales, examined the British Catholics' understanding of marriage in the 1990s and discovered the same difficulties. Buckley found that "[t]here is a growing number of people who will not petition for an annulment because they do not wish to establish that their marriage never existed."[23] They evidently understand the legal qualification of a marriage as null as a verdict about the

[21] See Canon Law Society of America, "Resolution 4," *Canon Law Society of America Proceedings* 45 (1984), 324–326; Canon Law Society of America's Annulment Language Committee, *Annual Report*, October 1985 (unpublished); idem, *Annual Report*, October 1986 (unpublished).

I am grateful to the Archives of the University of Notre Dame, which keep the Canon Law Society of America's Records, for granting me access to the documentation of the committee's work (see CLSA 12/28 Folder: Annulment Language Committee 1984–1986).

[22] Canon Law Society of America's Annulment Language Committee, *Annual Report*, October 1986, 7.

[23] Buckley, *What Binds Marriage*, 2nd edn, London, Geoffrey Chapman, 2002, 157.

social reality of the former bond. Buckley quoted a litigant's typical objection, "[A]lthough it was a washout, we all did our best; we did have some good times, so how can you say it has never been a marriage over 29 years?"[24] This challenge, in any case, does not merely apply to the English nullity terminology. It similarly applies with regard to German terminology. "*Annullierung*" ("annulment") and "*Nichtigkeit*" ("nullity") are similarly problematic and received as such by most listeners. Canonist and ecclesiastical judge Engelbert Frank emphasized this issue in two articles.[25] Correspondingly, many German Catholics who were asked about their marriage and family conceptions in the run-up to the Synod of Bishops in 2014 expressed their disapproval of nullity procedures because they did not regard a marriage, which had been a reality that had lasted for some time, as invalid, but as broken. As a result, they considered annulling a marriage to be dishonest, as it seems to deny the affected couple's past life.[26]

Substance and Accidents

I do not wish to go any deeper into potential strategies for avoiding this misunderstanding or into discussing which terminology would be better suited to communicate what is really meant by "annulment"; the Canon Law Society of America's Annulment Language Committee has in fact made some suggestions which are well worth considering. Neither do I want to speculate whether this would make Catholics feel any better about the nullity procedures or if their crisis —terminology apart—has its roots in the unsettling idea of making a marriage—a deeply personal reality—an object of forensic scrutiny. My point in this study is merely to illustrate that the annulment terminology is one example of how legal communication fails to convey the legal meaning of a term to non-expert listeners. I would like to suggest that it is not in the least surprising that it fails to do so, particularly when it comes to the deceptive term "annulment." My explanation is an ontological one, but it is easier than it may sound, as it is quite intuitive at least for readers with a Western cultural background. This is the case because Western thought, in accordance with Greek ontology, tends to comprehend objects as substances with one or more accidents. This idea can also be applied to marriage and, as I wish to argue, is applied to it by many Western

24 Ibid., 158.

25 See Frank, "Die Sprache kirchlicher Ehegerichte und ihre Wahrnehmung durch Betroffene," in Puza/Weiß, eds, *Iustitia in caritate*, Frankfurt am Main, Peter Lang, 1997, 463–473; idem, "Ehenichtigkeitserklärung," in Weiß/Ihli, eds, *Flexibilitas Iuris Canonici*, Frankfurt am Main, Peter Lang, 2003, 501–514.

26 See German Bishops' Conference, "Press Release: Die pastoralen Herausforderungen der Familie," February 3, 2014, 11, https://www.dbk.de/fileadmin/redaktion/diverse_downloads/presse_2014/2014-012a-Fragebogen-Die-pastoralen-Herausforderungen-der-Familie.pdf.

thinkers. Marriage, as a legal institution, is therefore seen as a substance, an invisible bond formed by the law that unites two individuals. Nevertheless, this abstract entity only becomes real by the accidents which bring it to life: love, living together, sharing time, and looking back on a shared history. I would consequently like to suggest that many individuals understand the legal reality of marriage as the substance, and the social reality of married life as its accidents. If I am right, it becomes rather understandable why many individuals regard a nullity verdict not solely as a verdict about the legal reality of marriage but as one about its social reality as well. And this is a rather natural conclusion, as I want to argue. If the legal substance is null, the accidents attached to that substance can hardly claim to exist. Taking away the substance also annihilates the accidents. If the legal reality of the marriage is nonexistent, this is automatically taken as a nullity verdict on its accidents, the social reality of a marriage. The parties concerned consequently understand "annulment" as a denial of their past lives. They accuse the church of pretending that there was "nothing," no legal and consequently no social reality to the marriage. Many Catholics therefore call "annulment" a dishonest and hypocritical move for dealing with broken marriages. They would prefer to opt for a divorce, thus acknowledging that while the marriage has been terminated, it still actually existed as a legal substance which provided a foundation for a social reality. Divorce is taken as a more honest step toward acknowledging the social reality of marriage, whereas "annulment" has a "fake" sound in many hearers' ears. In their interpretation, annulment, as an attempt to erase the past, is the church's version of "alternative reality."

A Grin without a Cat

A vivid picture painted by legal and literary scholar Sebastian McEvoy might help to illustrate the problem more clearly.[27] McEvoy once compared a related question—the relation between subjects and predicates in legal language—with the Cheshire Cat, the cat mentioned in Lewis Carroll's book *Alice's Adventures in Wonderland*. The Cheshire Cat is famous for its capacity to disappear, while only its grin remains visible. This cat is a good example of the impression that ecclesiastical nullity theory leaves in many individuals' heads. If the legal institution of marriage is the cat, thus the essence, and all the "other" features of marriage—its reality—are the cat's grin, hence the accidents, it comes as no surprise that individuals have a hard time imagining a grin without a cat. Alice commented on the disappearance of the Cheshire Cat with similar bafflement when she remarked,

[27] See McEvoy, "The Grin's Cat," in Freeman/Smith, eds, *Law and Language*, Oxford, Oxford University Press, 2013, 164–186.

"Well! I've often seen a cat without a grin, . . . but a grin without a cat! It's the most curious thing I ever saw in all my life!"[28] Alice stands for most people. Imagining a collection of accidents, the reality of married life, without its substance, marriage itself, seems like a catless grin to most of us.

If one takes into account that most individuals are better Aristotelians than we might suspect, the misunderstanding connected with "annulment" seems fairly logical. In this light, it is actually easier to understand the misunderstanding than to expect individuals to understand the legal term correctly. Having thought about the problem, it makes me all the more surprised when Western individuals actually comprehend "annulment" correctly, as I expect them to misunderstand it, based on their cultural knowledge of interpreting legal concepts in Aristotelian terms.

To sum up in brief: the example mentioned, I find, is helpful inasmuch as it points at two problematic aspects of transfer between legal and common language and knowledge. It shows that legal miscommunications happen and it is hard to avoid them. As long as the law uses specialist language, and as long as the legal and common meanings of terms differ, there will be communication problems between legal and common language. The example, nevertheless, also shows that transfer problems usually have a reason which can be detected by dedicating some study to it. This reason might be hard to find from time to time, as it might lie buried deep in cultural soil, the history of ideas, and everyday ontology. But it might be well worth unearthing it in order to understand misunderstandings and improve comprehension. In some cases, as in the example of "annulment," there might even be an answer to solving the transfer problem, for instance, by revising the language of the law. The amendment proposal made by the Canon Law Society of America's Annulment Language Committee shows that many transfer problems can be addressed if they are understood properly.

4.3 Blending Literary Genres

Another of the five requirements for making sense of legal language which Dietrich Busse mentioned is having a sense for intertextuality, as legal speech becomes understandable only in the light of the diverse genres which contribute to its meaning. Legal terms often only disclose their specific meaning to those who know how to decode a statute, study the judicial decisions that are based on it, and consult the relevant legal commentaries. However, intertextual study also relies on keeping the single legal genres clear. The language of a statute is different to the language of judicial decisions and again different to that of scholarly

[28] Carroll, *Alice's Adventures in Wonderland*, New York, The Macmillan Company, 1920, 94.

comments. Consequently, it is confusing and even misleading when genres are mixed up. Scholarly texts do not settle legal issues, even if they sometimes sound like they do. Judges are frequently angered when expert opinions dictate a judgment to them—which psychological experts in fact often do in ecclesiastical marriage procedures, making the judges grumble over this "border transgression." It is confusing when statutes suddenly turn into arguments presenting various opinions. The saying "*lex iubeat non doceat*" is one piece of advice given in many texts on how to design legal norms in civil law cultures, expressing the rule that the law is to command and to order a matter, not to teach and explain it.[29] Statutes are particularly delicate in this respect, as linguist Andreas Lötscher notes. While other legal genres often serve many different purposes, statutes are mono-functional, as he explains, as they primarily have an illocutionary function.[30] Their command has the purpose to impact our legal world and to change our reality by bringing about legal effects. This performative function of statutes is easily obscured whenever descriptive elements are added. Keeping legal norms widely free from any explanations or added information is therefore vital for preserving their illocutionary power. It is also a matter of authority, as Lötscher contends. A statute speaks for itself; it does not have to be justified by any further information. Adding to this, he observes, is that legal certainty requires legal norms to be kept free from any unnecessary trimmings, so that it is clear which components of a text are the legal rule and which are nonbinding elements.

Theological Trimmings

The reasons I have mentioned show how important it is to respect the different genres of legal texts, particularly where legal norms are concerned. Accordingly, canonist Remigiusz Sobański also presented the *lex iubeat* maxim as a rule for canon law.[31] Nevertheless, the ecclesiastical legislator did not strictly adhere to the rule when composing the 1983 Code. Legislation mostly refrained from inserting unnecessary "ornamental" terms into the law which Rudolf Köstler detected in the old Code, where terms like "*sacer*" and "*sanctus*" ("sacred," "holy"), or unnecessary double expressions, like "*ediximus et sanximus*" (both meaning "commanding," "ordering") were cluttering up the legal text.[32] Yet while

[29] See Lötscher, "Gesetze als Texte," in Lerch, ed, *Recht vermitteln*, Berlin, Walter de Gruyter, 2005, 189–190.

[30] See ibid., 190.

[31] See Sobański, "Der neue Codex des kanonischen Rechts als kirchliches und rechtliches Ereignis," *Österreichisches Archiv für Kirchenrecht* 35 (1985), 18.

[32] See Köstler, *Wörterbuch zum Codex Iuris Canonici*, Munich, Josef Kösel, 1927, 11.

Similar doublings also appear in secular legal languages; the English legal languages contain quite a few, like "fit and proper," "null and void," "rest, residue, and remainder," "last will and testament," "give, devise, and bequeath," "aid and comfort," "faith and credit," "had and received," or "force and

the new Code contains fewer ornamental trimmings, it is rather infamous for its blend of different textual genres, which, even more confusingly, include not only legal genres. Besides distinct legal rules with an illocutionary function, the Code contains descriptive texts, which are somewhat perplexing in this context. Canonist John P. Beal identifies this genre mix in the Code as a typical characteristic of premodern codifications and calls it "the same sort of potpourri that was characteristic of earlier patriarchal codifications"[33] like the Prussian General State Laws. Standing out from this potpourri in canon law are theological statements, about which Ladislas Orsy noted, "The content of the Code can be divided into literature that is proclamation of doctrine and literature that intends to give norms of action."[34] One can find proclamations of doctrine mainly in the sacramental law of the church. The law of the sacraments even contains some purely theological sentences, which one would rather expect in the Catechism, liturgical books, or papal encyclicals. The sacramental law starts off with canon 834 §1 CIC/1983, for instance, a canon describing the church as performing

> its sanctifying function in a particular way through the sacred liturgy, which is an exercise of the priestly function of Jesus Christ. In the sacred liturgy the sanctification of humanity is signified through sensible signs and effected in a manner proper to each sign. In the sacred liturgy, the whole public worship of God is carried out by the head and members of the mystical body of Jesus Christ.

Surely, this content is relevant to understanding the sacramental law of the church on the background of sacramental doctrine. However, besides providing an explanation of why the legislator saw a need to organize the liturgies and the sacraments as central actions of the church with the help of the law, the whole canon has no direct legal effect and thus disturbs the illocutionary mono-function of sacramental law. This problem is exacerbated when it comes to another genre mix common in the law of the sacraments. The law also integrates legal rules *into* theological sentences (for instance, see canons 840, 849 CIC/1983), thus obscuring—bearing Lötscher's critique in mind—which components of the text are legally binding and which are not. This insertion of nonlegal segments into the law is by no way coincidental, as canonist Stephan Haering pointed out,

effect." David Mellinkoff—and many scholars agreeing with him—called this practice "worthless doubling," Mellinkoff, *The Language of the Law*, Boston, MA, Little, Brown and Company, 1963, 349.

33 Beal, "Something There Is That Doesn't Love a Law," in Lacey/Oakley, eds, *The Crisis of Authority in Catholic Modernity*, Oxford University Press, Oxford, 2011, 147.

34 Orsy, "The Interpreter and His Art," *The Jurist* 40 (1980), 33. Orsy then goes into a detailed systematic of the doctrinal texts, which I do not wish to recall here at length; see 33–37.

but is often because these texts were indeed taken out of nonlegal, mostly doctrinal contexts and inserted into the law.[35] Haering refers to insertions of conciliar texts into the Code, as can be seen in canon 838 CIC/1983, which quotes a line taken from the Constitution on the Liturgy *Sacrosanctum concilium*, stating, "Regulation of the sacred liturgy depends solely on the authority of the church, that is, on the Apostolic See and, as laws may determine, on the bishop."[36] In this or a similar fashion, other statements of doctrinal origin became part of the law. In any case, many of these doctrinal and legal blends are confusing for readers, particularly for those without a legal training. They are also debatable insofar as they beg the question why the law of the church mixes theology and law. The answer usually given is that it reminds receivers of canon law that the law has to be interpreted in the light of theology. But this is a reminder that may also be given differently, without stuffing canonical statutes with theological assertions. In doing so, legislation in fact reinforces the impression that it wants to juridify theology—which it is indeed doing formally by inserting theological sentences into law—a practice seen rather critically by many church members. So there are reasons to doubt whether the integration of theological declarations into legal norms is of any value, or is even harmful for the Catholics' understanding and acceptance of canonical rules.

A Custom Commercial

Theological statements squeezed into ecclesiastical statute law are maybe the most manifest example for literary blends in canon law. However, there are other examples as well. One can be found in canon 27 CIC/1983. The canon reads, "Custom is the best interpreter of laws." At first sight this statement does not resemble a legal rule. The reason for this is that it was originally not a rule but a legal maxim, taken from Justinian's *Digest*.[37] Now part of the canons of the Code, the question arises whether the old legal maxim has become a legal rule in its new embedding. Describing custom as the best interpreter of laws is a descriptive articulation. Yet the sentence can be turned into a rule by rephrasing, "When interpreting a law consult custom first." Thus, one could reinterpret the statement as a rule of interpretation, commanding the interpreters of canon law to refer to custom when interpreting ecclesiastical laws. That this was not the legislator's intent is apparent, though, when studying those norms of the Code

[35] See Haering, "Konziliare Ekklesiologie und kanonische Sprache," in Güthoff/Haering, eds, *Ius quia iustum*, Berlin, Duncker & Humblot, 2015, 65–66.
[36] Article 22 no. 1, *Acta Apostolicae Sedis* 56 (1964), 106.
[37] See book 1, title 3, no. 37, *The Digest of Justinian*, Cambridge, Cambridge University Press, 1904, 23.

which clearly contain rules of interpretation. The key norm on interpretation, canon 17 CIC/1983, obliges the interpreter of ecclesiastical laws first to consider the proper meaning of the words used in a law with regard to text and context, and then to look for parallel places, purpose and circumstances of the law, and the intentions of the legislator. I will comment on this canon in greater depth in chapter 7. In light of the statement contained in canon 27 CIC/1983 praising custom as the best interpreter of laws, it is noteworthy that canon 17 CIC/1983 does not even mention custom as one source of legal meaning. So canon 27 CIC/1983, with its beautiful tribute to custom, has no actual legal relevance for the interpretation of canonical norms. It is not a legal rule. Instead it is somewhat of a garnish-type sentence, sounding respectful with regard to local traditions and usages without having too much of a legal impact. With regard to the practical insignificance of the canon, Ladislas Orsy once remarked, "'Custom is the best interpreter of laws.' But there is also a latent irony in the fact that our legal system goes a long way to inhibit the emergence of customs."[38] As the ecclesiastical legislator tends to answer open legal questions authoritatively and to clarify uncertain norms by himself, he leaves only a small space for the development of customary law at all, as Orsy also noted, "If all doubts are decided by decrees, how could the community ever contribute? What would be the purpose of canon 27 at all?"[39] The canon thus seems to be rather pointless. It serves as a political statement or a catchphrase, making use of the culturally sensitive tune that rings with local "custom," without attributing any power to custom in interpreting the law. Andreas Lötscher's critique of nonlegal insertions into statutes suggests that its inclusion into the Code is misleading and should be avoided for the sake of clarity. I would like to add to this and suggest avoiding purely "ornamental" rules particularly when they are actually a sham. The custom commercial that the legislator sends in canon 27 CIC/1983 is after all little more than a bluff that the ecclesiastical legal subjects do not deserve.

[38] Orsy, *Theology and Canon Law*, Collegeville, MN, The Liturgical Press, 1992, 116.
[39] Ibid., 116 fn. 22.

5
Challenging Legal Incomprehension

In the previous chapter I listed several reasons that impede the understanding of legal language. However, comprehending legal texts is generally challenging. Legalese is a specialist language; its comprehension requires specialist knowledge and training. For individuals who do not possess these skills, deciphering Legalese is virtually impossible. One of the most prominent writers to examine the struggles connected with understanding Legalese was David Mellinkoff; he inspired countless lawyers and linguists to engage in the debate on the language of the law. Mellinkoff attributed to the law an "uncommon touch,"[1] as he called it, as the law makes use of many features—common terms with uncommon meanings, words in foreign languages, formal words, or mannerisms—which make it harder to comprehend for the common listener or reader. In his book *The Language of the Law* Mellinkoff gave numerous examples of these peculiarities in the English legal languages, which capture the problem vividly. After Mellinkoff, many lawyers and linguists started collecting reasons why legal language is difficult to understand. Taking into account the characteristics of legal language, legal scholar Robert Benson observed that law leads to incomprehension thanks to its style, stating,

> There exist scores of empirical studies showing that most of the linguistic features found in legalese cause comprehension difficulties. Legalese is characterized by passive verbs, impersonality, nominalizations, long sentences, idea-stuffed sentences, difficult words, double negatives, illogical order, poor headings, and poor typeface and graphic layout. Each of these features alone is known to work against clear understanding.[2]

5.1 Exclusivism and Elitism

The composition of legal texts is therefore bound to result in incomprehension among those who are not trained to read and hear Legalese, and this is exactly what happens, as legal scholar Brian Tamanaha noted, maintaining,

[1] Mellinkoff, *The Language of the Law*, Boston, MA, Little, Brown and Company, 1963, 11.
[2] Benson, "The End of Legalese," *N.Y.U. Review of Law & Social Change* 13 (1984), 531; see also Tiersma, *Legal Language*, Chicago, IL, The University of Chicago Press, 1999, 203–210.

The Language of Canon Law. Judith Hahn, Oxford University Press. © Oxford University Press 2023.
DOI: 10.1093/oso/9780197674246.003.0005

> Lay people do not understand legal jargon. Employees lack the capacity and freedom to negotiate the details of employment contracts set by employers (and unions). Consumers do not read sales and service contracts they enter, signing away legal rights through waivers of liability and accepting mandatory arbitration should dispute arise. People have little choice in the matter other than to not take the job or engage in the transaction at all, and available alternatives frequently impose the same standard terms.[3]

Tamanaha's critique also alludes to the social costs of incomprehension. As the members of society have no choice other than be a party to legal transactions, they have to play their role as legal agents without truly mastering its legal side. They are either ignorant of their rights or cannot lay claim to them without professional help. So they are largely at the mercy of legal experts. This problem also applies to canon law. Most Catholics do not comprehend the unique mysteries of canon law language. They are usually not very well informed about the rights they possess in the church and how to claim them. However, the social costs of incomprehension are certainly not as high in the church as they are in other social arenas. As the church today has a restricted role in society, it also has a more limited part to play in the lives of the church members. Their incomprehension of canon law is therefore usually socially less costly than their unfamiliarity with state law. However, one matter in which their lack of legal literacy can be costly for legal subjects, both with regard to state law and canon law, is when it becomes necessary to organize the help of experts who function as translators of the law. To partake effectually in the legal debates of secular or canon law, legal laypeople frequently need the assistance of legally trained experts to "decode" the law for them. The caste of lawyers serve as legal professionals whose main duty is to convert Legalese into common language and back, as Harold Berman contended when writing, "The lawyer likes to translate, if he can get the layman's ear. Indeed, much of his professional work itself requires such translation—to clients, to juries, to legislative committees, and even to judges in oral argument."[4] Berman's words, as true as they are, suggest that it is normal and necessary that understanding the law requires professional assistance. However, this proposition has been subject to criticism over recent decades, particularly by scholars with a law and language proficiency. Accepting the law as a cryptic code or a secret language unknown to many is critical for several reasons. One main reason, which I will introduce in the following section, is that legal incomprehension is not only socially costly, as it excludes most members of society from engaging in the debates of one of society's most relevant normative systems, but that it becomes even

[3] Tamanaha, *A Realistic Theory of Law*, Cambridge, Cambridge University Press, 2017, 140–141.
[4] Berman, *Law and Language*, Cambridge, Cambridge University Press, 2013, 104.

pricier by allowing this status quo to persist, as incomprehensible law becomes an exclusivist and elitist project, used by a legal elite to dominate other members of society. This is hardly a satisfactory state of affairs for a modern society.[5] The debates on the incomprehensibility of the law are therefore closely connected with the social debates. They revolve around the question of what form modern societies and communities should take and what a law should look like that corresponds with modern democratic, liberal, and egalitarian ideals. A law that—via language—excludes most and includes but a few members of a group obviously presents a dilemma for modern concepts of social life and socialization.

Language Weapons

The critique of Legalese is usually pragmatic, as it wants the law to become more comprehensible in order to reduce social costs. But it can also become emotional, particularly when the language of the law is criticized for its exclusivist and elitist effects. Some scholars such as Robert Benson make no secret of the fact that they despise Legalese not only because it sounds ridiculously out of date but also because of the consequence of its outdated sound, namely, the formation of a legal elite and the exclusion of all who are not members of the legal guild. Benson ridicules the sound of the law, but at the same time points at its dark undertone, stating,

> Even tolerant, pluralistic publics would twitter or raise their eyebrows at persons who, in the latter half of the twentieth century, seriously insist upon wearing medieval coats of armor to work. And if these modern-day medievalists were members of an exclusive club wielding considerable power over the public, their armor would understandably provoke fear or resentment. Legalese, the medieval armor of lawyers, has precisely that effect. It is not merely different as prose styles go; it is strange in the extreme, off the edge of the range of normal prose styles even in a diverse society. It is so out of touch with ordinary language that—in the hands of a powerful, exclusive profession—it becomes at best a symbol of alienation and at worst a tool to intimidate and exploit the public.[6]

Benson not only shows sympathy with those nonspeakers of Legalese who are faced with their nonunderstanding, but he also expresses anger from his own professional point of view. It is evident that he as a legal scholar feels uncomfortable

[5] On the several post-Enlightenment attempts to make law more understandable, see Lerch, "Gesetze als Gemeingut aller," in idem, ed, *Recht verstehen*, Berlin, Walter de Gruyter, 2004, 225–237.
[6] Benson, "The End of Legalese," *N.Y.U. Review of Law & Social Change* 13 (1984), 522.

being part of the legal guild, which he envisages as a somewhat ridiculous parade of dressed-up pranksters equipped with the weapons of the law. They do not merely provoke social disapproval or even public antipathy but also pose a threat to the other people on the street. Certainly, at the heart of Benson's analysis lies once again the problem of incomprehensibility, as the dressed-up medievalists provoke fear and resentment particularly because they wield powerful weapons beyond the control of anyone else, as the right spells which perform legal magic are known only to them. Words are powerful, and words that others do not understand give those who know them power over those who do not. Benson explains this phenomenon again in a vivid depiction of a child learning just how powerful words are, writing, "But just as it is obvious to every school child who has ever scrawled a dirty word on the chalkboard that language is power, so it ought to be obvious to all of us that lawyers' language is power exercised by a power elite and that the stakes in it are very real and very high."[7] So the language of the law is power, but it is also a power reserved to a few, a chosen elite capable of participating in Legalese discourses. In consequence, Benson's critique is not only about incomprehension but also about the exclusivism and elitism that goes hand in hand with a secret language. Legal experts, in Benson's view, form a secret society based on their language, which excludes those who are unable to understand it. They also, he contends, use their secret language as an instrument of social control over those who do not understand it. Benson is highly self-critical in this respect when admitting,

> Every lawyer's personal experience bears witness to the fact that legalese can be a weapon. Is there a lawyer among us who has not employed the magic of legal language as a psychological device to dominate some lay person? I confess I have done so many times—particularly when dealing with recalcitrant bureaucrats and corporate clerks—and I have frequently seen my comrades-in-law do the same. If there breathes a lawyer who is free from this taint, I shall immediately nominate him or her to receive the next Saint Thomas More Award from my law school.[8]

Hence, as Benson illustrates, the temptation is strong to make use of legal magic to exclude others. And there is also a temptation to use shady tricks instead of real magic, to remain with Benson's picture. In this sense, he elsewhere refers to Legalese as the lawyers' "hocus-pocus."[9] The parallel which I have already discussed in this study, between the law and the sacraments, between the duty of lawyers and that of priests, becomes visible once again in this context. The

[7] Ibid., 520.
[8] Ibid., 530.
[9] Ibid., 531.

language of the law is both: it is a sacramental language, capable of effectually changing reality by using sacramental signs ("*Hoc est enim* . . ."), and it is the language of pretension and superstition ("*hocus, pocus*"), as no outsider can tell how the law effectuates what it achieves. This example shows that sacraments can turn into superstition if they are clothed in a penumbra of ignorance and half-truth. Whereas comprehension lays open the performative power of the law, incomprehensible Legalese turns legal sacraments into shady sorcery.

Linguistic Distinction

As the church now has less power than it had over Catholics' lives in the past, its law is not as powerful as it used to be. The language of canon law is a powerful tool, ready to perform legal magic, yet—at least for most church members—seldom any longer a threatening weapon. Due to this, the incomprehension of many church members might provoke less fear today than it used to in past times. In any case, it is common to find irritation and anger among many Catholics about a law composed with the purpose of avoiding debate and criticism due to its incomprehensibility. Many members of the churches from high-income countries are reacting negatively to the exclusivism and elitism within the church. The heated debates on clericalism that are currently rocking the German church are addressing both of these "-isms" as factors which have allowed abusive structures to grow in the church.[10] Secret societies, be they clerical or legal societies, are therefore much out of favor. In consequence, so are secret languages as instruments of social control. When it comes to the language of canon law, this problem is exacerbated by the widespread use of Latin. The use of Latin further detaches the law of the church from the everyday language of ordinary Catholics. And it serves as a symbolic marker of exclusion, excluding ordinary church members from the legal debates. Legal scholar and anthropologist Ransford Pyle observed with regard to the use of Latin as a marker of distinction,

> "Today the use of Latin and its English derivatives carries especial prestige for the very reason that Latin is no longer a spoken language. Acquisition of Latin terms, therefore, is a nearly exclusive product of formal education. Realistically, I hope we can acknowledge that access to extensive formal education is open first to those of wealth and high status."[11]

[10] E.g., Jansen, "Was ist Klerikalismus?," September 10, 2018, https://www.katholisch.de/aktuelles/aktuelle-artikel/was-ist-klerikalismus; Löbbert, "Sündenbock gesucht," September 28, 2018, https://www.zeit.de/2018/40/klerikalismus-sexueller-missbrauch-selbstkritik-katholische-kirche; Stewen, "Klerikalismus," October 8, 2018, https://www.feinschwarz.net/klerikalismus-wie-das-amen-in-der-kirche.

[11] Pyle, "Law, Ritual and Language," *American Legal Studies Association Forum* 8 (1984), 387.

Hence, Pyle is highly critical of the use of Latin as a marker of distinction in many specialist contexts, as he finds it to be an exclusive language, creating an elite identity by "othering" those who do not speak Latin. In the church, it explicitly indicates legal questions as requiring expert knowledge, thereby disengaging most members of the church from understanding or interpreting the law. Having said that, as vernacular translations of the Code exist, there is a chance for most church members to access canonical rules in a language they actually speak. But the authentic text of the Code is the Latin version and thus reserved for an elite which understands legal Latin well enough to get the message.

Preventing Legal Heresy

Excluding the majority of legal subjects from accessing the law seems to have been at least partially intended by the legislator, as indicated in 1985 by an argument put forward by canonist and civil attorney Peter Shannon. Shannon commented on the vernacular translations of the 1983 Code by noting that translating the law enabled a great number of individuals to read and understand the new canons who otherwise would be prevented from doing so. Shannon did not view an increased comprehension of canon law merely as progress but also as a danger, as he sensed there were among his fellow American civil lawyers a good number of attorneys who might come up with the idea of making a living off canon law. Shannon explained this problem by referring to canon 127 CIC/1983, suggesting,

> Some attorneys will read, for example, canon 127 which describes the necessity of consultation for the validity and liceity of juridic acts, and will use canon 127 and other canons in attempting to undo certain transactions. In a word, you can expect dozens of lawsuits, which would never have been filed, absent ready access to a vernacular code.[12]

While Shannon's caveat that canon law might become a bonanza for zealous lawyers might have seemed reasonable from his 1985 point of view, his argument is nevertheless perplexing, as it at least implicitly seems to suggest that laws that are incomprehensible to basically everybody could be a good option for the church. This argument is not so far distant from the idea that a legal order might be better off by obscuring its laws deliberately to avoid tempting anybody to actually make use of them. In premodern times, this idea was not uncommon.

12 Shannon, "Canon Law/Civil Law," *The Jurist* 45 (1985), 621.

Edward Coke, the most famous Elizabethan jurist, noted with regard to the use of Law French in Norman England,

> "It was not thought fit nor convenient, to publish either those, or any of the Statutes enacted in those dayes in the vulgar tongue, lest the unlearned by bare reading without right understanding might sucke out errors, and trusting to their owne conceit might endamage themselves, and sometimes fall into destruction."[13]

Both David Mellinkoff and Peter Tiersma took up this quotation as one striking example of how legal experts promote the idea of protecting the public from the law—and likewise the law from the public.[14] The thinking behind this approach is reminiscent of the attempt to prevent medieval Christians from reading the Bible, as Tiersma notes. Just as the Latin Bible prevented most medieval individuals from committing heresies by misunderstanding the biblical texts, law in foreign tongues prevented them from committing legal "heresies." Potential legal "heresy," in any case, and this also seems to be the cause of Shannon's objection, not only seems to lie in the danger of legal laypeople misinterpreting the law but also in tempting them to make use of it. Shannon's caution that the vernacular translations of the Code issued after 1983 could make many Catholics aware of their rights and competencies and encourage them to claim them has the flavor of preventing legal heresy. While this might sound stunning to anybody who cherishes the law and the possibilities that it offers as a tool of justice, it is worth noting that canon law traditionally used to be more a tool of hierarchical domination and less one of empowering the ordinary church members. So reactions such as Shannon's were probably not rare after 1983. They might even be at the root of some arguments today praising Latin as the one and only language of the church and its law. The less understandable it is, the more the law remains an elitist matter. As long as the authentic legal text is in Latin, the reception of canon law by the legal subjects remains difficult. So Latin, while being called the "language of the church," is rather the language of the *official* church or an ecclesiastical elite. It is a Romanized clerical elite in particular that is more familiar with Latin than most other church members, as Latin still plays a key role in the education of clerics. This also connects the question of ecclesiastical Legalese with the debates on clericalism. Clericalism—as the specific ecclesiastical form of exclusivism and elitism—finds expression in legal Latin which is far apart from the language of the ordinary church members.

[13] Coke, *The Selected Writings and Speeches*, vol. 1, Indianapolis, IN, Liberty Fund, 2003, 76.

[14] See Mellinkoff, *The Language of the Law*, Boston, MA, Little, Brown and Company, 1963, 123; Tiersma, *Legal Language*, Chicago, IL, The University of Chicago Press, 1999, 28–29.

5.2 Endorsing Plain Language

The strong criticism of Legalese which has developed over the past fifty years has encouraged many legal scholars and linguists to think about alternative ways of communicating legal content. A growing number of scholars and legal experts share the belief that while legal matters tend to be complex, this does not necessarily imply that they have to be expressed in difficult terminology and style. In the Anglo-American legal cultures, this belief has given rise to the *Plain Language Movement*, the supporters of which are called "plainers."[15] With the help of plain language organizations, the plainers campaign for simple language to be employed to express legal facts. They support "simplification" more than "translation" to make legal content available to legal laypeople more easily.[16] Their work has been received favorably in many legal orders. So what began in Anglo-American legal contexts has become an idea which has spread out across the borders of legal traditions.[17] The Legalese of European law, for instance—one major obstacle for many European citizens on their way to embracing an ever closer union in legal terms—has come under increased scrutiny over the past couple of years.[18]

Avoiding Useless Precision

There are several arguments in favor of plain language, inter alia, that it is more precise, less prone to errors, and more elegant than Legalese, but most importantly that it is more democratic to phrase legal ideas in terms that legal subjects actually understand.[19] Some of the arguments in favor of plain language have nevertheless been refuted by legal scholars who are skeptical whether plain language can achieve what was usually accomplished by complex language. Harold Berman, for instance, alluded to the limits of conveying all legal meaning in plain terms. He noted, "We can unfreeze the legal terms, but we cannot replace them. The pragmatist's view that the particular words do not matter so long as

[15] See Adler, "The Plain Language Movement," in Solan/Tiersma, eds, *The Oxford Handbook of Language and Law*, Oxford, Oxford University Press, 2012, 67–83. For a good and short overview of the history of the movement, see Williams, "Legal English and Plain Language," *ESP Across Cultures* 1 (2004), 115–117.

[16] See Tiersma, *Legal Language*, Chicago, IL, The University of Chicago Press, 1999, 201–202, 211–230.

[17] For the German debates, see Lerch, "Verständlichkeit als Pflicht?," in idem, ed, *Recht verstehen*, Berlin, Walter de Gruyter, 2004, 239–283.

[18] E.g., Grasso, "Plain English and the EU," in Marino et al., eds, *Language and Law*, Cham, Springer Nature Switzerland, 2018, 359–376.

[19] E.g., Adler, "The Plain Language Movement," in Solan/Tiersma, eds, *The Oxford Handbook of Language and Law*, Oxford, Oxford University Press, 2012, 71–72.

you get the same practical consequences neglects the stubborn fact that you never do get the same practical consequences when you use different words."[20] So Berman, like many others, was convinced that the language of the law, despite the prospect of making it better, could not fully abstain from being a specialist terminology.[21] A language of the law with no specialist elements is therefore presumably unachievable. But a language of the law which is more understandable seems within reach.

Another argument which is sometimes espoused in favor of Legalese is that plain language could never be as precise. Robert Benson parries this argument by making the point that precision with regard to the law is not about exact terminology, but about the reliability with which a legal communication successfully conveys a specific message. As an enthusiast of lively metaphors and vivid pictures, Benson explains his problem with Legalese's claim to precision with a story, retelling

> the tale of the Swiss clockmaker who installed his most perfect clock in the tower on the town square. "But Johann," complained the mayor, "the clock has no hands or numbers and the citizens cannot tell the time!" "I give you the finest precision-instrument in Europe," grumbled Johann, "and you are ungrateful. Besides, if the citizens want to know the time, they can pay me to climb the tower, inspect the workings, and announce it."[22]

Benson accuses Legalese of "unintelligible, and therefore useless, precision"[23] and on occasion, no precision at all. And he accuses it of cultivating useless precision as a selling point, as it serves to pay those who perform the translations for others. Certainly, Benson's view on Legalese is extremely negative. But even those who do not fully share his skepticism might see some good reasons for considering the use of plain language in legal contexts, whenever and as far as possible. This view is shared by many scholars, particularly in the law and language field. Today it is sometimes connected with the motto of "linguistic democracy."[24] While this term was initially used to campaign for equal rights for

[20] Berman, *Law and Language*, Cambridge, Cambridge University Press, 2013, 104.

[21] See also Benson, "The End of Legalese," *N.Y.U. Review of Law & Social Change* 13 (1984), 561–562; Neumann, "Juristische Fachsprache und Umgangssprache," in Grewendorf, ed, *Rechtskultur als Sprachkultur*, Frankfurt am Main, Suhrkamp, 1992, 118–120.

[22] Benson, "The End of Legalese," *N.Y.U. Review of Law & Social Change* 13 (1984), 560.

[23] Ibid.

[24] E.g., Mattila, "Legal Vocabulary," in Solan/Tiersma, eds, *The Oxford Handbook of Language and Law*, Oxford, Oxford University Press, 2012, 35.

minority languages,[25] it is also used today in the debates on legal participation in general. As the complex language of the law can be identified as a key barrier to equality with regard to the law, the plain language campaign has become interwoven with some aspects of the linguistic democracy movement. So on the whole, Mark Adler identifies "a strong wind in favor of plain language," while at the same time noting, "There has been much change but progress is slow."[26]

Simple Structure and Style

The question of how legal language could be made easier was addressed back in the 1970s by Robert and Veda Charrow in their famous study on jury instructions. In analyzing how to simplify the complex directions issued by judges, Charrow and Charrow developed a catalog of general tools which help to make Legalese more comprehensible. They suggested using the active instead of the passive voice whenever possible; avoiding "whiz deletions" and using relative pronouns and copulas; replacing nominalizations with verb phrases; avoiding multiple negatives and unclear prepositional phrases ("As to . . ."); avoiding complex embeddings (mainly of subordinate clauses); and, last but not least, replacing difficult terms with easier ones.[27] In particular, the idea of substituting difficult terms has revived the campaign which was launched in the nineteenth century to replace the relics of Law Latin and Law French with vernacular terms. However, the campaign is now based on a different set of motivations. Instead of nationalist reasons, a change to the vernacular is now frequently favored as a step which might make the law more democratic. During the last couple of decades the Anglo-American plain language movement has been advocating the abolition of the French and Latin terms from legal English to make it less exclusive and more understandable throughout the legal community.[28] A similar tendency can be observed in civil law countries, where the aims of the plain language campaign are also under discussion, albeit with less passion than in common law. But there are also growing reservations to Law Latin, as Heikki Mattila notes, "As a result, it can generally be said that today Latin expressions and maxims appear

[25] E.g., Rodríguez, "Language and Participation," *California Law Review* 94 (2006), 687–767; Schmidt, "Democratic Theory and the Challenge of Linguistic Diversity," *Language Policy* 13 (2014), 395–411; Kibbee, *Language and the Law*, Cambridge, Cambridge University Press, 2016.

[26] Adler, "The Plain Language Movement," in Solan/Tiersma, eds, *The Oxford Handbook of Language and Law*, Oxford, Oxford University Press, 2012, 70.

[27] See Charrow/Charrow, "Making Legal Language Understandable," *Columbia Law Review* 79 (1979), 1328–1329; see also Williams, "Legal English and Plain Language," *ESP Across Cultures* 1 (2004), 117–123.

[28] See Tiersma, "A History of the Languages of Law," in idem/Solan, eds, *The Oxford Handbook of Language and Law*, Oxford, Oxford University Press, 2012, 22–23; Hiltunen, "The Grammar and Structure of Legal Texts," in Solan/Tiersma, eds, *The Oxford Handbook of Language and Law*, Oxford, Oxford University Press, 2012, 50.

less frequently than earlier in legal and administrative texts."[29] However, Mattila also detects a countertrend when it comes to Eastern European civil law. After the fall of the Iron Curtain, the legal languages of some former socialist countries increased their use of Latin legal terminology to identify with Western civil law, as Mattila assumes, "In this way, lawyers from these countries emphasize that they belong to the old legal culture of Europe with roots in classical Roman law."[30]

Modernizing Legal Speech

The plainers' attempt to erase unnecessarily difficult terms and phrases from the law is not restricted to loan words from foreign languages, such as Law Latin and Law French, in any case, but also applies to terms in vernacular languages which have become outdated. Robert Benson's critique of the archaic sound of Legalese that he compared with the sound of "modern-day medievalists"[31] not only relates to the old-fashioned sound of medieval Latin or Norman French but also to the demerit that legal texts in general tend to make heavy use of an outmoded vernacular. This is not surprising, considering that many legal texts are indeed very old or are based on some older sources, but it is nevertheless an obstacle to understanding them. This challenge is exacerbated by the fact that everyday language is in a process of permanent change and is evolving quickly, whereas the language of law is evolving less rapidly, which makes it always somewhat outdated and tends to increase the gap between common and legal language even more over time. This is not per se a problem, as Peter Tiersma finds, but it usually becomes one over a certain period of time. Tiersma elucidates this by referring to prepositional prefixes like "where-," "here-," or "there-," common in bygone days, yet unusual today, as in "herewith" ("with this") or "whereunder" ("under what"). Both prepositions are still commonly used in legal English. They are, as Tiersma contends, "generally still comprehensible to Shakespeare scholars and, perhaps, lawyers. Most individuals today, however, have real difficulties understanding such formations."[32] Tiersma illustrates this by taking an example from Shakespearean prose, a passage from *Romeo and Juliet* which is celebrated for its power and beauty, yet is challenging for modern comprehension, stating,

29 Mattila, "Legal Vocabulary," in Solan/Tiersma, eds, *The Oxford Handbook of Language and Law*, Oxford, Oxford University Press, 2012, 35.

30 Ibid.

31 Benson, "The End of Legalese," *N.Y.U. Review of Law & Social Change* 13 (1984), 522.

32 Tiersma, "Reforming the Language of Jury Instructions," *Hofstra Law Review* 22 (1993), 66.
David Mellinkoff goes one step further in claiming that words such as "aforesaid," "forthwith," "hereafter," "hereby," "herein," "hereinafter," and "heretofore" are not only hard to comprehend today

> I sometimes ask people what Juliet meant when on her balcony she pined: "O, Romeo, Romeo! wherefore art thou Romeo?" Respondents almost invariably think that Juliet cannot spot her lover in the garden below, and that she is asking, "Where, oh where, are you, Romeo?" In fact, "wherefore" is the interrogative form of "therefore" and means "why" or "for what reason." The common misinterpretation obscures the whole point of the scene. Juliet is asking Romeo why his name is Romeo Montague, marking him as a member of the Montague clan with which her family is feuding, and thus preventing them from being together.[33]

As people today tend to read less Shakespeare—and likewise less of the King James Bible as a similar good practice of listening to a somewhat outdated language, as Tiersma suggests—he proposes reforming the language of the law before it becomes fully incomprehensible to legal laypeople. These examples of outdated prose which are unfamiliar to our modern ears and echoed in legal language all refer to examples taken from the English language. Nevertheless, one can doubtlessly find slightly different but comparable examples in most non-English legal languages, too.

5.3 Plain Canon Law?

In light of many convincing reasons for making the language of the law easier to understand, the language of canon law is faced with the same question of how to respond to the plain language claim. Canonists like Remigiusz Sobański leave no doubt that it is essential for canon law to be understood by its legal subjects.[34] The 1983 Code and its language, I would like to suggest, can be interpreted as a first step in the ecclesiastical legislator's acceptance of the need to make canon law more comprehensible to the church members. A first obvious sign of this insight is that the Code was issued in most of the common global languages, even though these translations only serve as working aids. Furthermore, the revised Code was purged of many unnecessary regulations which were cluttering up the old Code. With its 1752 canons, it is now considerably reduced in comparison to the 2,414 canons of the old Code. Many unnecessary ornamental terms, like *sacer* and *sanctus* were also eradicated from the text.

but usually fully useless in legal texts; see Mellinkoff, *The Language of the Law*, Boston, MA, Little, Brown and Company, 1963, 305–317.

33 Tiersma, "Reforming the Language of Jury Instructions," *Hofstra Law Review* 22 (1993), 66.

34 See Sobański, "Der neue Codex des kanonischen Rechts als kirchliches und rechtliches Ereignis," *Österreichisches Archiv für Kirchenrecht* 35 (1985), 15–16.

Simplifying Constructions

Nevertheless, the style in which the canons are drafted remained largely unaltered. The authentic text of both Codes is drafted in Canon Law Latin. It makes heavy use of the passive voice and of nominalizations. It also often employs "whiz deletions," as subordinate clauses are often introduced without an introductory phrase or squeezed into participial constructions. Canon 6 §1 CIC/1983 may serve as a typical example of a text that shows several of the characteristics mentioned. The canon reads in its English translation,

> When this Code takes force, the following are abrogated: 1° the Code of Canon Law promulgated in 1917; 2° other universal or particular laws contrary to the prescripts of this Code unless other provision is expressly made for particular laws; 3° any universal or particular penal laws whatsoever issued by the Apostolic See unless they are contained in this Code; 4° other universal disciplinary laws regarding matter which this Code completely reorders.

The English text is largely plain and clear. In contrast, the original Latin grammar and structure is more complex than the translation suggests. The canon starts off with a whiz deletion replaced by a participial construction in the present tense ("*Hoc Codice vim obtinente*"), followed by a passive verb "*abrogantur.*" This is followed by the lists of abrogated laws. In no. 1 of the paragraph, the 1917 Code is simply marked as "*anno 1917 promulgatus*," a whiz deletion again replaced by a participial construction in the perfect tense. In no. 2 other universal or particular laws are abrogated if contrary to the new law. The phrase "*praescriptis huius Codicis contrariae*" is a truncated relative clause, containing a whiz deletion, an adverb, but no auxiliary verb. It is followed by a "*nisi*"-prepositional phrase stating an exception to the aforesaid, the whole sentence ending in the passive voice ("*caveatur*"). Much the same structure can be found in no. 3 ("*leges poenales quaelibet, sive universales sive particulares a Sede Apostolica latae, nisi in ipso hoc Codice recipiantur*"); a similar one follows in no. 4, albeit without the "*nisi*"-exception in the second part ("*ceterae quoque leges disciplinares universales materiam respicientes, quae hoc Codice ex integro ordinatur*"). Instead, the legislator has inserted a "*quae*," making use of a real relative pronoun, so no whiz deletion this time! Without evidencing this any further, I guess it has become clear that the legislator, with some simple adjustments to grammar and structure, could vastly improve the comprehensibility of many canonical norms.

Replacing Outdated Terms

That the language of the law usually carries with it terminological relics of the past is also true for canon law. Besides the fact that Canon Law Latin as such is a derivative of medieval Law Latin and therefore has an ancient sound to it, it also employs specific terms which today defy common understanding. These specific terms, as I want to show, are not merely used to denote issues of minor relevance, but in fact touch upon key matters of the ecclesiastical legal order such as its adjudication. I would like to mention by way of example one technical term which I have already referred to briefly which describes the standard of proof used in canonical adjudication, namely, the term "moral certitude" (see canon 1608 CIC/1983). It refers to the certitude necessary for the judge to decide a case against the burden of proof, which is the conviction the judge arrives at after overcoming any reasonable doubts. To modern ears, the term sounds strangely outdated. Historian Barbara Shapiro agrees when observing,

> Only a few quite well-educated older people who have read a great deal of nineteenth-century literature are likely even to have said, "I am morally certain that you left your coat in the restaurant" or "Are you morally certain that you came into the room before he did?" It is the kind of phrase that a screenwriter might put in the mouth of a country storekeeper to suggest a slightly bookish, straight-laced, religious old man still living in an earlier age.[35]

However, this outdated sound is not only a matter of fashion but also of comprehension. The term "moral certitude," as I also mentioned earlier in chapter 3, section 3.2, also served to denote the standard of proof in British and American criminal trials until the twentieth century, but was then widely replaced by the standard of "beyond a reasonable doubt," which carries roughly the same meaning but is slightly easier to understand.[36] "Moral certitude" fell into disuse, mostly due to misunderstandings about its meaning. William Atkins already raised doubts about the use of the term in Anglo-American criminal trials before a jury in the 1960s, doubting the jurors' comprehension of the term, as he found, "[t]o understand the difference between certainty and 'moral certainty' requires a knowledge of semantics seemingly beyond the grasp of the average juror. Therefore, elusive words such as 'moral certainty' and 'abiding conviction,' which tend to befog the jurors should be replaced with simpler language."[37] In a

[35] Shapiro, "To a Moral Certainty," *The Hastings Law Journal* 38 (1986), 153.
[36] See Hahn, "Moral Certitude," *Oxford Journal of Law and Religion* 8 (2019), 300–325.
[37] Atkins, "Evidence—Moral Certainty—Reasonable Doubt," *Howard Law Journal* 1 (1955), 121.

similar vein, legal scholar James Whitman called "moral certitude" a term "that we find baffling and troubling today."[38] One major misunderstanding associated with it is that it is easily mistaken for a certitude that is based on a *moral* judgment. Only just recently, a renowned German newspaper which investigated the cover-up of a major case of abuse by a cleric wrote that canon law is a legal order which does not aim at justice but at moral certitude.[39] Hence, the journalists evidently mistook "moral certitude" as proof that the legal order of the church is in fact not guided by legal principles but by moral beliefs, a dangerous misapprehension for the law. Jurisprudence, particularly common law criminal trials before a lay jury, therefore widely erased speaking of "moral certitude" to avoid this misinterpretation by jurors feeling obliged to deliver a moral judgment about the perpetrator and her or his deeds. This misunderstanding, which most legal laypeople would probably stumble over, is a valid reason to rethink the use of the term in the church as well. At a time when the church is suffering from some major credibility problems with regard to its moral judgments anyway, there is no need to discuss the problem of a morally judgmental church in those matters in which it is actually *not* judging morally.

Besides the public being tempted to suspect the church of judging morally in legal matters, the trouble is exacerbated by the fact that "moral certitude" might also cloud the understanding of ecclesiastical judges. Arthur Caron identified this problem in the late 1960s. He found that "not a few judges have failed to reach a conclusion or have lost precious time, pondering the pros and cons of a case before coming to a decision, simply because the concept of moral certitude has never been very clear in their mind."[40] Today's professional full-time judges certainly know how to make their decisions, even though this does not necessarily mean that they are certain about the precise meaning of "moral certitude." However, many local churches still employ honorary judges who might be uncertain about the standard of proof itself. In saying this, I do not wish to imply that they are unsure of their duties. Yet I would expect some of them to be unfamiliar with "moral certitude." I was certainly unsure about the meaning of the term even after having received my degree in canon law. Finding a term so difficult to understand and evidently prone to provoke major misapprehension is a good reason to reconsider its use.

[38] Whitman, *The Origins of Reasonable Doubt*, New Haven, CT, Yale University Press, 2008, 204.

[39] Original quote, "Es geht nicht darum, Gerechtigkeit herzustellen, sondern moralische Gewissheit," Löbbert/Löwisch, "In der Verantwortung," *Die Zeit*, January 5, 2022, 55.

[40] Caron, "The Concept of Moral Certitude in Canonical Decisions," *The Jurist* 19 (1959), 12.

Challenging Law Latin

The previous section has shown that the ecclesiastical legislator could vastly improve the comprehensibility of the law with some adjustments to grammar and structure and with a revision of the terms employed by canon law. Nevertheless, this advice does not address the elephant in the room, namely, the fundamental issue lurking behind many of the considerations on how to improve canon law language. This elephant is evidently the question whether it is wise after all to abide with Canon Law Latin as the primary language of ecclesiastical statute law. Interestingly, letting go of Latin hardly seems to be a serious option for most canon lawyers. There are many critical voices on single aspects of canon law language and terminology, as has been shown in the previous sections, but barely any criticism of using Latin as such. For many canonists in the twentieth century, the use of Latin in ecclesiastical law never seemed to be doubtful. Klaus Mörsdorf, for instance, when addressing the language of the old Code monographically, seemed to have taken for granted that the language of canon law was Latin. He referred to Latin outright as a "dead language," yet without taking this as a reason to challenge its use. Mörsdorf even noted that secular law was rightly striving to establish vernacular legal languages, but promptly added that because canon law was composed in dead Latin this aim could not be achieved for the ecclesiastical legal order.[41] Mörsdorf did not see this as a problem, as the old law mostly addressed the "leading church," a church led by clerics with a proficient knowledge of Latin. Hence he and his contemporaries did not see the point in debating the use of Latin. However, there has been a growing sensitivity toward this matter in canon law scholarship. The use of Latin is explicitly touched upon as a topic, yet most surprisingly, it is not usually questioned fundamentally. On the contrary, many canonists praise Latin as the unique legal language of the church. In an article which provides a good overview of the history of Canon Law Latin and the advantages of its use, Stephan Haering argues in favor of Latin as it shows the unity of the church and its law, privileges none of the modern languages, marks the difference between canon law and secular law, and expresses the continuity of canon law with its tradition.[42] Haering's arguments are somewhat typical of those put forward by canonists in favor of Latin. I do not therefore want to dismiss them out of hand, but prefer to discuss them somewhat more intensively to assess whether they are convincing enough to attribute a dead language with the

[41] See Mörsdorf, *Die Rechtssprache des Codex Juris Canonici*, 2nd edn, Paderborn, Ferdinand Schöningh, 1967, 18.

[42] See Haering, "Lateinische Sprache und Kanonisches Recht," *Seminarium* 43 (2003), 244; consenting Zeller, "Die Terminologie der kirchlichen Gesetzbücher," in Ohly et al., eds, *Theologia Iuris Canonici*, Berlin, Duncker & Humblot, 2017, 145.

key role as the principal language of canon law, particularly as its use is unfavorable for comprehending the law.

Intelligibility over Distinction

Admittedly, the use of one language for its law is a strong indicator of the unity of the church. It is not only symbolic in an institutional sense—in the sense of "one church, one law, and one language"—but is also plausible when it comes to the theory of authority behind the law, as one of legal scholar Christoph Möllers's observations helps to understand. Möllers emphasizes the significance of the language chosen by the legislator with regard to the authority of the law.[43] A legal norm is always authorized in a certain language, and it is only the text in this language which directly profits from the legislator's authority. The choice of a single legal language serves to connect a norm with a specific legislator's will; this connection fades away with translations. By choosing one language, the legislator expresses his control over the content of the law and its meaning. This voluntarist moment also has its place in ecclesiastical legal theory, in which the supreme legislator functions as the central instance of canonical lawmaking and of creating legal meaning. Thus, the choice of Latin that echoes the supreme legislator's will in the ears of the legal subjects is a strong symbol of the centralist Roman authority. However, this symbolic function of expressing the church's unity by choosing one language to allude to the origin of canon law in one source of authority does not necessarily depend on Latin. It could also be fulfilled by a modern language, giving at least some more church members the chance to understand the law of the church.

In any case, it is also worth discussing more profoundly whether a uniform language as a marker of formal unity and symbolic distinction is a true value for global Catholic canon law. One could, for instance, oppose this argument by claiming that global legal norms expressed in the myriad of local languages which Catholics speak around the world is an even stronger symbol of the church's unity, as a unison of plural voices and languages would represent the inclusive power of the law more convincingly than a dead language expressing the mere formal authority of a distant Roman legislator. This in mind, there is good reason to ask if abiding with dead Latin has the desired symbolic value. For the very same reason one might also debate Haering's argument in favor of Canon Law Latin insofar as it signifies a difference between canon law and secular law. Undoubtedly, canon law *is* different from secular law. It is the law of a religious community in comparison to the laws that regulate secular societies and, thus,

[43] See Möllers, *The Possibility of Norms*, Oxford, Oxford University Press, 2020, 173–174.

differs in some respects with regard to its scope and purposes. However, it is debatable if marking this difference formally and symbolically representing it with the help of a distinct language is of any particular value. And, even if one finds this to be the case, one may ask if this difference is adequately represented by using a language which is incomprehensible to most of the church members.

Comprehension over Tradition

Throughout the Middle Ages and into modernity it was indeed Latin that served as the lingua franca of the church and allowed the church to develop a global legal order, communicating across language borders. That it is currently Latin that occupies the role of the one principal language of canon law is owed to the tradition of ecclesiastical law, with its roots in the ancient Roman law of late antiquity. This attributes the language of canon law with some eminence drawn from its history. Ransford Pyle alludes to the "aura of prestige that Latin has always enjoyed,"[44] noting that it is a legacy owed to the past, "Its prestige is derived from a history of ecclesiastical and legal domination and several neoclassical scholarly renascences which have cloaked the Roman epoch with great prestige."[45] Most secular legal orders also look back on a Latin tradition, as has been shown. However, at one point in history the secular legislators decided to turn to the vernaculars as legal languages, as this would grant the legal subjects more comprehension. The argument of tradition is evidently hard to defend against the argument of comprehension. I find it difficult to argue anyway that tradition has its own inherent merit. Pyle rather ironically remarks, "I find no reason to believe that God prefers Latin to other languages."[46] In a similar vein, David Mellinkoff, in his fierce critique on Legalese, criticizes the tendency of legal languages to rely on old terms and ancient languages—"[t]he deader the better"—as a misconception that traditional language is a better guarantor of meaning than modern language. In response to the idea that "anything that old must be good," he sharply replies, "Not so. Many words that old have simply been bad longer."[47] While this is not necessarily the case, Mellinkoff rightly notes that traditional language does not per se guarantee precision. This notwithstanding, the tradition argument still seems to carry weight with many canonists. Klaus Zeller, for instance, praises the

44 Pyle, "Law, Ritual and Language," *American Legal Studies Association Forum* 8 (1984), 386.
45 Ibid., 386–387.
46 Ibid., 386.
47 Mellinkoff, *The Language of the Law*, Boston, MA, Little, Brown and Company, 1963, 304.

use of Latin in canon law as safeguarding the "diachronic communicability"[48] of the law, thereby placing the diachronic fit of legal language over synchronic understanding. While I do not seek to devalue diachronicity, I find it hard to argue that it triumphs over synchronic communicability. If law is communication, communicating the law is key. A legal language that supports communication is therefore a value that the tradition argument cannot replace.

Supporting Equal Comprehension

Haering's argument in favor of Latin as the legal language of a truly global church which does not privilege any of the modern languages and their speakers is, as I find, the most interesting proposition when it comes to promoting Canon Law Latin. As Latin is a dead language, and therefore not spoken in any of the local churches, no local Catholics have an advantage over any others in understanding ecclesiastical law. This argument, which considers the equal disadvantages of the church members to be a sign of their equality, is indeed intriguing. However, I find it only partially convincing. While it is true that most members of the church are not overly comfortable with Latin, there is, in any case, a Romanized, mostly clerical elite in the church which is more familiar with Latin than most others, particularly as Latin is still present in clerical formation (see canon 249 CIC/1983). So the idea of an egalitarian disadvantage for all is a somewhat veiled argument for supporting a Latinized elite culture in the church. I have already mentioned this exclusivism and elitism in connection with the use of the Latin language and find it rather disadvantageous for canon law. Canon Law Latin thus proves to be less the language of the church, and more the language of a clerical church, the "leading church," as Mörsdorf saw it.[49] It excludes the majority of the church members from the official legal debates. This is certainly questionable, as it implies that the legal comprehension of the laity is of lesser importance than the understanding of the clergy. This imbalance not only obstructs the equality argument but also poses a question to ecclesiology. If the church—as is one key motif of the Second Vatican Council—consists of both clergy and laity as two ways of life of equal dignity and value in serving the church, then it is difficult to defend a structural imbalance with regard to understanding the law of the church. As a matter of fact, the use of Latin as the principal language of canon law not only symbolizes a neglect of the laity's importance in partaking in the

[48] Original quote, "diachrone[n] Kommunikationsfähigkeit," Zeller, "Die Terminologie der kirchlichen Gesetzbücher," in Ohly et al., eds, *Theologia Iuris Canonici*, Berlin, Duncker & Humblot, 2017, 145.

[49] See Mörsdorf, *Die Rechtssprache des Codex Juris Canonici*, 2nd edn, Paderborn, Ferdinand Schöningh, 1967, 18.

legal discourses of the church, but even evokes the culture of the "perfect society" of the nineteenth century, in which the ability to partake in legal discourses was regarded as sufficient for the higher clergy, whereas ordinary members of the church were not expected to discuss the law but simply to obey it. Modern canon law language should avoid this pitfall. The language of current canon law should consequently be a modern language which most individuals speak and understand. This would certainly not solve all problems, but could send the message that the legal subjects' comprehension is of central value to the legislator. Clearly, reshaping a global law in a modern vernacular presents challenges of its own. I will discuss these challenges in the next chapter and also suggest a model for how the church, as a global institution, might address the multi-language issues of its law.

6
A Global Law and Its Language

To a greater extent than history has ever demanded before, legal systems today are confronted with the challenge of organizing a complex and truly global world by means of law, as Lawrence Solan and Peter Tiersma have pointed out, "[W]e live in a time of unparalleled effort to create supranational legal systems that cut across legal cultures and national boundaries, and to harmonize the laws of individual legal systems so that cross-border transactions are not impeded by the fact that the participants do not communicate in the same language, and at times do not even share the same legal concepts."[1] These challenges to the law in modernity are not unknown to canon law, even though canon law is less concerned with national boundaries than is state law. However, as universal canon law endeavors to give a legal frame to the global church, it is permanently crossing national boundaries as well as borders of language and culture. It attempts to integrate the local churches worldwide, churches influenced by different legal cultures, communicating in multiple voices and legal languages. Shaping a global canon law is therefore a cross-cultural challenge which has to answer to the problem of how to develop legal concepts which are acceptable in all local churches. And it is likewise a linguistic challenge, as it calls for a language which is understandable across the globe.

Legal communications across language borders are therefore clearly a difficulty for the global church. Nevertheless, they are not solely a burden for the church but increasingly a challenge that law generally faces in modernity. Globalization is challenging the law to transcend the borders that separate cultures and languages. In light of the uncertainty whether a global legal order is even conceivable with regard to language and culture, linguist Jan Engberg asks, "Is law necessarily tied to a national jurisdiction and its national culture, or is it possible to also have law at a supranational level, without direct recourse to any one national culture?"[2] This question is raised particularly with regard to language, as Engberg states, because "when attempting to achieve a globalized legal order it is essential to guarantee a common basis of interpretation across

[1] Solan/Tiersma, "Introduction," in idem, eds, *The Oxford Handbook of Language and Law*, Oxford, Oxford University Press, 2012, 6–7.

[2] Engberg, "Word Meaning and the Problem of a Globalized Legal Order," in Solan/Tiersma, eds, *The Oxford Handbook of Language and Law*, Oxford, Oxford University Press, 2012, 182.

The Language of Canon Law. Judith Hahn, Oxford University Press. © Oxford University Press 2023.
DOI: 10.1093/oso/9780197674246.003.0006

languages and cultures in order to make the semiotic process work in a satisfactory way."[3] It is exactly this "common basis of interpretation across languages and cultures" which is disputable. Modern scholarship has learned that this common basis cannot be a neutral supercultural substrate. A supercultural law does not exist and cannot exist. Law is always a product of a specific culture. Above all, this has to do with the language of the law, as language sets much of the cultural frame for legal concepts and ideas.

6.1 Linguistic Relativity

Linguistic scholarship describes the fact that language impregnates the way we think in the so-called hypothesis of "linguistic relativity." It exists in weak and in strong versions, the weak versions claiming that language influences the way we think, the strong versions that it fully determines our thought. Theories of full determination at present tend to be received unfavorably by many scholars, but different shades of linguistic relativity, some stronger, some weaker, are a matter of constant debate by linguists. That language indeed influences the way we perceive reality is beyond doubt.

Perceiving Reality via Language

The hypothesis of linguistic relativity has sparked empirical research on the influence of language on how individuals experience the world. Some research directly relates to the law and language debate, particularly to the *adjudication and language* strand, insofar as the question of how individuals perceive reality has huge repercussions for the judiciary, for instance, when it comes to witness testimonies. They are of major concern for a number of reasons. For example, we may assume that language affects cognitive processes such as recollection, which is highly important for witness testimonies. One famous experiment from the 1970s dealt with these questions. Psychologists Elizabeth Loftus and John Palmer made test persons watch films of car accidents and afterward interrogated them about the content of the videos, using different verbs in their questions to describe the accidents, namely, "hitting" or "smashing." The test persons who were asked questions which suggested that a car had "smashed" into another car estimated the speed of the cars to be higher than those test subjects who had read "hit" before. The test persons thus evidently associated "smashing" with a higher speed than "hitting." When questioned again about the same film a week later

[3] Ibid.

those test persons who had answered questions which included the verb "smash" were more likely to recall that the accident had broken glass, even though there was no breaking of glass in the video. Hence, the test persons apparently associated the verb "smash" not merely with more speed but in consequence also with a more serious accident. Loftus and Palmer noted, "These results are consistent with the view that the questions asked subsequent to an event can cause a reconstruction in one's memory of that event."[4]

Their findings about the role language plays in recollection have motivated many scholars of psychology and linguistics to study the link between language, perception, and recollection ever since. Some of these experiments are directly linked with law and language issues. Language and cognition scholar Luna Filipović, for instance, experimentally compared witness testimonies given by English and Spanish speakers and found that they differed to a great extent due to the different structure of the respective languages. When asked about a scene with protagonists in motion, English witnesses made use of the various verbs available in the English language for different ways of moving—such as "running," "jumping," or "sneaking"—whereas Spanish witnesses were more restricted in this respect, as the Spanish language does not provide as many different verbs to describe different ways of moving. Filipović observed,

> As a result of these linguistic differences monolingual speakers of English tended to provide more detailed information about the manner of motion than their Spanish peers and they also had better memory for manner. Furthermore, the task was much more taxing for Spanish speakers, who had to remember these complex motion events without labelling them efficiently with singular verbs, as English speakers did.[5]

So with regard to scenes of motion, English enabled the native speakers to remember more and remember it more easily, because English provides verbs describing distinct types of movement, whereas Spanish requires the speakers to record "extra information," such as adverbs to specify the movement, to get the types of movement right. As the linguistic reconstruction of the events in Spanish is more complex than in English, Spanish native speakers, as expected, remembered less and made more errors when recalling the scene. However, this is by no means proof that Spanish witnesses are less reliable than English ones. Filipović showed this by repeating the experiment and showing the test persons another scene which was not about movement but about causation. She had the

[4] Loftus/Palmer, "Reconstruction of Automobile Destruction," *Journal of Verbal Learning and Verbal Behavior* 13 (1974), 585.

[5] Filipović, "The Role of Language in Legal Contexts," in Freeman/Smith, eds, *Law and Language*, Oxford, Oxford University Press, 2013, 336.

test persons watch a video of people dropping objects and afterward asked them what had happened, namely, whether a person had accidentally or intentionally dropped an object. In this experiment, Spanish witnesses could recall the scene more accurately than English witnesses. Filipović explained the difference with the fact that this time the English language made it harder for witnesses to remember the scene correctly. The English verb of "dropping" something, namely, does not differentiate between whether the dropping happens accidentally or on purpose, so that the English witnesses had to remember this information expressly, and managed to do so only 75 percent of the time. As the Spanish active and passive verbal constructions make a clear distinction between accidental happenings and intentional acts, all of the Spanish witnesses remembered the scene correctly. Thus, the experiment showed that cognition and recollection is strongly determined by language. Filipović deduced, "we can conclude that speakers whose languages oblige them to pay attention to an event component (e.g. manner of motion) may have an advantage in how much and how well they remember it."[6] If a language provides a special term for a thing, a person, or an event or an expression that contains detailed information about it, details relating to that thing, person, or event are easier to perceive and to remember.

Relativity of Legal Concepts

How strongly our perception of the world is influenced by our language and, consequently, how radically our ideas, such as legal ones, are linguistically influenced is another aspect of linguistic relativity which is of crucial relevance for the law and language debate. For canon law, it was particularly the merit of John Huels who, in a groundbreaking article, alluded to the culturality of legal concepts and to the language responsible for their differences.[7] Huels pondered the intricacies of interpreting canon law in the light of the diverse cultures which make up the global church. He asked himself how the church could act as if interpreting its global law was easy when local languages and the specific ideas that language evokes are obviously fundamentally different. Huels consequently picked up the hypothesis of linguistic relativity in its implications for canon law. If it is true, as he contended, that "the structure of language affects a people's fundamental ideas,"[8] then this has a formative relevance for the way individuals perceive legal ideas and understand legal concepts. To illustrate this, Huels referred to linguist Benjamin Lee Whorf's famous studies on the characteristics of the Hopi

[6] Ibid., 337.
[7] See Huels, "Interpreting Canon Law in Diverse Cultures," *The Jurist* 47 (1987), 249–293.
[8] Ibid., 252.

language[9] and discussed their propositions for canon law. Whorf had discovered that the Hopi language does not possess the typical European combination of mass nouns, describing a substance without a definite outline, such as "water," "fruit," or "grass," with container nouns which provide those substances with an outline, such as "glass" ("of water"), "piece" ("of fruit"), or "patch" ("of grass"). Whorf called this the "duality of formless item and form,"[10] something which is typically European yet unknown in the Hopi language. This European combination of formless item and form, as Huels found, is not a random phenomenon of European thought but deeply embedded in Aristotelian ontology. It stands for the typical European concept of substance and accidents, in this case the combination of a substance with the accidental category of quantity. European thought, as Huels noted, is deeply impregnated by this dualism. We interpret our world by structuring it with the help of this dualism, forming ontological ideas by dividing reality into substantial and accidental properties. I already mentioned this tendency in Western thought when I explained in chapter 4, section 4.2 the comprehension difficulty many individuals have with the Cheshire Cat appearance of marriage nullity. However, the dualism of substance and accidents in general was highly influential on theology and canon law, primarily because medieval Scholastic theology employed it to explain sacramental theology. To clarify what happens in the course of Eucharistic transubstantiation, Scholastic scholars referred to the Eucharistic matters of bread and wine as accidents which are connected with the substance, Christ's body and blood, when transubstantiated. In order to understand the church's approach to sacramentality, one therefore needs to be familiar with Aristotelian thought, as it is echoed in the European history of ideas. Huels consequently asked how the Catholic understanding of the sacraments and of sacramental law, which relies heavily on the ontological differentiation between substance and accidents, could be expressed in the Hopi language, which lacks a similar concept. He wondered, "Much of sacramental law is based on an Aristotelian-Thomistic philosophy of substance and accidents. . . . What meaning can this philosophy have in a culture whose language and thinking have no comparable concepts?"[11] Huels expressed doubt that Hopi thought could embrace European sacramental theory by referring to the western legal concept of marriage. As I mentioned in chapter 4, section 4.2,

[9] See Whorf's articles collected in his book *Language, Thought, and Reality*, Cambridge, MA, The Technology Press of Massachusetts Institute of Technology, 1956, particularly "The Punctual and Segmentative Aspects of Verbs in Hopi" (1936), 51–56; "Discussion on Hopi Linguistics" (1937), 102–111; "Some Verbal Categories of Hopi" (1938), 112–124; "The Relation of Habitual Thought and Behaviour to Language" (1939), 134–159; "Linguistic Factors in the Terminology of Hopi Architecture" (1940), 199–206.

[10] Whorf, "The Relation of Habitual Thought and Behaviour to Language," in idem, *Language, Thought, and Reality*, Cambridge, MA, The Technology Press of Massachusetts Institute of Technology, 1956, 142.

[11] Huels, "Interpreting Canon Law in Diverse Cultures," *The Jurist* 47 (1987), 262.

marriage in Western legal thought is considered to be an institution. It exists autonomously from the concrete actions of a married couple, irrespective of whether they live together or part company. The legal entity of a marriage therefore exists independently of the social reality of marriage; I already discussed this in the mentioned section 4.2 with regard to the nullity issue. Huels related to this tension by noting, "Thus even a living relationship that is processual and changeable in nature, like marriage, is viewed as an objective thing, a substance that can perdure even when the former partners to the marriage are now long divorced and happily remarried to other partners."[12] Indeed, the way canon law approaches marriage shows that it does not see it as a fluid and procedural phenomenon—as one would if one understood marriage rather as a journey, a path that people share for part of their lives—but rather as a stable entity. This idea is expressed in canon law language by the term "*vinculum*," describing the marital bond between the spouses, which is understood as indissoluble and thus as a solid thing, which persists independently of the partners and their behavior toward each other.

However, the finding that marriage, as we know it, is a result of Western thinking, makes one wonder, as Huels acknowledged, whether it is truly a universal concept or rather a particular idea which makes more sense in some cultures and less in others. Huels even tentatively suggested that the Roman Catholic theology of marriage might be plainly a result of "limitations in our language and philosophy . . . based on a peculiar 'thought world' conditioned by a specific linguistic and cultural system that may have no basis in reality for other cultures, philosophies, and languages."[13] He shattered the universality of the concept by asking, "Can the 'essence' of marriage really be defined apart from the actual relationship of the persons involved?"[14] His observations made Huels wonder whether the church might need to find another construct to serve as the basis for its theory of the sacraments, when he asked, "Would it not be better to ground our sacramental law and theology on a firmer basis than one philosophical system rooted in a certain culture at a certain period in history?"[15] Yet he also admitted that it is impossible to find another basis that is not deeply cultural in itself, conceding, "There is no such thing as a law—or philosophy, theology, or language—that does not reflect the culture which gives rise to it."[16] Hence, whatever concept the church adopts in its theory and theology will always have a certain cultural impregnation. It seems necessary to become more aware of this fact and to keep it alive within theological thought. It was for this

[12] Ibid.
[13] Ibid.
[14] Ibid.
[15] Ibid.
[16] Ibid.

reason that Huels opted for developing and cultivating a "cross-cultural hermeneutic" for theology and canon law "that has the adaptability to apply a universal Catholic law in cultures that do not share the language, legal system, philosophical presuppositions, or perhaps even the way of looking at reality that are found in the culture that produced the canonical system."[17]

Cultural Conflicts in Global Law

Laws are always cultural artifacts; canon law is no exception. Canon law is part of civil law, which relies on dense bodies of written codified rules as the basis of legal orders. As civil law, canon law naturally causes some communication problems with common law cultures in the Anglo-American legal system, to which the statutory character of law as found in civil law is somewhat alien. John Huels maintained, "Catholics living in a society with a common law tradition and a literalistic attitude towards interpretation and observance of law often have difficulty comprehending the canonical system and sometimes experience canon law more as a source of conflict rather than as a source of unity in the community."[18] These challenges are becoming even greater nowadays in a church that is truly global. The culture clashes of the premodern era were mostly European conflicts. Today the tensions have a global nature and reveal fundamental cultural incompatibilities. Consequently, canon law as a typical European law is encountering reservations particularly in non-European churches. It is above all the non-Western countries without a civil law tradition that find it hard to accept Romanly impregnated ecclesiastical law. Besides Catholics from common law countries, this also includes Catholics from cultures which hold the law traditionally in lower esteem than do most Catholics of the West. Huels related to the example of China to explain how cultural differences can even lead to a negative response to the law as such. Confucianism, as he noted, had little esteem for law as a regulator of society, as it preferred virtue and morality over legal control. He discerned, "In Confucianism, a ruler must govern by means of virtue rather than law; the moral uprightness of the ruler serves as the example for the proper behavior of the subjects."[19] As a result, it is naturally difficult to communicate canon law to such a group, which holds the law as a medium of regulation in low esteem. That the church even attributes a salvific meaning to the law, as it helps to communicate the binding force of God's graceful acting toward humankind, may simply sound puzzling or even appalling to listeners

[17] Ibid.
[18] Ibid., 274.
[19] Ibid.

with a Confucian background. For this reason, Huels suggested increasing the freedom of local churches to implement global canon law. He evidently did not want to question the general validity of global canon law, but recommended giving the local churches more freedom in deciding *how* to adopt the law to avoid cultural dissonances. He proposed, "If Christianity is truly open to all cultures, it seems that the local church in such a society needs to 'interpret' the canonical requirements in a way that disruption to the people's language and way of thinking is minimized."[20] In saying this, Huels stressed that he does not restrict the term "interpretation" to the act of interpreting a norm in the strict sense, but that he comprehends it in a broader sense as the freedom to decide whether and how to apply global canon law locally, maintaining, "'Interpretation' of canon law, as used here . . . , is not limited merely to understanding the meaning of the words of a law in its text and legal context. Interpretation, rather, involves broader skills that include making judgments about the way that a law should be observed or whether it should be observed."[21] This broadened interpretive authority to decide whether and how the global law of the church is applied in a local church can, in certain cases, include the local appliers' decision not to refer to a certain law norm at all, as Huels proposed, "In some cases the best interpretation of a law might be that it should not be observed due to the particular circumstances of a culture or situation."[22] He even went one step further in doubting that the legal system of canon law could be established and inculturated in all places by claiming, "We must also acknowledge that no legal system, including the canonical, is entirely and uniformly suitable for every culture."[23]

6.2 Strong and Weak Language Theories

The culturality of each law is obviously a fact; yet at the same time it is a burden which makes it harder to communicate the law across cultural borders. For this reason, the law and language debate pays a great deal of attention to the question of whether cross-cultural exchanges on legal matters are really possible, and if so, how they might be addressed linguistically, as they call for a language of the law which is understandable cross-culturally. The debate revolves around several approaches to the problem, ranging from approaches which deem communication across language borders to be nearly impossible, to others which consider

[20] Ibid., 260.
[21] Ibid., 260 fn. 33.
[22] Ibid.
[23] Ibid., 290.

it possible even though it faces the challenge of how to transport a legal message from one language into another without losing its meaning.[24]

Language and Cultural Borders

Supporters of strong language theories tend to negate the idea that an understanding across language borders is truly possible, as Jan Engberg explains, "The common denominator of these approaches is that they see languages and their structural aspects at lexical and/or deeper typological levels as so deeply rooted in cultures that they prevent individuals from understanding each other at deeper levels across linguistic barriers. Language is thus viewed as a barrier, and one which is in principle insurmountable."[25] One prominent representative of a strong language theory is Pierre Legrand. He does not argue as a linguist but as a comparative legal scholar when approaching the question of whether legal terms expressed in different languages are comparable with each other. His considerations on comparability likewise contribute to the issue of communicability. Legrand is skeptical of both; he argues against their basic underlying premise, namely, that strong similarities between different laws exist which serve as connecting factors for understanding foreign law.[26] Legrand denies these similarities. Comparative legal scholars would praise them, but they are scarcely more than projections, as he sees them. He refers by way of example to attempts at understanding the German term "*Schuld*."[27] Sometimes its meaning is "fault," sometimes "transgression." That this makes true communication across language borders impossible is something which Legrand exemplifies by alluding to the use of the term which relates to *both* implications. There is no English term which carries both meanings of "*Schuld*." A translation expressing "*Schuld*" by referring to "fault" or "transgression" is therefore necessarily missing some of the original meaning. Legrand adds further examples by asking, "In other words (literally!), how does one say 'civil rights' in French or 'rule of law' in German?"[28] While I cannot contribute to solving the first riddle due to my own limited language skills, I can affirm that Legrand's second reference is indeed a challenge. "Rule of law" usually translates into "*Rechtsstaatlichkeit*." But the German term does not possess the exact meaning of the English term. One

[24] See Engberg, "Word Meaning and the Problem of a Globalized Legal Order," in Solan/Tiersma, eds, *The Oxford Handbook of Language and Law*, Oxford, Oxford University Press, 2012, 175–186.
[25] Ibid., 179.
[26] See Legrand, "Foreign Law," *Journal of Comparative Law* 6 (2011), 67–177, particularly 95; Glanert/Legrand, "Foreign Law in Translation," in Freeman/Smith, eds, *Law and Language*, Oxford, Oxford University Press, 2013, 513–532.
[27] See Legrand, "Foreign Law," *Journal of Comparative Law* 6 (2011), 92.
[28] Ibid., 102.

would get closer to "rule of law" with an approximation such as "a specific concept of *Rechtsstaatlichkeit* as the rule of law," yet without revealing to an English reader what "*Rechtsstaatlichkeit*" means precisely.[29] For Legrand these difficulties are not singular mishaps, but normal phenomena. He believes that there is no way to truly communicate law across language borders or comprehend the meaning of foreign law. So the comparatists' vision of mutual understanding is rather a fiction, as he finds—an "attempt to fit the square peg of similarity into the round hole of singularity,"[30] or a "frenetic search for commonalities-that-clearly-must-be-there-since-we-want-them-there."[31] Understanding and translating other legal languages can therefore never be really successful. While this does not mean that there can be no comprehension at all, it will only ever be possible to understand foreign concepts in a tentative and approximate way, as Legrand suggests,

> It is not that a Parisian can never understand the Canadian legal experience. Understanding there can be but, the self not being the other, a different understanding it will have to be since a Parisian cannot inhabit Canadian legal culture. Canadian law, for example, is that which a Parisian observes while it is that which a Montrealer lives through.[32]

While members of a certain legal culture experience their culture from within, those who are not part of that culture only observe it from the outside. And this is even the case according to Legrand, as his example shows, if the insider and the outsider share the same native language. As the law and its culture are different, there can never be a full exchange of experiences across these boundaries. As a consequence, legal communications across the borders of legal cultures are never entirely unobstructed, be it for reasons of language or of different cultural experience.

Reconstructing Meaning

In contrast to representatives of strong language theories, supporters of weak language approaches do consider it possible to transfer meaning across the

[29] When it comes to this particular example of "*Rechtsstaatlichkeit*," or "rule of law," it is striking to find that Canon Law Latin does not even bother to try. There is no conceptual and consequently no terminological equivalent to "rule of law" in canon law language to subsume ecclesiastical governance and canon law under modern principles of good governance, such as the separation of powers, free election of officeholders, or limited periods of office.

[30] Legrand, "Foreign Law," *Journal of Comparative Law* 6 (2011), 101.

[31] Ibid., 107.

[32] Ibid., 136–137.

boundaries of language. This requires them to explain how the reconstruction of meaning in the other language takes place. One representative of this idea for canon law is John Huels, who deems it possible to communicate across the borders of language and culture. He writes, "Although people have been variously socialized and have different ways of viewing reality, the structure of the mind itself is everywhere the same, so cross-cultural communication and understanding is possible, though difficult."[33] Huels is optimistic, for anthropological reasons, that cross-linguistic and cross-cultural communication can be successful. In his view, human beings have much in common, so that an exchange of experiences based on what all humans live through should be feasible. To explain the process of understanding other cultures, Huels refers to ethnologist Clifford Geertz's epistemological observations on how the social sciences can gain cultural knowledge. Geertz devoted intense study to the question of "how is anthropological knowledge of the way natives think, feel, and perceive possible?"[34] He answered this question by comparing the task of the anthropologist with the idea of putting oneself into someone else's skin, stating,

> To grasp concepts which, for another people, are experience-near, and to do so well enough to place them in illuminating connection with those experience-distant concepts that theorists have fashioned to capture the general features of social life is clearly a task at least as delicate, if a bit less magical, as putting oneself into someone else's skin.[35]

It would be misleading, though, to misunderstand this step as truly climbing into the other person's head. Geertz stressed that there always remains a distance to the other, which makes it actually impossible to see something through the eyes of the other person. However, he deemed it possible to grasp what moves the other, what makes him or her think the way he or she thinks, as he found, "The trick is not to achieve some inner correspondence of spirit with your informants. . . . The trick is to figure out what the devil they think they are up to."[36] In his reception of Geertz's theory, Huels takes up parts of this approach, as he proposes his own strategy for understanding other cultures, suggesting,

> Our "translation" of their culture is made possible by setting up a personal relationship with members of the other culture, not by the pure observation of a detached observer or a faraway student of human behavior with no contact with

33 Huels, "Interpreting Canon Law in Diverse Cultures," *The Jurist* 47 (1987), 289.

34 Geertz, "From the Native's Point of View," *Bulletin of the American Academy of Arts and Sciences* 28 (1974), 27.

35 Ibid., 29.

36 Ibid.

> the lived reality of the people. It must be a dialogical relationship, which means the peoples of other cultures are equal partners in the dialogue.[37]

For Huels, mutual understanding is possible based on a dialogue in which individuals attempt to understand each other. It is a difficult but feasible task, as he sees it, writing,

> Anthropology reveals that the task of understanding people in other cultures is very difficult. We need to know their language and other ways of communicating meaning, their perceptions of reality, and the social context in which meanings are transmitted. The difficulty in achieving such objectives is compounded by our own personal and cultural biases and the way we restructure or reinterpret meanings according to our own way of thinking.[38]

In the end, it seems that Huels is not so far away from Legrand, who doubts that it is possible to genuinely share legal experience across cultural and linguistic borders. Huels suggests that it is doable albeit extremely difficult. In any case, it remains doubtful if it can ever happen successfully because of the manifold preconditions upon which such cross-cultural communications rest. Genuine understanding not only requires a knowledge of the other language but also a full insight into the way the members of other cultures perceive reality to gain a comprehensive experience of their situation, including letting go of subjective personal and cultural biases. Taking these preconditions into account, it seems rather uncertain if it is in any way realistic to believe it possible to fully understand others. Ultimately, it is impossible to climb into other individuals' skins, think with their minds, and use their words with the exact meanings they attach to them. Yet if we need or want to communicate across language and cultural borders, there might be no other way than to pretend that it is actually possible somehow. It does not seem to be coincidental that Huels as a canonist supports a weak language theory. Global canon law tries to embrace all local ecclesial cultures. This endeavor only seems plausible to supporters of weak language theories who expect cross-cultural regulations to be somehow feasible and comprehensible at the very least. The great strength of weak language theories is therefore that they support cross-cultural communication, even though this endeavor never seems to be fully successful in fact. As cross-cultural communications seem essential in an increasingly global legal world, it is imperative to at least try to bring them about. This is encouraged by approaches which suggest that attempts may indeed prove successful. It remains disputable, though,

[37] Huels, "Interpreting Canon Law in Diverse Cultures," *The Jurist* 47 (1987), 271.
[38] Ibid., 288.

whether communication across cultural borders will ever be more than a way of moving toward mutual understanding. Having said this, this might in fact be true for all acts of communication, even between speakers of the same language and members of the same culture. As genuine and mutual comprehension is always doubtful, it might be wise to conceive of it in terms of approximation only.

6.3 Legislation for Multi-Language Groups

If we take it as given that communicating legal issues across language and cultural borders is difficult yet necessary, the question arises of how to put it into practice. This subject is particularly urgent for the church, as canon law not only attempts to connect a small number of legal languages and cultures but actually endeavors to organize a legal frame for all local churches which is efficacious across the globe. To understand how this might be achieved, it is helpful to consider how other legal communities deal with multi-language challenges. There are several potential approaches to assembling multi-language and multicultural communities under one law. Jan Engberg identifies four models.[39] The first option is choosing one language for the law; this is the model the church currently uses with Latin. The second approach is to accept one model law in one specific language, which serves as the original text from which translations are created. A third approach is to work with a limited number of official legal languages, such as the six official languages used by the United Nations or the two languages, English and French, used by the International Court of Justice, the Council of Europe, and the European Court of Human Rights. The fourth model is the one favored by the European Union, which publishes its core legal documents of relevance for the whole Union in all of the member states' official languages (see Treaty on European Union, article 55; Treaty on the Functioning of the European Union, article 358), with all versions serving as authentic texts.

Legal and Linguistic Colonialism

At present the model chosen by the church for its global law is the first one, to promote the official and authentic text of the law in one language, Latin. However, this concept is problematically hegemonic, as Engberg notes,[40] as it privileges one language and the culture connected with this language over others. In the

[39] See Engberg, "Word Meaning and the Problem of a Globalized Legal Order," in Solan/Tiersma, eds, *The Oxford Handbook of Language and Law*, Oxford, Oxford University Press, 2012, 182–185.
[40] See ibid., 183.

case of canon law, the prioritized culture is the Vatican's legal culture. Even though the law of the Code does not immunize itself against the local churches and their legal cultures—as canon 20 CIC/1983 shows, for instance, by protecting particular legislation from being overridden by acts of global legislation—the Romanocentrism of canon law nourishes a centralistic form of legal thinking which encourages a certain cultural, specifically Vatican view of the law. Laws shaped in the Vatican are exported into the culturally diverse local churches. This process has an imperialistic drift, as the legal transfer follows asymmetrical power relations between the Roman papal church and the local churches which result in the local legal cultures being superimposed by the imported law. The scholarly debates on legal politics use the term "legal colonialism" to describe this type of one-way imposition of culturally alien law onto a marginalized legal culture. John Huels suggests that the unilateral export of Vatican canon law into the Catholic legal cultures across the world shares at least some of the characteristics of legal colonialism. He calls the transfer of global canon law into the local churches the "imposition of a universal canon law."[41] This imposition is troublesome for several reasons. First, it cultivates cultural asymmetries. This practice is debatable also from a theological point of view insofar as ecclesiastical doctrine understands the Christian faith as a universal message, so that there is no culture which is naturally superior or better suited to express Christian thought. Second, the imposition cultivates power asymmetries, as the privileged culture continues to dominate the other cultures. This problem becomes particularly tangible in the field of language. Legal scholars Michael Freeman and Fiona Smith compared the imposition of one language on multilingual communities with the ancient Assyrian policy of subduing conquered peoples under the Assyrian language. They interpret the biblical Babel narrative to be a story criticizing exactly this practice, writing,

> The reference in Genesis (in the chapter before the Babel story) to "maritime peoples spread[ing] out into the lands in their clans within their nation, each with its own language" [Genesis 10:31] may be to what we now know as historical fact. It was the imperial practice of the neo-Assyrians to impose their language on peoples they conquered. An inscription of the time records that Ashurbanipal II "made the totality of all peoples speak one speech". A cylinder inscription of Sargon II says: "Populations of the four quarters of the world with strange tongues and incompatible speech . . . whom I had taken as booty at the Command of Ashur my Lord by the might of my spectre, I caused to accept a

[41] Huels, "Interpreting Canon Law in Diverse Cultures," *The Jurist* 47 (1987), 289.

> single voice". The neo-Assyrians asserted their supremacy by insisting that their language was the only one to be used by populations they had defeated.[42]

The Babel narrative, as Freeman and Smith suggest, is an "early critique of imperialism."[43] It opposes a centralism that forces one language upon multilingual communities. Similar stories have been told of other historical acts of land-grabbing, as David Mellinkoff showed with regard to the 1066 Norman Conquest of England. He identified the "tale that William made French the language of the law," that he subdued the conquered Saxons under one language, Norman French, as a "myth,"[44] namely, a narrative showing how Norman imperialism worked, whereas reality reveals the successive takeover of Norman French in politics and law as the "language of learning and gentility."[45] In any case, subduing foreign peoples under one language seems to be a plausible image to depict a colonialist approach to creating unity.

Structures of Dominance

Admittedly, the imposition of Canon Law Latin on the local churches cannot be compared to the force of Assyrian or Norman imperialism. Yet there is an analogy to it in that one language is superimposed on other cultures without too much attention being paid to the question of whether this superimposition is culturally acceptable. This practice points at power asymmetries, and it recreates them at the same time, as the members of the prioritized culture persistently benefit from their cultural advantage over others. This can become manifest in greater or smaller benefits. Legal scholar Mathilde Cohen, for instance, observed how international courts with French as the working language recruit their court staff from a small group of candidates, most of whom have a French background. The selection process, Cohen reviews, is more about finding personnel with French language skills than finding excellent legal experts.[46] This example of recruiting benefits for members of prioritized cultures might have some parallels in the church. It could be interesting to scrutinize the selection processes of ecclesiastical judges for papal tribunals with regard to this asymmetry. We scarcely know anything about the reasons and motives that move the pope and his

[42] Freeman/Smith, "Law and Language," in idem, eds, *Law and Language*, Oxford, Oxford University Press, 2013, 1.

[43] Ibid.

[44] Mellinkoff, *The Language of the Law*, Boston, MA, Little, Brown and Company, 1963, 63–65.

[45] Ibid., 70; see also Tiersma, *Legal Language*, Chicago, IL, The University of Chicago Press, 1999, 19–20.

[46] See Cohen, "On the Linguistic Design of Multinational Courts," *International Journal of Constitutional Law* 14 (2016), 508–510.

officials to hire somebody—it is not a transparent recruiting system. Anyhow, one may presume from the outside that being part of the curial culture and being proficient in Latin may help. So there is reason to believe that the power asymmetries that come with the dominance of Vatican canon law over the other local ecclesial cultures constitute a system that recreates itself by mostly featuring legal staff who represent exactly this culture and, inter alia, selecting them on the basis of language, namely, Latin.

Besides these and other practical imbalances and justice problems that go along with all concepts of legal imperialism, the imposition of "Roman" canon law on other ecclesial cultures is specifically debatable for the reason that it is also ecclesiologically dubious. A crucial question with regard to the legitimacy of the Roman dominance in canon law arises from the insight that the local churches are ecclesiologically more central than the Roman papal church. The local churches are true realizations of the Church of Christ and, as such, they participate in the universal church.[47] The Roman papal church, on the other hand, does not. It is not a realization of the universal church itself, but a historically contingent organization that serves the universal church. Thus, the cultures of the local churches have a genuine ecclesiological dignity that the Roman papal church and its culture do not. In fact, the Roman papal church serves the local churches. This duty to serve, in any case, is hardly consistent with a legal colonialism which marginalizes the local legal cultures and their languages.

For similar reasons, Engberg's second and third approaches to modeling a law for multilingual communities are also inappropriate for the church, as they too have their share of legal colonialism. The second approach, which accepts one model law in one specific language which is then translated into other languages has a hegemonic drift, as it privileges this model law—albeit less so than the first model, as the other languages also have their say in expressing the original text in translations. The third approach of working with a limited number of official legal languages might likewise be seen in a critical light, as Mathilde Cohen noted with regard to the languages used in European courts, "The choice of French and English at the old Permanent Court had a colonial—and later at the International Court of Justice, a postcolonial—flavor. These were the languages of the two leading imperial states."[48] While both models have less of a colonialist and imperialist flaw than the first one, they are still confronted with the problem of attributing hegemonic power to selected languages and their native speakers, without giving good reasons for marginalizing others.

[47] See Second Vatican Council, "Dogmatic Constitution *Lumen gentium* on the Church," nos. 23, 26, *Acta Apostolicae Sedis* 57 (1965), 27–29, 31–32.

[48] Cohen, "On the Linguistic Design of Multinational Courts," *International Journal of Constitutional Law* 14 (2016), 506.

Multi-Language Approaches

This problem is only avoided by the fourth model, which envisages publishing core legal documents in all languages officially used by the legal subjects. The European Union adopted this model despite its inherent problems, as translations necessarily create changes in meaning and ambiguities in legal texts. The Union tries to meet these challenges in order to assist the member states and their citizens in accepting the supranational law as binding for themselves. Making the national languages official languages of the Union "is the promotion of the democratic principle within the EU,"[49] as European law scholar Silvia Marino noted. Lawrence Solan suggests this step is motivated by the "respect for the equality and sovereignty of the individual member states."[50] The practice of the European Union is unparalleled with regard to the sheer number of languages—at present twenty-four official working languages—which have to be considered when shaping European law. Nevertheless, a micro-example of this practice can also be found in the church (surprisingly!), which has a long history of entering into concordats with foreign nations. The concordats usually exist in two languages, in Latin, Italian, or French as languages of the Apostolic See—which is, most interestingly, not necessarily the much vaunted church language Latin[51]—and in the national language of the other contracting party. This multi-language practice of the concordats was so remarkable for canon law that canonist Hans Barion dedicated an article to it in the 1940s. He observed that interpretation problems could arise from the fact that both language versions have to be regarded as equal expressions of the contracting parties' will.[52] As with other multi-language contracts between different nations, the question arises how to proceed in those cases in which both texts prove to be ambiguous with regard to a specific matter. Barion highlighted several terminological inconsistencies and ambiguities, translation errors, and even contradictions between the different language versions of the German concordats.[53] While some of them are unproblematic, some obscure the will of the contracting parties to the point where it appears doubtful whether there was actually a shared will between the parties. Barion had no clear suggestion on how to proceed in those cases. He

49 Marino, "Introduction," in eadem et al., eds, *Language and Law*, Cham, Springer Nature Switzerland, 2018, 1.

50 Solan, "Statutory Interpretation in the EU," in Olsen et al., eds, *Translation Issues in Language and Law*, London, Palgrave Macmillan, 2009, 36.

51 Latin is the language of the universal church, but not of the Apostolic See. Therefore, it is not always used in documents of the See; see Barion, "Über doppelsprachige Konkordate," *Deutsche Rechtswissenschaft* 5 (1940), 247.

52 See Barion, "Über doppelsprachige Konkordate," *Deutsche Rechtswissenschaft* 5 (1940), 228.

53 See ibid., 232–242.

discussed several models but was not convinced he had found the ideal solution. If conflict arises, he suggested, a one-off solution has to be found.

His considerations on the one hand show that creating multi-language contracts is a highly complicated business, as the outcome always suffers from ambiguities. Yet on the other hand, as Barion also confirmed, whenever contract law is concerned, a multi-language practice is the natural way to proceed, should the contracting parties speak different languages. So it is beyond any debate that two equal parties, such as nation states, are entitled to contract in their own respective languages when forming contracts. This is simply a matter of coming together on an equal basis. In any case, the church changes its policy when it comes to the implementation of statute law in the local churches. Global statute law is superimposed on the local churches in its authentic language, Latin, without any consideration being paid to the principle of equal basis. Surely, it is somewhat odd to compare the local churches with nation states. However, there is a parallel in the idea of sovereignty, insofar as ecclesiology understands the local churches as real and sovereign embodiments of the Church of Christ. All local churches are connected and constitute the one church under papal primacy, but are nevertheless still composed as sovereign entities with bishops leading the local churches like sovereign monarchs. This does not equate the churches with nation states, yet as with nation states, there is a need to respect their autonomy. Whenever the Roman papal church fulfills the service of contributing to the unity of the church, for instance, by providing the church with the homogenous legal frame of global canon law, this regulation should consider the autonomy of the local churches and symbolize it with regard to language. As shaping contracts in the languages of the contracting parties is a symbol of coming together on an equal basis in concordat law, statute law should by the same token symbolize the autonomy of the local churches by making use of their local languages, not as working aids only but also for official texts of the law. This makes the fourth model for multi-language communities the preferable model for canon law.

Creating Multi-Language Law

The next step in taking on a multi-language approach for the church raises the question of *how* to create the legal texts.[54] To design a procedure, it is of help to study other examples. In practice and merely with regard to producing multi-language law, as becomes clear when studying the example of the European Union, most multi-language approaches make use of the second approach of

[54] See Bratschi/Nussbaumer, "Mehrsprachige Rechtsetzung," in Felder/Vogel, eds, *Handbuch Sprache im Recht*, Berlin, Walter de Gruyter, 2017, 367–390.

first designing a monolingual model law from which translations are created in a second step. In this sense, legal scholar and expert for the language of the European Union, Karen McAuliffe, alludes to the fact that European law in the process of its making is usually formulated in English or French and then translated into the languages of the other member states, according to its own set of European rules.[55] So practically speaking, the Union is using a model law approach in shaping its law, but with the aspiration not to let the model become too dominant in any way. The degree to which this works successfully with regard to the outcome of European legislation is one of McAuliffe's research interests.

One much debated counterexample is Canada, with its innovative form of parallel text production in English and French. The Canadian model, drafted in the 1970s in the context of the equal rights debate, consists of "co-drafting, a form of simultaneous text production that goes beyond traditional translation,"[56] as legal language and translation expert Susan Šarčević explains. Both language versions of laws, the English and the French, are formed concurrently and follow the stylistic rules of the respective languages. The results, thus, may vary between the two to a considerable degree but embody a typical English or French law in style.[57] Nevertheless, however much as the Canadian model is praised for the way it respects the idiosyncrasies of the English and French language and their own legislative style, there is some doubt that this model might be applied in legal communities with a greater variety of official legal languages. While simultaneous text production might prove successful with two languages, it becomes increasingly difficult when three or more languages are involved. For the European Union and its twenty-four official languages, the Canadian example is not feasible. When forming multi-language law in this or similar dimensions, a model law procedure is the more obvious option.

Drafting in Foreign Languages

A similar decision to somehow restrict the multi-language practice was made for European jurisprudence. The European Court of Justice accepts cases in the languages of all member states and publishes its decisions in all of their languages, but internally proceeds in French as its working language, as Mathilde Cohen affirms in her empirical studies on the court, writing, "French remains

[55] See McAuliffe, "Language and Law in the European Union," in Solan/Tiersma, eds, *The Oxford Handbook of Language and Law*, Oxford, Oxford University Press, 2012, 201 fn. 4.

[56] Šarčević, "Challenges to the Legal Translator," in Tiersma/Solan, eds, *The Oxford Handbook of Language and Law*, Oxford, Oxford University Press, 2012, 188–189.

[57] See Bratschi/Nussbaumer, "Mehrsprachige Rechtsetzung," in Felder/Vogel, eds, *Handbuch Sprache im Recht*, Berlin, Walter de Gruyter, 2017, 376–377.

the language of deliberation and the language in which internal documents are drafted. Advocates general retain some discretion as to the language of their opinions, but judges and their legal assistants (the *référendaires*) are still required to draft judgments in French."[58] This has an effect on the decisions of the court and their sound, as Karen McAuliffe notes, "The case law of the ECJ is shaped by the language in which it is drafted—that is French. Because French is rarely the mother tongue of those drafting that case law, the texts produced are often stilted and awkward."[59] So there is native French and European "Court French," a revenant of the old English "Law French." However, that nonnative speakers have to draft texts in French ist not merely worth mentioning because of the awkwardness of the outcome, as McAuliffe observes. She deems it noteworthy that the thinking process that precedes the drafting of a legal document is regularly done in a different language. From her empirical research, she reports that many officials working at the European Court of Justice admit drafting legal texts in their mother tongue before having them translated into French.[60] So much of the conceptual work is done in different languages before it is rephrased in French. It would be interesting to analyze the decisions of the Roman Rota in comparison. Those decisions are drafted in Latin. As there are no judges with Latin as their mother tongue, it is highly likely that most of the drafting takes place in the different mother languages of the Rota judges before being translated into Latin. Like the texts in European "Court French," Rota decisions probably have a stilted formal sound. Yet it is hard to prove their awkwardness, as dead Latin does not really allow us to tell how "proper" native Latin should sound.

Another observation that McAuliffe and Cohen made in their empirical studies at international courts is that many officials admitted to frequently using "copy and paste" when drafting texts, particularly when composing texts in nonnative languages.[61] This leads to a high level of redundancy of legal arguments as phrases are borrowed from previous cases. It is interesting to read Rota decisions in light of this phenomenon, too. It is rather apparent that these decisions, which also all revolve around marriage cases, contain many redundancies due to the practice of borrowing passages from older decisions. Cohen adds that in courts

[58] Cohen, "On the Linguistic Design of Multinational Courts," *International Journal of Constitutional Law* 14 (2016), 502–503.

[59] McAuliffe, "Language and Law in the European Union," in Solan/Tiersma, eds, *The Oxford Handbook of Language and Law*, Oxford, Oxford University Press, 2012, 203; see eadem, "Precedent at the Court of Justice of the European Union," in Freeman/Smith, eds, *Law and Language*, Oxford, Oxford University Press, 2013, 485.

[60] See McAuliffe, "Language and Law in the European Union," in Solan/Tiersma, eds, *The Oxford Handbook of Language and Law*, Oxford, Oxford University Press, 2012, 205.

[61] See ibid.; McAuliffe, "Precedent at the Court of Justice of the European Union," in Freeman/Smith, eds, *Law and Language*, Oxford, Oxford University Press, 2013, 487–490; Cohen, "On the Linguistic Design of Multinational Courts," *International Journal of Constitutional Law* 14 (2016), 515–516.

with French as a working language, copy and paste is used not only because it prevents nonnative speakers making mistakes when writing in French but also because it accords to the French style of drafting judgments,

> French judgments constantly quote precedents, but they typically do so word for word, without quotation marks or even pinpoint citation. The language of the controlling precedents is simply reproduced as is. Because at multinational courts judges and the support personnel involved in the drafting of opinions do not always use their native tongue, they have an increased incentive to follow the French practice of reproducing the exact wording.[62]

For Cohen, this proves how using a certain language also introduces the specific techniques of the language's legal routines. The use of French in international courts therefore supports the use of French legal techniques even though the French legal culture as such is not highly influential in itself on a global scale. With regard to the European institutions and the influence of French judicial style on them, Cohen speaks of "The French capture" allowing the "French judicial culture to disproportionately influence the courts' inner workings."[63]

Multi-Language Canon Law

The examples mentioned show that even though the European Union follows the fourth model of publishing core legal documents in all official languages of the member states, there is always a tendency to rely on the second model in practice. Texts are written in a specific language—which in the European Union is often French. Translation into the other languages of the Union takes place in a second step. Thus, a multi-language approach in theory is in practice usually a monolingual drafting process with subsequent translation. This would be no different if canon law were to convert to the fourth model as well. The drafting of the legal documents would usually take place in one specific language, only to be translated into the language of the local churches in a second step. In practice, this results in a blend of the second and the fourth model. However, this blend would allow the new model to be implemented easily, adding to what is already standard practice in the church. At present, global canon law is drafted in whatever language its drafters are speaking—Italian mostly—then translated into Latin. The Latin text then serves as the authentic text. Translations made by

[62] Cohen, "On the Linguistic Design of Multinational Courts," *International Journal of Constitutional Law* 14 (2016), 515.
[63] Ibid., 498.

many bishops' conferences or local canon law societies in the respective local vernaculars serve as working aids to help local Catholics make sense of the Latin original. So, practically, when it comes to a reformed ecclesiastical multi-language legislation, not much needs changing. The Latin text—or the Italian draft—could serve as the "model law" which could be used as the reference text from which the translations are produced. However, these translations should be more than just working aids. To express the ecclesiological status of the local churches, the languages of the local churches should have an official status as languages of canon law. So instead of treating the translations issued by the bishops' conferences with the help of local canon law societies as working aids only, they should be attributed authentic status, and should serve as authentic versions of the law in the local churches. This would potentially result in many of the languages spoken in the local churches becoming official languages of global canon law. While it seems barely feasible to provide texts in all global languages,[64] relying on the bishops' conferences to provide vernacular versions would ensure that a great variety of languages are represented. Compared to the present situation, this requires virtually no extra effort at the stage of text production. The translations already exist; all that has to happen is that they are treated differently, attributing them with an official status as legal sources. This is neither as innovative nor as risky as it may sound. The church has gained some experience in accepting local translations as official texts since the Second Vatican Council. What functions well with Bible translations and liturgical texts could likewise be suitable when it comes to the law. In my short overview of ecclesiastical media law in the introduction, I referred to the system of local translation and the necessary approval of the Apostolic See which is in use for liturgical books (see canon 838 CIC/1983). A similar procedure could be applied to creating vernacular versions of global ecclesiastical laws.

Of course, one objection that might be raised against this suggested approval of the translations as official texts is the inevitable problem of ambiguity. Translations necessarily create divergences, and these are specifically challenging in legal documents; I will come back to this issue shortly when speaking about *interpreting* multi-language law. So the objection is certainly justified that following the European example and creating a multi-language canon law increases

[64] For secular law, Solan and Tiersma likewise admit that it is often impossible to provide a legal text in all of the languages spoken within a legal community. This is a particular problem for ethnic minorities and has to be recognized as part of the minority rights debate; see Solan/Tiersma, "Introduction," in idem, eds, *The Oxford Handbook of Language and Law*, Oxford, Oxford University Press, 2012, 7. For the European Union, for instance, it has to be noted that some of the languages spoken in the European countries did not become official languages of the union, including languages that are official languages of member states. Turkish, the official language of Cyprus along with Greek, is not an official language of the European Union; for an overview of the language practice of the European Union, see Doczekalska, "Legal Languages," in Marino et al., eds, *Language and Law*, Cham, Springer Nature Switzerland, 2018, 165–168.

the ambiguity dilemma of many legal norms. The problem is there, and it is serious. Yet I do not consider it as a valid argument for carrying on regardless. It is hard to argue that the Latin dominance over the local churches, which cannot be justified either culturally or theologically, is a feasible model even though it avoids uncertainties that come with multi-language practice. While ambiguity is troubling for the law, it is a difficulty which may be addressed through interpretation. So there barely seems to be a way around the finding that the culturally blind imposition of "Latin" canon law onto the local churches needs to stop and be replaced with a multi-language practice.

Literalistic and Free Translations

Nevertheless, taking on the fourth model requires the church to invest more thought in the task of translating the law into the local languages. This task is particularly difficult because while the creation of the language versions is in fact an act of translating from a model law, it should not result in a simple translation, as Silvia Marino emphasizes, stating, "[T]he output is legally not a translation, but an official version of the act."[65] It is for this reason that Marino demands the translation "be as accurate as possible."[66] Her demand certainly begs the question what "accuracy" actually is. Hence, before translating legal texts into the diverse languages of a legal community, there is a need to debate whether to prioritize the spirit of the model text or the letter of the source text, thus going more for a literalistic approach. Each option represents a different strategy for translating legal texts into other languages. Translations preserving the spirit rather than the letter of the original wording generally fit better into the receiving language cultures while somewhat loosening the link with the source text. Literalistic word-for-word translations, on the other hand, stay closer to the source text, yet at the cost of sounding stilted and sometimes even awkward. The translated text might be difficult to understand, as it does not have a familiar "sound" to the local readers or listeners. The benefit of literal translations is, in any case, that the formal sound of the text exposes its alien origin, which can be a helpful hint for local receivers when interpreting the law. The debate about choosing a more literal or a freer approach to translating texts is as old as the task of translation itself, as translation scholar Christiane Nord explains. She writes,

[65] Marino, "Introduction," in eadem et al., eds, *Language and Law*, Cham, Springer Nature Switzerland, 2018, 3.
[66] Ibid.

> The dichotomy between "literal" and "free" . . . has been a constant in the history of translation. From Cicero, who made a distinction between translating "ut interpres" (like a translator) or "ut orator" (like an orator), and St. Jerome (verbum e verbo/sensum de sensu), to Schleiermacher (taking the reader to the text/taking the text to the reader) and Nida (formal vs. dynamic equivalence . . .), Venuti (foreignising/domesticating translation) and many others, translators of all centuries found themselves confronted with this "eternal dilemma." Usually, they give preference to one of the two basic strategies, sometimes even declaring it to be "translation proper" as compared to the other one (e.g. Schleiermacher).[67]

The centuries prior to the twentieth century showed a tendency to prefer literal approaches, as Susan Šarčević points out, "For centuries the primary task of legal translators was to preserve the letter and form of the original by 'faithfully' reproducing the words and even syntax as closely as possible, often resulting in a translation that could be 'understood' only by reference to the source text."[68] However, in the twentieth century, with the rise of minority rights, the idea of formulating more readable texts became more prominent, thus moving away from a strictly literal approach. "Today translators of legally binding instruments are generally allowed to reconstruct the target text in the spirit of the target language, provided the substance remains unaltered,"[69] Šarčević observes. Multi-language communities like Canada, Switzerland, Ireland, and Wales[70] which follow the *equal authenticity rule* (that is taking all language versions of the legal text as equally authentic)[71] aim to achieve authenticity by providing multi-language legal documents that breathe the same spirit of the law without mistreating the language. This tendency is also connected with the rise of hermeneutics, as hermeneutic thought deconstructed the idea of translating as a literalistic endeavor. Scholar of comparative law Alberto Vespaziani contends,

[67] Nord, "Function + Loyalty," *Open Theology* 2 (2016), 569.

[68] Šarčević, "Challenges to the Legal Translator," in Tiersma/Solan, eds, *The Oxford Handbook of Language and Law*, Oxford, Oxford University Press, 2012, 191.

[69] Ibid., 192.

[70] On the Welsh situation, see Fflur Huws, "(Language + Law)2 = ?," in Freeman/Smith, eds, *Law and Language*, Oxford, Oxford University Press, 2013, 400–416.

[71] For the Canadian example, see section 133 of the British North America Act 1867, which reads, "Either the English or the French Language may be used by any Person in the Debates of the Houses of the Parliament of Canada and of the Houses of the Legislature of Quebec; and both those Languages shall be used in the respective Records and Journals of those Houses; and either of those Languages may be used by any Person or in any Pleading or Process in or issuing from any Court of Canada established under this Act, and in or from all or any of the Courts of Quebec. The Acts of the Parliament of Canada and of the Legislature of Quebec shall be printed and published in both those Languages."

> As anyone who has crossed the shadowy valley of translation knows, translating a phrase from one language to another is nothing like taking apart a mosaic and putting the pieces back together somewhere else; translating a legal concept from one cultural context to another is more like transplanting a whole tree in a different soil.[72]

For the tree to grow—the legal concept to be received fruitfully in the receiving culture—the process of transplantation requires cultural sensitivity that a literalist word-for-word translation usually does not provide. This shows that approaches to translating texts more freely are typically more concerned about the receiving community. They want to provide the community with texts that suit their language, even if this leads to an increase in ambiguity between the different language versions. Yet this tendency to prefer freer translations is not followed across the board, as the European example shows. Karen McAuliffe, in her empirical research at the European Court of Justice, found that lawyer-linguists,[73] when translating the court's decisions, usually translate rather literally to avoid altering the judges' arguments.[74] So when it comes to judicial decisions, a more literalistic approach seems to be favorable to allow readers to get as close to the original argument of the court as possible, even at the cost of making the argument sound slightly awkward or stilted. The literal approach is therefore obviously more concerned about the intent of those who have made the decision. While freer translations are more concerned about the receiving community, literal approaches to legal texts are often more protective of the authorities'—the legislator's or the judges'—intent. They are not only concerned about conveying a meaning in another language but about conveying exactly the meaning that the legislator or the judge connected with a legal text so that the text expresses precisely the same content after it has been translated.[75]

Intermediate Approaches

This idea has a familiar ring for canonists, as canon law is highly protective of intent. I will come back to this in the following chapter on interpreting the law.

[72] Vespaziani, "Towards a Hermeneutical Approach to Legal Metaphor," in Bustamante/Onazi, eds, *Human Rights, Language and Law*, Franz Steiner Verlag, Stuttgart, 2012, 80.

[73] Lawyer-linguists are members of the language service of the European Court of Justice, "experts with adequate legal training and a thorough knowledge of several official languages of the European Union" (Rules of Procedure of the Court of Justice, article 42).

[74] See McAuliffe, "Language and Law in the European Union," in Solan/Tiersma, eds, *The Oxford Handbook of Language and Law*, Oxford, Oxford University Press, 2012, 213–214.

[75] See Šarčević, "Challenges to the Legal Translator," in Tiersma/Solan, eds, *The Oxford Handbook of Language and Law*, Oxford, Oxford University Press, 2012, 189.

So choosing a somewhat more literal approach to translating the model text could be a suitable way of reconciling the old canonical model of one authentic Latin text with the new model of providing multi-language versions of the law. The model of promulgating only one authentic Latin text was a radical attempt to protect the legislator's intent by allowing his letters only to be taken as law. Allowing multi-language versions of the law to serve as law is, apparently, a step that loosens the link between the legislator and his wording. To create translated versions in such a way that they stay literally close to the source text could be a compromise that meets both concerns. This decision is in any case evidently a compromise only as it comes at the cost of the local churches and the local Catholics' comprehension and familiarity with the texts. Translations that are more literal will have a somewhat alien sound and will not fit into the local language as smoothly as freer translations.

Interestingly, when the 1983 Code of Canon Law was published and then translated into diverse world languages, the same questions were already being addressed by those canon lawyers undertaking the translations. The working group that created the German translation on behalf of the German-speaking bishops' conferences followed the self-imposed rule to translate as literally as possible and as readably as necessary, as Winfried Aymans noted in the preface to the first Latin-German edition of the Code.[76] As the German text serves only as an aid to understanding the authentic Latin text, aesthetic arguments were seen to be only of secondary importance. This practice was at the expense of establishing a thoroughly homogenous and understandable German language of canon law, as Aymans acknowledged. In the second and third editions of the translation, the authors sought to harmonize Canon Law German somewhat more, as Aymans conveyed.[77] He cited the example of finding an adequate German translation for the three ways of official recognition, which the Latin calls "*recognoscere*," "*probare*," and "*approbare*." In the third edition of the Latin-German translation of the Code these ways were harmonized and translated into German consistently as "*überprüfen*," "*billigen*," and "*genehmigen*,"[78] whereas the English translation still tends to translate "*recognoscere*" as "recognize," but both "*probare*" and "*approbare*" as "approved," as can be shown in most English translations of canons 117 and 119 no. 3 CIC/1983. So with regard to the existing translations of the Code, it is interesting to note that the translators did not follow a purely literal approach or one mainly following the spirit of the source

[76] See Aymans, "Aus dem Vorwort zur ersten Auflage," in *Codex des Kanonischen Rechts*, 7th edn, Kevelaer, Butzon & Bercker, 2012, II.

[77] See Aymans, "Aus dem Vorwort zur zweiten Auflage," in *Codex des Kanonischen Rechts*, 7th edn, Kevelaer, Butzon & Bercker, 2012, IV; idem, "Aus dem Vorwort zur dritten Auflage," in *Codex des Kanonischen Rechts*, 7th edn, Kevelaer, Butzon & Bercker, 2012, V.

[78] See Aymans, "Aus dem Vorwort zur dritten Auflage," in *Codex des Kanonischen Rechts*, 7th edn, Kevelaer, Butzon & Bercker, 2012, V.

text, but mediated between both approaches to achieve a text which is as close to the original as possible but is also understandable in the local churches.

Achieving Legal Equivalence

This somewhat mixed model is backed theoretically by functional approaches that try to overcome the tension between literal and freer translations. These approaches are not radically dedicated to either literal or freer translation, but focus more on purpose, hence permitting the translator to be guided more by the purpose of the law, as Christiane Nord explains, "In functional translation theory, translating is regarded as a 'purposeful activity.' A translation process does not automatically lead from a source to a target text. The translator is an expert of intercultural communication carrying out a communicative activity directed at a particular communicative purpose or various purposes."[79] In a similar way, Susan Šarčević, from the practical perspective of translation studies, suggests always asking what a translation is seeking to achieve. One key question guiding these decisions is asking whether it is the translator's job to achieve linguistic equivalence or legal equivalence. With translations of legal sources, such as statutes, Šarčević sees the purpose of translations as producing texts which express the same legal consequence as the original text. A translation of legal texts fulfills its purpose if it results in the same legal outcome. Translating laws therefore, as Šarčević finds, is not about linguistic equivalence but about legal equivalence.[80] Because of their openness for a purpose, functional approaches are well suited to serve as theories for translating the law. They might prevent overly literal translations as well as overly free ones. However, it is apparent that this requires the translators to possess enormous skills. There is a danger inherent in these approaches that the translators' interpretation of the purpose of a law becomes dominant in the translations. It is difficult to avoid this, as translating is always and by necessity a way of interpreting a text. Šarčević, in this sense, rightly remarks that translating is not an exact science but always an approximation.[81] It is achieved best by experts who know a maximum of the law and a maximum of language. This reflects the urgent need for "lawyer-linguists," experts trained legally as well as linguistically who possess the essential prerequisites to translate the law with a maximum of legal knowledge and linguistic skills. If canon law proceeds with the fourth model of providing authentic legal texts in the languages of the local churches, it consequently has to invest in the training of

[79] Nord, "Function + Loyalty," *Open Theology* 2 (2016), 569.
[80] See Šarčević, "Challenges to the Legal Translator," in Tiersma/Solan, eds, *The Oxford Handbook of Language and Law*, Oxford, Oxford University Press, 2012, 192–193.
[81] See ibid., 192.

canonical lawyer-linguists. This seems necessary, as translating canon law for use in a multilingual church is especially difficult, because the translation process is not only about bridging language borders but also about crossing the borders of legal systems. Translation scholar Peter Sandrini observes that there is a growth in complexity from translating legal texts for use in one multi-language legal community, to translating texts for another legal order within the same legal system, to translating them for members of a different legal order of another legal system.[82] While canon law formally embraces members of the same legal order only, namely, the ecclesiastical order, the situation is in fact more complicated, as the local churches are part of the different legal cultures around the globe. Translating canonical statute law for use in common law cultures, for instance, requires a specific sensitivity for phrasing civil statute law to be received by individuals who are used to common law and who will subject canon law to interpretation following common law standards of interpretation. For the church as a legal community operating across the borders of legal systems, it is a challenge to deal with these ruptures in theory and in practice. As there is hardly any law that oversteps the boundaries of legal cultures so radically as global canon law—on a small scale Canada is in a similar situation of referring to the English and French language *and* of having a mixed legal system of common and civil law—canon law studies have plenty to offer to the general debates on law and language on how to shape cross-cultural legal communications. Investing more thought into translating canon law would therefore not only be profitable for the law itself—which with the improvement of local comprehension stands a fair chance of increasing its acceptance—but also for canon law studies, which could be an important voice in the debates on creating multi-language and cross-cultural law.

[82] See Sandrini, "Translation zwischen Kultur und Kommunikation," in idem, ed, *Übersetzen von Rechtstexten*, Tübingen, Narr, 1999, 17–19.

7
Interpreting the Law

Whenever it comes to acts of communication, there is an ideal model of an undisturbed meaning being conveyed between sender and receiver, a mutual exchange of signs uninterrupted by the problem of uncertainty. This is the ideal. It is fulfilled for the law whenever its meaning is clear, whenever the sense and purpose of legal communication is evident for those who deal with the law. When the law makes use of words that carry a distinct meaning, there is no need for further debate. The meaning is at hand, conveyed by the ordinary literal sense of the terms and structure used in legal statements.

7.1 Plain and Proper Meaning

Whenever this happens, there seems to be no need for further interpretation. The United States Supreme Court expressed this idea in its *plain meaning rule*, also called the *literal rule*, as a basic rule for understanding the constitution. The court stated, "Where language is plain and admits of no more than one meaning the duty of interpretation does not arise, and the rules which are to aid doubtful meanings need no discussion."[1] The literal rule expresses the vision that words used in legal texts might carry a plain, an ordinary meaning that is apparent to any ordinary speaker on the street or can be found in any dictionary. This ordinary literal sense of legal terms makes it easy to apply the law, as it renders interpretation superfluous. A rule similar to plain meaning can be found in canon law. It is the codified law itself that contains a norm, canon 17 CIC/1983, on how to understand the law of the church. While most legal orders contain some rules on how to interpret the law, these rules are usually not part of the law. However, they are in canon law. Richard Posner once noted, "[A] hierarchical church, like the hierarchical judiciary, has better prospects for circumscribing interpretive freedom than a nonhierachical professional community has."[2] This does seem to have more than a grain of truth to it when it comes to ecclesiastical interpretation rules. The circumscription of interpretive freedom in the hierarchical church

[1] The United States Supreme Court, "Caminetti v. United States," decided January 15, 1917, *United States Reports* 242 (1917), 485.
[2] Posner, *Law and Literature*, 3rd edn, Cambridge, MA, Harvard University Press, 2009, 321.

The Language of Canon Law. Judith Hahn, Oxford University Press. © Oxford University Press 2023.
DOI: 10.1093/oso/9780197674246.003.0007

goes so far as to take on the form of legal rules contained in canonical statute law. This reveals something of the strictness with which the supreme legislator wanted his rules on interpretation to be observed.

No Meaning without Context

The first sentence of canon 17 CIC/1983 reads, "Ecclesiastical laws must be understood in accord with the proper meaning of the words considered in their text and context." The canon shares the idea that there is a proper meaning of words, a "*propria verborum significatio*," which in some cases can be found by considering the wording of a text alone. However, it also takes into account that the meaning of terms used within legal rules might often be discovered only by considering not only the wording but also its context. The norm therefore in fact reflects two theoretical approaches to interpretation, *literalism* and *contextualism*, as two subsequent steps in the process of discovering textual meaning. This is surprising insofar as literalism and contextualism are usually understood as antagonists. While literalists are reluctant to draw on the context to discover the meaning of terms, as the literal meaning stands for itself, most contextualists do not see a sense in searching for a chimera-like literal meaning. Meaning, they reckon, can only be found by considering the context. Legal scholars Larry Alexander and Saikrishna Prakash give one example for the dependence of meaning on context when asking what to give to a customer who walks into a bar and demands "chips."[3] They suggest that the costumer would probably like tortilla chips or potato chips if he or she sounds American, but French fries if he or she sounds British. Yet it is only context which helps to decipher which "chips" are meant. The meaning of terms, so it seems, is seldom as plain or proper as the idea of *propria verborum significatio* implies. For this and for other reasons, the doctrine of a plain meaning of legal terms has been the target of scholarly criticism, among others, by scholars participating in the law and language debate.[4] These scholars express their general doubts over whether a plain meaning exists in connection with terms. Taking into account the achievement of hermeneutics, Alberto Vespaziani speaks of the "myth or prejudice of literal interpretation," as "from the hermeneutic perspective, it is clear that there is literally no such thing as a literal interpretation. The sequence of l-e-t-t-e-r-s does not produce nor

[3] See Alexander/Prakash, "'Is that English You're Speaking?'," *San Diego Law Review* 41 (2004), 975.
[4] E.g., Marmor, "The Immorality of Textualism," *Loyola of Los Angeles Law Review* 38 (2005), 2063–2079; McGinnis/Rappaport, "The Constitution and the Language of the Law," *William & Mary Law Review* 59 (2018), 1330–1331, 1347–1353.

does it evoke meaning."[5] In a similar vein, constitutional scholar Steven Winter speaks of

> the fundamental and conventional tendency to hypostatize and fetishize meaning—that is, to assume that meaning is "in" the words we use and, then, to endow those words with causal efficacy. But meaning is not "in" the words; meaning is in the mind. Words are at best tokens or stimuli that activate the mental processes that constitute and create meaning.[6]

Winter suggests meaning is always a result of "complex processes of cognition and categorization"[7] which we simply happen to miss when "plain" terms are concerned, as their meaning seems to come naturally to us. Nevertheless, even the meaning of "plain" terms results from communication and depends on the context in which sender and receiver exchange their conversation. So there is no meaning apart from context and no meaning that is not a result of the mental processes which create it. Winter gives one example that he picks up from reading legal philosopher Ronald Dworkin's book *Law's Empire*, namely, the term "bachelor."[8] Dworkin noted that "bachelor" refers to an "unmarried man."[9] So one could suggest that there is a literal meaning connected with the term "bachelor." Yet Winter objects that it is not that easy. The term "bachelor," as he sees it, cannot be applied to all unmarried men alike without creating confusion. To call the pope a "bachelor" would at least raise some eyebrows. This is the case because the term "bachelor" only makes sense in a *context* in which marrying is the social norm. Hence, individuals who are not expected to marry are not accurately described as "bachelors," except as a joke. Of course, it may be funny in some contexts to call a community of cloistered nuns a "flat share of bachelorettes," but it is context then as well that makes the joke a good one (or raises some eyebrows). So Winter and others show, I believe convincingly, that it is context and the mental processes of creating meaning that make meaning, and never a pure and plain connection between a word and its predefined meaning.

[5] Vespaziani, "Towards a Hermeneutical Approach to Legal Metaphor," in Bustamante/Onazi, eds, *Human Rights, Language and Law*, Franz Steiner Verlag, Stuttgart, 2012, 80.

[6] Winter, "Frame Semantics and the 'Internal Point of View,'" in Freeman/Smith, eds, *Law and Language*, Oxford, Oxford University Press, 2013, 117.

[7] Ibid., 115.

[8] See ibid., 118.

[9] See Dworkin, *Law's Empire*, Cambridge, MA, Belknap Press, 1986, 72.

Challenging "Plain" Meaning

To these doubts regarding the merit of plain meaning Lawrence Solan adds the problem of practically identifying whether a meaning is plain, as what seems clear to one person might be ambiguous to another.[10] So even when a term seems plain in its meaning at first sight, this does not guarantee that this opinion is shared by everyone and at all times. I want to elucidate this with an example from canon law, which I stumbled over when reading John Coughlin's comparative study *Canon Law* on canon law and common law. Coughlin asks whether canon 915 CIC/1983 on refusing communion to certain Catholics, the applicability of which is often critically questioned by canon lawyers and Catholic bishops alike, provides its readers with an unambiguous meaning. He approaches this question with the intense debate between the United States' Catholic bishops in mind, who in the 2004 electoral campaign discussed whether Catholic public officials running for office, including the then Democratic candidate for presidency John Kerry, should be excluded from receiving the Eucharist if they supported pro-choice policies; the debate is recurrent at present, as the bishops discussed the same issue again in 2020 with regard to the now-president Joseph Biden. The critical part of canon 915 CIC/1983 reads, "Those . . . obstinately persevering in manifest grave sin are not to be admitted to holy communion." Coughlin is convinced that the meaning of the norm is clear. He divides the canon into three parts and discusses each part.[11] The phrase "are not to be admitted" ("*ne admittantur*"), as he sees it, clearly states an imperative meaning. The phrase "obstinately persevering" ("*obstinate perseverantes*") relates to the fact that somebody fails to correct himself or herself after having received a pastoral warning. Regarding the phrase "in manifest grave sin" ("*in manifesto gravi peccato*"), Coughlin discusses whether the public support of abortion or euthanasia, as upheld by many Catholic politicians, has to be considered as gravely sinful. He concludes that supporting those positions is undoubtedly a grave sin, as it has to be interpreted as a formal cooperation in these sinful acts. The sin is manifest, whenever it is generally known to the public. So when it comes to plain meaning, Coughlin believes the case of canon 915 CIC/1983 is easy to decide. I find this rather debatable. While I agree that the phrases "are not to be admitted," "obstinately persevering," and "manifest" appear unambiguous, I doubt whether the term "grave sin" provides any clarity, particularly in a legal context. For Coughlin, the answer seems at hand. The church was always clear that abortion and euthanasia were gravely sinful and that

[10] See Solan, *The Language of Judges*, Chicago, IL, The University of Chicago Press, 1993, 93–94.
[11] See Coughlin, *Canon Law*, Oxford, Oxford University Press, 2011, 151–155.

formal cooperation in these acts was gravely sinful as well. Whoever supports pro-choice positions is therefore objectively transgressing a church's moral norm. This objective state of not according with the moral standards of the church places a person in a state of grave sin. This is undoubtedly a position which can be derived out of the church's tradition. Yet it provides only a very narrow and restricted answer to what "sin" means today. Modern theology, both academic and magisterial theology, has raised doubts about whether a purely objective approach to sin may explain its nature convincingly. To many contemporary theologians, it provides only half the answer. Francis emphasized, for instance, in his 2016 document *Amoris laetitia* that it is possible that divorced and remarried couples, who live in an objectively sinful situation according to traditional church teaching, are nevertheless not subjectively in a situation of sin but in fact "can be living in God's grace,"[12] which might even qualify them to receive the sacraments. Hence, to count as sin, an objective act of doing evil must also include a subjective side, namely, the subjective factor of being guilty, of being aware of doing wrong and transgressing a moral norm. Abortion and euthanasia, in this sense, are sinful only if a person is aware that they are acting wrongly. To talk about sin in a purely objective sense has become largely theologically implausible according to present-day moral theology. Well, that is theology, one could object. It does not necessarily determine the meaning of the term "sin" when used in a *legal* context. But it is similarly impossible to argue that the law uses the term "sin" to describe the objective side of doing wrong only. That the subjective dimension of sin has found its way into ecclesiastical legislation is manifest in canon 916 CIC/1983, the canon directly following the critical canon 915 CIC/1983. Here the legislator speaks about individuals "*conscious* of grave sin" who have to abstain from receiving the Eucharist because they are aware that they are unready to receive it. This is obviously a subjective approach toward sin. In the light of these debates on the nature of sin, it is hard to defend the idea that the meaning of canon 915 CIC/1983 is plain. To state that the canon simply refers to an act objectively transgressing an ecclesiastical moral norm, as the church's tradition understood sin, brushes aside modern considerations of what sin is and how the term can be interpreted as a consequence. "Sin" is not a plain term at all. Due to the use of this highly ambiguous term, the meaning of canon 915 CIC/1983 is not easy to determine, and the norm can hardly be applied to cases by using the plain meaning rule.

12 Francis, "Post-Synodal Apostolic Exhortation *Amoris laetitia* on Love in the Family," March 19, 2016, no. 305, *Acta Apostolicae Sedis* 108 (2016), 437.

Open Texture of the Law

So there is reason to suspect that plain meaning is at hand less often than the plain meaning rule seems to suggest. As law operates with words, the meaning of which is often vague and indeterminate, it is mostly open to interpretation. In fact a great deal of effort used by those who work in the legal system is dedicated to interpreting the law. Ralf Poscher observes, "Significant portions of the institutional legal system, especially courts at the appellate level and supreme courts, are for the most part concerned not with disentangling the facts of cases but with the indeterminacies of the law."[13] H.L.A. Hart identified this phenomenon as a consequence of what he called the "open texture" of the law, stating, "Whichever device, precedent or legislation, is chosen for the communication of standards of behaviour, these, however smoothly they work over the great mass of ordinary cases, will, at some point where their application is in question, prove indeterminate; they will have what has been termed an *open texture*."[14] This open texture is owed to the fact that law operates with language and employs general terms to convey a legal message. With the use of language, the law also adopts the vagueness of terms, as Hart explains, "[U]ncertainty at the borderline is the price to be paid for the use of general classifying terms in any form of communication concerning matters of fact."[15] He explicates this with his famous example of the rule that "vehicles" are not allowed in the park. This rule raises the question of what can be classified as a "vehicle." One may wonder whether toy trucks are "vehicles" and consequently not allowed in the park. And one can discuss how the rule relates to bicycles. While there are objects which are evidently included in the term "vehicle" in the mentioned example—Hart calls them the "paradigm, clear cases (the motor-car, the bus, the motor-cycle)"[16]—there are other objects, such as the toy truck or bicycle, the "vehicle-ness" of which is less clear, at least when it comes to the rule of not taking them into the park. This uncertainty is owed to the "fuzziness" of terms, as Lawrence Solan calls it. Many terms are fuzzy, when it comes to their margins. Solan explains this by referring to color. While a bright red object is obviously "red" and a purely white object is clearly "not red," there is less clarity with regard to the question how "red" orange, purple, or pink objects are.[17] Such fuzzy edges of terms also play a role when it comes to understanding

[13] Poscher, "Ambiguity and Vagueness in Legal Interpretation," in Tiersma/Solan, eds, *The Oxford Handbook of Language and Law*, Oxford, Oxford University Press, 2012, 128.

[14] Hart, *The Concept of Law*, 3rd edn, Oxford, Oxford University Press, 2012, 127–128; on Hart's theory, see Bix, *Law, Language and Legal Determinacy*, Oxford, Clarendon Press, 1993, 7–35; Charnock, "Hart as Contextualist?," in Freeman/Smith, eds, *Law and Language*, Oxford, Oxford University Press, 2013, 128–150.

[15] Hart, *The Concept of Law*, 3rd edn, Oxford, Oxford University Press, 2012, 128.

[16] Ibid., 129.

[17] See Solan, *The Language of Judges*, Chicago, IL, The University of Chicago Press, 1993, 97.

legal terms. Sanford Schane clarifies this with an example from judicature, the case *Interstate Commerce Commission v. Allen E. Kroblin, Inc.*[18] In this case, the litigants in fact quarreled over the meaning of the term "manufacture." The concrete question was whether dressed and eviscerated chickens are manufactured goods (and thus to be transported in specific certified carriers). The question did not arise from an ambiguity of the term "manufacture" itself, as the meaning of the term is quite clear, but from the fact that "manufacture" has fuzzy margins. It is obvious that a whole chicken with feathers, head, and feet is not manufactured, and it is likewise clear that a ready-made chicken dinner is manufactured. Yet there is less clarity when it comes to all states of chicken in between those two margins. There are no clear margins to determine when treating a good becomes "manufacture," so that there is no clear line but rather a scale of "manufacturedness." Schane calls this problem the "vagueness of categorization."[19] This vagueness makes it difficult to determine and consequently debatable how dressed and eviscerated chickens are to be treated legally—as manufactured goods or as goods at a lower level of manufacturing, so that the legal rule on manufactured goods does not apply.

7.2 A Matter of Interpretation

The court opted for the last mentioned alternative. By interpreting "manufacture," it came to the conclusion that dressed chickens are not to be treated as manufactured goods. This result was not easily at hand but the fruit of the court's interpretation—and it is quite obvious that the court could also have interpreted differently and could have arrived at a different verdict. So whenever interpretation takes place, its outcome is uncertain. This can hardly be avoided. It is impossible to employ terms which only carry a plain and unambiguous meaning in legal texts. And it is also largely unfeasible to regulate in a determining density that leaves no doubt about the meaning of terms used in legal texts. So interpretation, as uncertain as it may be, is usually the only way to discover legal meaning. Andrei Marmor notes, "Judges typically need to interpret statutes—and cases get to higher courts precisely because the meaning of the relevant statutory provision is not clear enough to yield a particular outcome."[20] As interpretation is one key task of everyone in the legal business, the literature on the

18 United States District Court for the Northern District of Iowa, "Interstate Commerce Commission v. Allen E. Kroblin, Inc.," decided June 30, 1953, *Federal Supplement* 113 (1953), 599–631.

19 Schane, "Ambiguity and Misunderstanding in the Law," *Thomas Jefferson Law Review* 25 (2002), 178.

20 Marmor, "The Immorality of Textualism," *Loyola of Los Angeles Law Review* 38 (2005), 2065.

methods and methodology of the law is largely focused on legal interpretation. The same applies to canon law. Even though linguistic issues of the law have not attracted vast attention, there are several authors who deal with the interpretation of canon law, as already mentioned.[21]

However, the challenges connected with interpretation when it comes to the law go deeper than merely searching for meaning in a concrete legal case. They actually touch upon fundamental topics. The dispute about what interpretation actually is alludes to debates on how to understand interpretation on an essential level. One can conceive of it to be more of a *reconstruction*, the finding of a sense in a legal text that is already there. Or one can perceive it to be more of a *construction*, the making of a sense where otherwise there is none.[22] While in German "meaning" is often combined with terms like "recognizing" ("*erkennen*"), "discovering" ("*entdecken*"), or "finding" ("*finden*"), English legal interpretation theory and its language—realistically, as I find—seem to be entirely comfortable with "constructing" meaning. That the US rules on interpreting statute law, to which I will return later in this chapter, are called "canons of *construction*" is in any case a valuable hint that there is good reason to understand interpretation essentially as the generation of meaning, even though one may argue about the proportions of reconstruction and construction that take place whenever meaning is elaborated. These struggles regarding how to interpret interpretation methodologically have further consequences for methodical issues of legal interpretation. How interpretation works, by focusing on the text itself or by searching for extra-textual sources which help to see sense in a text, is an object of an elemental debate. I will try to sketch out the answers canon law offers to these queries in the following subsections.

(Re)constructing Meaning

For canon law, Ladislas Orsy gives a definition of interpretation in which he relates to the "task of the interpreter. He must find the truth of the law. That is, he must find out the objective meaning of the norm. In reality, this means to generate a meaning on the basis of the text in its doctrinal and cultural context."[23] This is an interesting definition, as it points at two rather different angles. On the one hand, Orsy understands interpretation to be an objective task. For him

[21] Two of the most prominent being Ladislas Orsy and Helmuth Pree: see Orsy, "The Interpreter and His Art," *The Jurist* 40 (1980), 27–56; idem, "Models of Approaches to Canon Law and Their Impact on Interpretation," *The Jurist* 50 (1990), 83–101; Pree, *Die evolutive Interpretation der Rechtsnorm im Kanonischen Recht*, Vienna, Springer, 1980.

[22] On these general questions, e.g., Marmor, *Interpretation and Legal Theory*, 2nd edn, Oxford, Hart Publishing, 2005.

[23] Orsy, "The Interpreter and His Art," *The Jurist* 40 (1980), 50.

there is a truth within legal norms which is readily found. On the other hand, he admits that "finding" the truth is "to generate a meaning," and is therefore also a way of constructing it. This ambivalence might be somewhat typical for canonists. As theologians, canonists tend to speak of the "truth," even the "truth of the law." But whether there is such a thing as a "truth of the law" is a difficult and hotly debated question in its own right.[24] I do not wish to go any deeper into the philosophical debates on this matter at this stage, but would like to emphasize that canon law has yet to face the puzzle whether it is convincing to speak of the law by using the category of "truth." In any case, the majority of canonists seem to accept a connection between truth and law. As a consequence, when speaking about interpretation, canonists tend to search for a truth that precedes the act of its "finding," although they might be well aware that there is also a great deal of constructing taking place whenever this "finding" happens. But these elements of construction are interpreted more as epistemological challenges and less as ontological ones. Interpreters are not perfect in detecting the truth, therefore there is always some cultural blurring or contextual fuzziness. The resulting difficulties in detecting the "true" legal meaning, in any case, do not seem to discourage most canonists from assuming that it in fact exists. "There is an enduring core-meaning in the law,"[25] Ladislas Orsy insists, which may be discovered by the interpreter, besides all "relativity" that comes with interpretation.

Purposeful Interpretation

Like any other texts, legal norms are regularly open to interpretation, so that their meaning needs reconstruction or rather construction to become clear. Yet unlike many texts, interpreting the law is not free but has a specific purpose, as Orsy contends. He scrutinizes two alternative approaches to interpreting legal texts, particularly legal norms, only to discard the first one immediately, "Legal texts can be approached either as literary productions with a myriad of meanings, or as norms which intend to determine specific actions."[26] Orsy believes that legal texts cannot be taken as sources with a possible multitude of meanings because they follow

[24] E.g., Neumann, "Wahrheit statt Autorität," in Lerch, ed, *Recht verhandeln*, Berlin, Walter de Gruyter, 2005, 369–384; Bix, "Linguistic Meaning and Legal Truth," in Freeman/Smith, eds, *Law and Language*, Oxford, Oxford University Press, 2013, 34–44; Marmor, "Truth in Law," in Freeman/Smith, eds, *Law and Language*, Oxford, Oxford University Press, 2013, 45–61; Halpin, "Language, Truth, and Law," in Freeman/Smith, eds, *Law and Language*, Oxford, Oxford University Press, 2013, 62–78.

[25] Orsy, "The Interpreter and His Art," *The Jurist* 40 (1980), 50.

[26] Orsy, "Models of Approaches to Canon Law and Their Impact on Interpretation," *The Jurist* 50 (1990), 90.

> an overriding intention: to impose a specific course of action. That is, the aim of the law-maker (be it a constitutional legislator, be it the people through customs) is not to communicate knowledge through an elaborate text, but to convey a decision in view of an action. This intention then must become a primary hermeneutical factor in interpretation.[27]

This clear focus on the intention of the legislator, as typical as it is for canon law, is a bone of contention in the general debates on legal interpretation.[28] These debates revolve around the core disagreement of how important intentions are exactly for interpreting a legal norm. This relates to the underlying issue of where the meaning of a norm comes from, from the text itself or rather from the intentions of those who shaped it. These different approaches to finding legal meaning constitute the fundamental conflict in interpretation theory of *textualism* versus *intentionalism*, which is most prominently visible in the Anglo-American disputes between textualist and intentionalist legal scholars.

Textualist Approaches

One specific strand of the debate consists of approaches to constitutional interpretation with the antipodes of *living constitutionalism* versus *originalism*.[29] All theories, of course, exist in different degrees of purity. One example of a radical textualist is the late Supreme Court Justice Antonin Scalia, who has become an icon of textualism and a role model for many textualists. Scalia became famous for his catchy and emphatic statements advocating the derivation of legal meaning from the words of the law. He wrote, for instance, "It is the *law* that governs, not the intent of the lawgiver. . . . A government of laws, not of men. Men may intend what they will; but it is only the laws that they enact which bind us."[30] When it comes to constitutional interpretation, textualism is usually coupled with the approach of living constitutionalism. Defenders of living constitution interpret the text of the constitution in the light of current legal questions and present needs, thus understanding meaning as a dynamic phenomenon. However, other constitutional scholars, such as the aforementioned Antonin Scalia, do not support the idea of a fluid living constitution and stick to the concept of originalism in its subtype of *original meaning*. This approach tries to grasp the meaning that

[27] Ibid.

[28] For the manifold critical questions that intentionalism has to answer, see Marmor, *Interpretation and Legal Theory*, 2nd edn, Oxford, Hart Publishing, 2005, 119–139.

[29] E.g., Bennett, "Constitutional Interpretation," in Solan/Tiersma, eds, *The Oxford Handbook of Language and Law*, Oxford, Oxford University Press, 2012, 114–127.

[30] Scalia, "Common-Law Courts in a Civil-Law System," in idem, *A Matter of Interpretation*, Princeton, NJ, Princeton University Press, 1997, 17.

reasonable individuals would have attributed to the constitution at the time of its design and implementation. Textualism and original meaning have in common that they do not care much about the intentions of the drafters of a law. Whereas textualism is about the meaning that a text presents in the here and now, originalism is concerned with a meaning from the past. Both approaches, in any case, are concerned with the *objective* content of a statute or the constitution. The objective content is what a reasonable hearer would derive from the text, be it a reasonable hearer of bygone days or of the present day. Textualism, nevertheless, finds its natural limits when it comes to deriving the proper meaning of terms. As discussed earlier, the idea that a proper meaning can be detected easily by interviewing a reasonable hearer or by consulting a dictionary might work in many but not all cases. Understanding terms, even for a textualist, often depends on the context, as it is frequently only their embedding that reveals the meaning of words that carry several meanings. It is only the context that reveals whether the term "apple" refers to a fruit or a computer. Textualism thus often takes a peek at *contextualism* to determine the meaning of terms.

Intentionalist Interpretations

Yet even the context frequently offers little help in determining the meaning of a term. This is why many scholars argue that it is not overly helpful to speculate about the meaning of words used in legal norms, and more helpful to ask which purpose or intention they want to express.[31] This is the stance referred to as *intentionalism*. It mostly focuses on the intention of the legislator or of the ratifier who took on a certain law for a specific group of legal subjects. At the level of constitutional interpretation in the United States, intentionalism is met by the approach called *original intent*. It attempts to derive the meaning of constitutional texts by investigating the intent of the so-called "Framers of the Constitution." At present, there is, for instance, an intense debate over whether the Framers used plain language or legal language to compose the US Constitution. Against the widespread presumption that the Constitution is written in plain language, legal scholars John McGinnis and Michael Rappaport just recently devoted a study to showing that the Constitution was in fact shaped by legal experts as a legal text by making use of legal terminology.[32] Approaches dealing with constitutional interpretation that search for the Framers' intent to decipher the meaning of terms should therefore be aware of this. Hence, intentionalists tend to look

[31] E.g., Posner, *Law and Literature*, 3rd edn, Cambridge, MA, Harvard University Press, 2009, 274.

[32] See McGinnis/Rappaport, "The Constitution and the Language of the Law," *William & Mary Law Review* 59 (2018), 1321–1411.

back and try to discover the intentions that were connected with the law at the time of its formation and implementation. In an intentionalist view, this binds all interpreters of the law, as Richard Posner explicates, "For an intentionalist judge, the task in interpreting a statute is to figure out from its words, structure, and background how the legislators whose votes were necessary for enactment would have answered the interpretive question had it occurred to them."[33] Posner also explains intentionalism with a practical example, a transmission model, stating,

> A command is a communication, to be decoded in accordance with the sender's intentions. If a message is garbled in transmission you ask the sender to repeat it; that is intentionalism in practice. If you cannot reach the sender you try to glean from everything you know about him and the circumstances of the failed message what he would have done had he been on the spot.[34]

Relevance of the Author

As intentionalism is usually all about the author and his or her intentions, the intentionalist scholars Larry Alexander and Saikrishna Prakash advocate the slogan "no author, no meaning."[35] Alexander and Prakash illustrate their opinion by giving the example of rain dripping from the roof which just randomly happens to form letters and words on the ground. According to them, these words can have no meaning, irrespective of how intentionally they seem to have been written. For words to have a meaning, there needs to be an author somewhere. The text cannot be considered in isolation from his or her intentions. Their approach does, however, merit critical discussion. While it seems broadly convincing that meaning depends on intention, one might still discuss whether it is always the intention of the author that makes a meaning. When it comes to the law, particularly to very old law, one must admit that the author's intentions are not always of help in discovering a meaning that solves present-day legal problems. Ancient intentions do not necessarily address current legal issues adequately. German "textualists" (the term is not really common, but suitable to describe a certain approach to legal theory) often provoke their intentionalist colleagues by remarking that the text of the law is sometimes smarter than the legislator had been, and that it often in fact must be smarter in order to adapt the law to the legal needs of the here and now. So both textualist and intentionalist

[33] Posner, *Law and Literature*, 3rd edn, Cambridge, MA, Harvard University Press, 2009, 287; critical toward this approach of hypothetical intention is Marmor, *Interpretation and Legal Theory*, 2nd edn, Oxford, Hart Publishing, 2005, 130, and with regard to original intent, 155–160.

[34] Posner, *Law and Literature*, 3rd edn, Cambridge, MA, Harvard University Press, 2009, 308.

[35] Alexander/Prakash, "'Is that English You're Speaking?'," *San Diego Law Review* 41 (2004), 977.

approaches have their evident limits. While textualism revolves around the words of the law, ignorant of the fact that there is no meaning in words but only in the minds of individuals who utter or receive those words, intentionalists frequently overstretch the original intentions connected with a law, as if those intentions necessarily guarantee the best understanding of a law once and for all. This raises the question whether it is indeed possible or helpful to draw a clear line between pure textualism and intentionalism. While the heated arguments between radical textualists and intentionalists seem irreconcilable, it often seems as though their approaches are not as far apart as their dispute suggests. Lawrence Solan observed that textualists usually also have the intent of a legal text in mind when interpreting the words of a text, whereas intentionalists regularly turn to the text itself to discover its intent.[36] I therefore also support a mixed model. Notwithstanding the fact that canon law likewise promotes a mixed approach in its interpretation theory, as I will show in one of the following subsections, there are historical reasons for seeing textualism and intentionalism as being closer together than their present collisions suggest. David Frank points at Rabbinic interpretation theory to show that interpretation according to intention in Rabbinic times was regularly understood not as asking for the intention of the original speaker, but asking for the intention of the text. Frank explicates, "In other words, authorial intent was not the governing factor in scripture interpretation (not 'What does the prophet mean?'), but rather the text itself ('What does the prophecy itself mean?'), including how these words might apply to a new situation."[37] The focus on the author's intention, as Frank works out, is rather a modern idea which came into being during the Enlightenment and which revolved around the presumption that the authors had the right to determine what their creation was about and what it was saying to their audience. This shift was connected with a certain turn toward honoring the human mind and its products, as Frank explains, writing, "A reason for focusing on authorial intent in the Modern worldview has to do with the elevation of the human mind as being the thing we can be most sure of and rely upon."[38] The idea of authorship which contained the right of an author to determine the meaning of her or his creation was supplemented by the idea that a fixed meaning given by the author could provide a text with a reliable and hence objective meaning, as Frank contends,

[36] See Solan, *The Language of Statutes*, Chicago, IL, The University of Chicago Press, 2010, 51–52; idem, "Linguistic Issues in Statutory Interpretation," in Tiersma/Solan, eds, *The Oxford Handbook of Language and Law*, Oxford, Oxford University Press, 2012, 87–88.

Ronald Dworkin, in any case, is highly critical of these inconsistencies, particularly of Antonin Scalia's surprising references to intention; see Dworkin, "Comment," in Scalia, *A Matter of Interpretation* Princeton, NJ, Princeton University Press, 1997, 115–127.

[37] Frank, "Do We Translate the Original Author's Intended Meaning?," *Open Theology* 2 (2016), 656.

[38] Ibid., 659.

> Another rationale for focusing on the meaning that an author intended for his or her text has to do with the Modernist drive toward objectivity, including objective meaning, and the concern that if a text does not have a meaning that is unified by whatever the author intended it to mean, then its meaning is subjective and indeterminate.[39]

In any case, this idea was deconstructed in the twentieth century by many authors, as Frank notes, "However, both the traditional Hebrew approach to textual meaning and the Postmodern approach accept the fact that meanings are not objective and not fixed, and that the unifying element of hermeneutics is not the author's intention, but rather the text itself, as it is interpreted in various contexts."[40]

The Death of the Author

One author who set out this postmodern theory in one of its more radical versions was philosopher Roland Barthes, who proclaimed "The Death of the Author."[41] For Barthes, "the modern scriptor is born simultaneously with the text."[42] He or she does not precede the text but becomes the author with the formation of the text. The text stands for itself. The author is merely the person who collects ideas and groups them together, ideas that he or she finds in the culture that surround her or him, as Barthes maintained, "The text is a tissue of quotations drawn from the innumerable centres of culture."[43] The author's intention is therefore of no further relevance for the meaning of the text. His or her intentions are no worthier than those of other persons, namely, of those authors who created the bits and pieces that the author then unites to form a new text, as well as of those who read the text and interpret it. Barthes eventually summed up, "[T]he birth of the reader must be at the cost of the death of the Author."[44] I do not wish to discuss Barthes in depth here, but I do believe that he touched upon a significant point by claiming that the author and her or his intentions are less central to interpretation than modern intentionalism sometimes suggests. I would never call for the death of the author, as the author's intentions, as I see them, may indeed be a help in interpreting a text, although they cannot be the sole approach to finding a meaning. A text stands for itself. It is the text that speaks in the mind of its readers

[39] Ibid.
[40] Ibid.
[41] See Barthes, "The Death of the Author," in idem, *Image—Music—Text*, New York, Hill and Wang, 1977, 142–148.
[42] Ibid., 145.
[43] Ibid., 146.
[44] Ibid., 148.

or listeners. It might tell a story in the light of the author's intentions, but it also does so in the light of the intentions of present-day readers and interpreters, who might not even know much about the author's intentions in the first place. The Rabbinic approach of considering intentions but not necessarily those of the drafters and makers of a text, even including those which might be connected with a text today, provides us with helpful advice on how to combine a textualist with an intentionalist point of view. This somewhat premodern mixed approach has also survived in parts in the interpretation theory of canon law, as I will show in the next subsections.

Canons of Construction

The debates on how to interpret legal norms with an unclear meaning have left their mark on legal methodology. Many legal orders provide the appliers of the law with rules on how to interpret the law. British law suggests the *golden rule* and the *mischief rule* whenever the plain meaning rule does not help its appliers to derive a reasonable meaning from a statute. The golden rule prevents a literal interpretation in those cases in which a literalistic approach would lead to absurd results. The mischief rule seeks to identify the mischief a statute was designed to cure and interprets the statute in the way that best supports that purpose. The legal tradition of the United States, particularly its textualist strand, follows the so-called *canons of construction* guiding the courts to interpret statute law. The most prominent canons are *Eiusdem generis* (of the same kinds, class, or nature—a term is interpreted to correspond to other terms used in the same context), *Expressio unius est exclusio alterius* (the explicit mention of one matter excludes other matters that are not mentioned), *In pari materia* (upon the same matter—ambiguous statutes are interpreted in the light of other statutes on the same matter), *Noscitur a sociis* (understanding a term by its company), *Reddendo singula singulis* (referring each to each, each phrase or expression to its corresponding object), and *Generalia specialibus non derogant* (the general does not detract from the specific). These canons are supplemented by further rules like the *rule of lenity*—or *strict construction*—obliging the court to interpret unclear criminal law in the way most favorable to the defendant.

In a similar way, canon law provides its appliers with rules on the interpretation of unclear ecclesiastical law. These rules are also contained in canon 17 CIC/1983. As I said in section 7.1, the first part of canon 17 CIC/1983 contains the canonical version of the plain meaning rule, yet the second part of the canon goes on to add several further rules guiding ecclesiastical interpretation. It reads, "If the meaning remains doubtful and obscure, recourse must be made to parallel places, if there are such, to the purpose and circumstances of the law, and to the mind of the legislator." These rules are supplemented by canon 6 §2 CIC/1983, obliging interpreters to consider former law when interpreting present norms in the light of tradition. The canon reads, "Insofar as they repeat former law, the canons of this Code must be assessed also in accord with canonical tradition." Another rule on interpretation—the ecclesiastical version of the rule of lenity—is found in canon 18 CIC/1983, which directs, "Laws which establish a penalty, restrict the free exercise of rights, or contain an exception from the law are subject to strict interpretation."

It is well worth discussing what these norms tell us about the interpretation of canon law. It was H.L.A. Hart who formulated the wise words that "[c]anons of 'interpretation' . . . cannot, any more than other rules, provide for their own interpretation."[45] As the canons are made of words as well, they are open to interpretation just like every text. And this is also true for the canons mentioned, and particularly obvious when it comes to canon 17 CIC/1983, as its meaning is pretty obscure. Here, I want to attempt to shed some light on the bundle of rules contained in the ecclesiastical canons of construction. First of all, canon 17 CIC/1983 refers the interpreter of ecclesiastical norms, whenever their meaning is unclear, to parallel places, norms in the Code or in other ecclesiastical texts which correspond to the unclear passage of the norm and which might help to explain it. Likewise, the purpose of the law might help to discover its meaning. Asking what a norm was designed for, what good is to be achieved by its observation, often reveals a certain interpretation best suited to fulfilling that purpose. Similarly, the circumstances of the law—that is the historical context of its genesis, the historical reasons that moved the legislator to formulate the law, or the process of its formation—may be of help in discovering its meaning. This rule of historical interpretation is supplemented by canon 6 §2 CIC/1983, obliging the interpreters to consider the canonical tradition when interpreting norms that repeat former law. Finally but no less importantly, the "mind of the legislator" (*mens legislatoris*), the ecclesiastical version of intentionalism, is of help in finding out how the law is supposed to be interpreted. Part of the legislator's intention is the concrete intention connected with the respective norm but also more general intentions connected with canon law as such. The "mind of the legislator" provides canonical interpretation theory with the voluntarist flavor that pervades ecclesiastical legal theory, as the legislator proves responsible not only for making the law but also for producing much of its meaning. I will return to this tendency of canon law to rely heavily on the legislator shortly.

[45] Hart, *The Concept of Law*, 3rd edn, Oxford, Oxford University Press, 2012, 126.

Blending Interpretation Rules

Just as the US canons of construction have been criticized for not solving the problem of interpretation,[46] so has been canon 17 CIC/1983.[47] The response canon law gives to the restricted service of single interpretation rules is in any case interesting in this respect inasmuch as the law attempts to balance the weaknesses of the diverse approaches by making use of various approaches to interpretation. Canon 17 CIC/1983, first of all, presents a plain meaning rule. It then opens up the literal approach to contextual insights. This is supplemented by the four rules on interpretation which put forward comparatist, teleological, historical, and intentionalist strategies to discovering the meaning in question. By taking up a grammatical (or literal), systematic (that is context-related), historical, and teleological method of interpretation, canon law obviously revives the traditional canons of legal interpretation which legal scholar Friedrich Carl von Savigny developed in the nineteenth century[48] and which became tremendously influential not only for German interpretation theory in Savigny's home country but for many European legal orders as well. In receiving Savigny's theory, modern canon law proves to have been inspired by European civil law, imitating state-of-the-art interpretation theory—from the late nineteenth and early twentieth centuries. Some canonists have commented upon this decision critically. They note that canon law when developing its interpretation theory before 1917 (the norms on interpretation in the present Code are identical with those created for the 1917 codification) was presenting an up-to-date interpretation theory then, but while secular interpretation theory has developed over the past hundred years, ecclesiastical interpretation theory has not.[49] It is high time to revise it, they suggest, according to the standards of secular civil law on interpretation theory, freeing it in particular from its positivistic, static, and nonhermeneutical taint.

However, canon law never received Savigny's canons purely but added the intentionalist *mens legislatoris* as early as 1917. Any purist in the field of interpretation theory probably finds this mix of interpretive approaches abhorrent. A confessed textualist to whom the church's plain meaning rule *propria*

[46] E.g., Marmor, "The Immorality of Textualism," *Loyola of Los Angeles Law Review* 38 (2005), 2075; Stewart, "The Rhetorical Canons of Construction," *Michigan Law Review* 116 (2018), 1485–1514; in defense, Scalia, "Common-Law Courts in a Civil-Law System," in idem, *A Matter of Interpretation*, Princeton, NJ, Princeton University Press, 1997, 25–27.

[47] E.g., Drössler, "Bemerkungen zur Interpretationstheorie des CIC/1983," *Archiv für katholisches Kirchenrecht* 153 (1984), 3–34; Neudecker, *Ius sequitur vitam*, Münster, LIT, 2013, 613.

[48] See Savigny, *System des heutigen Römischen Rechts*, vol. 1, Berlin, Veit und Comp., 1840, 213–216.

[49] E.g., Drössler, "Bemerkungen zur Interpretationstheorie des CIC/1983," *Archiv für katholisches Kirchenrecht* 153 (1984), 14–15, with further references in fn. 48–49; Neudecker, *Ius sequitur vitam*, Münster, LIT, 2013, 613–614.

verborum significatio would certainly appeal could hardly support the use of the intentionalist *mens legislatoris* in cases where plain meaning fails to provide a clear meaning. Staunch intentionalists, on the other hand, can barely relate to the overriding belief in the ordinary literal sense of words in the first place. While interpreters preferring original intent might be happy with the "mind of the legislator" and the historical context, presentist intentionalists concerned with the intention of the law for the here and now would object to precisely that approach, but could still relate to finding meaning in parallel norms or the purpose of a law. The church's approach to interpretation is therefore influenced by most interpretation theories being debated in secular jurisprudence without seeing any need to make a clear-cut decision. Ecclesiastical interpretation amalgamates textual, contextual, and intentionalist theories, merges objectivist and subjectivist approaches, and takes on a historical and presentist perspective.

What seems undecided and arbitrary—or theoretically weak—at first glance proves to be surprisingly pragmatic upon closer inspection. The church's mixed method concords to the finding that (re)constructing meaning is challenging and therefore best approached pragmatically.[50] If a clear meaning is not at hand, there are several ways of unearthing meaning. Context might help, as do parallels in other norms or related texts. In some cases, meaning might be found by examining the purpose of law. Considering the history of a norm might also be wise, as might trying to identify what the legislator intended. Sometimes the answers found by applying these methods are somewhat random; sometimes it might be hard to decide which interpretation to follow when the methods result in contradictory interpretations. This requires decisions on prioritization. Nevertheless, I find the mixed methods approach congenial in its modesty. While I find the primary reference to plain meaning misleading, ecclesiastical interpretation theory in a second step confronts its own ideology of plain meaning with context and parallels.[51] And it defies the absoluteness of historical arguments and the dogma of intentionalism with teleology. This mix seems to acknowledge the constraints of finding meaning in texts and the limits to what rules of interpretation can contribute to this problem. In its pragmatic attitude of giving every approach a go, the mixed methodology of canon law interpretation is closer to hermeneutics than one would presume at first sight. It defies plain textualist or intentionalist

[50] For a positive judgment on mixed approaches, see also Solan, *The Language of Statutes*, Chicago, IL, The University of Chicago Press, 2010, 51–52.

[51] For a hermeneutical critique of the ideological programme behind plain meaning, see Vespaziani, "Towards a Hermeneutical Approach to Legal Metaphor," in Bustamante/Onazi, eds, *Human Rights, Language and Law*, Franz Steiner Verlag, Stuttgart, 2012, 80.

answers, allowing the unfolding of a complex process of discovering meaning between history and the present day, between subjectivism and objectivism.[52]

Borders of Interpretation

However, even though I have expressed my sympathy for the church's mixed approach on interpretation, it is far from having been thought through sufficiently. There is an urgent need to do more research in this field and to discuss canonical interpretation theory in the light of the findings provided by linguistic theory and modern interpretation theory. I cannot perform this task in this context, as it requires a study of its own. Nevertheless, it would be a highly worthwhile endeavor, maybe even contributing to the current debates on interpretation in general, as canon law in its plural approach to interpretation relates to the full spectrum of theories on legal interpretation currently under discussion. I want to mention at least one more aspect at this point in my study which requires further scrutiny. It connects with the finding that particularly pragmatic approaches like the one promoted by the church face some difficulties in defining the *borders* of interpretation. Employing diverse approaches to discovering the meaning of legal texts raises the question of what counts as interpretation and what transcends interpretation to become steps in the *development* of the law. German legal methodology responds to this doubt by introducing the idea of the "*Wortlautgrenze*,"[53] the "border of the wording," referring to the semantic boundary that divides those meanings contained from those meanings not contained in legal texts and their terms. Whenever a fact may be subsumed under the law, when it may be understood as having been included in the terms used in the legal text, legal interpreters operate within the boundaries of its wording. If a fact is not included in the terms used by the law, yet the law is applied to the fact anyway, this is not interpretation but development of the law. The *Wortlautgrenze* is therefore what distinguishes between interpretation and legal development. It is evidently hard to determine this border in practice. The margin between meanings included in a term and those excluded from it is often more of a gray zone than of a clear line, as I showed in section 7.1 with the examples of terms with fuzzy margins, such as "vehicle," "red," or "manufacture." Dietrich Busse therefore called it a juridic "fetish" to think that a division between interpretation

[52] Highly critical of this "results-oriented jurisprudence" and "reminiscent of the 'legal realism'" is John P. Beal, see Beal, "Something There Is That Doesn't Love a Law," in Lacey/Oakley, eds, *The Crisis of Authority in Catholic Modernity*, Oxford University Press, Oxford, 2011, 149.

[53] See Klatt, "Die Wortlautgrenze," in Lerch, ed, *Recht verhandeln*, Berlin, Walter de Gruyter, 2005, 343–368; Christensen, "Die Wortlautgrenze," in Felder/Vogel, eds, *Handbuch Sprache im Recht*, Berlin, Walter de Gruyter, 2017, 187–205; Zumbült, "Ordnen," in Meyer/Wichard, eds, *Sprachen der Kirche*, Munich, dkv, 2018, 182.

and legal development is possible by recourse to linguistics.[54] Nevertheless, many legal scholars do not want to give up on the *Wortlautgrenze*. However difficult or impossible it might be to determine the border in practice, this does not devalue the idea of using semantic boundaries to define the margin of interpretation, as legal scholar Matthias Klatt states.[55] He regards the *Wortlautgrenze*, however impossible it is to trace clearly, as one semantic approach which is helpful in distinguishing legal interpretation from legal development, albeit one approach faced with the unavoidable gray zone between the two. Despite all its limitations, the *Wortlautgrenze* can also therefore be used for canon law at least as a fiction, to demarcate the dividing line between interpretation and legal development.

Multi-Language Interpretations

If the church does indeed take the step of broadening its official language use with regard to global canon law, as I suggested in chapter 6, section 6.3, this transformation also requires consideration with regard to interpretation theory. The object of interpreting the Code of Canon Law is currently the Latin text only. If canon law becomes a multi-language law, publishing its official legal texts in the multiple languages of the local churches, the difference between these various language versions of legal texts will give rise to the need for a revised methodology of approaching meaning. However skillfully multiple language versions of legal norms are made, they always pose the problem of dealing with inevitable discrepancies between the different versions. Laws promulgated in various languages unavoidably contain ambiguities due to terms or sentence structure used in different languages.[56] If there is one authentic text translated into different languages, the problem may be solved easily: one can turn to the original text to discover the meaning of the ambiguous part. Yet if there is no single authentic text, the challenge has to be addressed differently. This problem is well known in the European Union, as all of the multi-language versions of its legal documents are considered to be authentic versions. As a result, interpreting European law has to embrace the idea of equal authenticity.[57] It is therefore necessarily a comparatist

[54] See Busse, "Was ist die Bedeutung eines Gesetzestextes?," Müller, ed, *Untersuchungen zur Rechtslinguistik*, Berlin, Duncker & Humblot, 1989, 144–147.

[55] See Klatt, "Die Wortlautgrenze," in Lerch, ed, *Recht verhandeln*, Berlin, Walter de Gruyter, 2005, 366.

[56] For practical examples from European competition law, see Sosoni, "Language and Translation in EU Competition Law," in Marino et al., eds, *Language and Law*, Cham, Springer Nature Switzerland, 2018, 179–205; more examples given by Bajčić/Martinović, "A Mutual Learning Exercise in Terminology and Multilingual Law," in Marino et al., eds, *Language and Law*, Cham, Springer Nature Switzerland, 2018, 207–223.

[57] See Doczekalska, "Legal Languages in Contact," in Marino et al., eds, *Language and Law*, Cham, Springer Nature Switzerland, 2018, 172–175.

task. This is naturally challenging. But moreover, it requires clarification regarding how to proceed in those cases in which the various language versions offer their interpreters different and equally plausible meanings. One methodology of dealing with these challenges discussed by Lawrence Solan is the "Augustinian approach," so called by Solan, which he discovered when studying the interpretation practice of the European Court of Justice.[58] Solan associates the court's approach with interpreting the multi-language versions of European regulations with the exegetical work of Augustine of Hippo, one of the key Church Fathers of the Latin Church, who traced the meaning of biblical terms by comparing different Bible translations, Hebrew, Greek, and Latin versions, with each other. In doing so, Augustine discovered convincing conformities and implausible variances. His approach profits from the plausibility of the majority and its opinion on the meaning of a certain term or a passage. As "human beings have the capacity to form similar concepts from similar experiences,"[59] as Jan Engberg sums up the key assumption behind Solan's approach, concordant translations may be considered to reflect the original idea more accurately. Yet, again, one can also scrutinize majoritarian readings critically to find more convincing interpretations. This approach, as Solan suggests, is also helpful today in trying to discover the meaning of legal terms expressed differently in different languages. When confronted with unclear bits of European legislation, the European Court of Justice compares the various language versions of the law to find its meaning. Having diverse language versions at hand does not therefore make interpretation more difficult but easier, according to Solan, who praises the European Union for providing this insight into the clarifying function of plurality when stating, "Babel is not punishment, it is a gift."[60] His Augustinian view on interpreting the law could also be of help for multi-language canon law. The complex task of finding meaning in canon law, currently addressed by the legislator's employment of all approaches to interpretation that he could find, could become easier with a comparatist method like the Augustinian approach.

7.3 Competent Interpreters

As interpretation is a natural process within each act of learning and understanding, everybody reading a legal text with the purpose of comprehending it is

[58] See Solan, "Statutory Interpretation in the EU," in Olsen et al., eds, *Translation Issues in Language and Law*, London, Palgrave Macmillan, 2009.

[59] Engberg, "Word Meaning and the Problem of a Globalized Legal Order," in Solan/Tiersma, eds, *The Oxford Handbook of Language and Law*, Oxford, Oxford University Press, 2012, 181.

[60] Solan, "Statutory Interpretation in the EU," in Olsen et al., eds, *Translation Issues in Language and Law*, London, Palgrave Macmillan, 2009, 43.

engaged in interpretation. Consequently, interpreting the law takes place whenever readers or listeners attempt to discover meaning in legal norms. The interpretations resulting from these processes are manifold, as are the perspectives of the subjects engaging in the task of interpretation. Interpretations differ depending on the point of view of the interpreter. John Huels, by referring to canon 218 CIC/1983, gives one example of how canonical norms might be construed depending on the interpreters' perspective. The canon reads, "Those engaged in the sacred disciplines have a just freedom of inquiry and of expressing their opinion prudently on those matters in which they possess expertise, while observing the submission due to the magisterium of the church." Quite naturally, as Huels contends, a theological scholar and a Vatican official tend to interpret this norm differently. He states, "Such a law is likely to be restructured much differently by an American university professor who highly esteems academic freedom than by a Vatican official charged with protecting unity of faith and discipline."[61] This evidently raises the question of whose interpretations to follow. So whenever differing interpretations arise, concomitantly the question of who is authorized to place her or his interpretations over those of others becomes relevant.

Binding Interpretations

Consequently, every legal order is tasked with identifying who is authorized to interpret the law bindingly, to derive a meaning out of a legal norm which not only serves as a private opinion but as an official understanding of the text, legally binding others and other interpreters of the law. Common law countries mostly attribute the task of legally binding interpretation to judges, providing that the interpretations of the higher courts have a precedential function for the lower courts. Civil law traditions also refer to the interpretations of courts, albeit usually without attributing to them precedential effect. The judges' interpretations are official interpretations, binding on the litigants, yet regularly not binding on other judges. In this respect, canon law is a typical representative of civil law. Its canon 16 §3 CIC/1983 regulates the competence of ecclesiastical tribunals and administrative deciders when interpreting the law of the church as one of primary relevance with regard to the respective parties concerned, directing, "An interpretation in the form of a judicial sentence or of an administrative act in a particular matter, however, does not have the force of law and only binds the persons for whom and affects the matters for which it was given." This regulation first of all notes the restricted effect of judicial or administrative interpretations.

[61] Huels, "Interpreting Canon Law in Diverse Cultures," *The Jurist* 47 (1987), 254.

They do not have the same general effect that comes with law, but help to settle an individual case, a specific matter only. Ecclesiastical tribunals do not therefore have the power to set precedents, but "make law at least for the parties who are seeking justice,"[62] as Ladislas Orsy explains. This approach limits the tribunals' power to shape canon law sustainably, as shown in detail in a bulky volume written by canonist Gerhard Neudecker.[63] But Orsy also reminds his readers that this is a rather theoretical view of the role and function of ecclesiastical tribunals. In practice, many local ecclesiastical tribunals take a peek over Rome's shoulder to adopt interpretations set out by the papal tribunals. So despite the restricted effect of judicial interpretations according to canon 16 §3 CIC/1983, higher ecclesiastical tribunals fulfill a precedential service in practice, at least when it comes to marriage cases as the main task of ecclesiastical tribunals. This practice is in any case ambivalent, to say the least. There is some learning from each other; but at the same time there is also a ready willingness by the local ecclesiastical tribunals to ignore those decisions which do not seem to do justice to local cases. So while there are some interrelations between the ecclesiastical tribunals and their judicature for sure, there is also a tendency to decide cases independently.

Authentic Interpretations

The restricted interpretive competence of the ecclesiastical tribunals and administrative deciders with regard to the power to establish precedents does not stand for itself, but has a counterpart. This counterpart is authentic interpretation, which describes the official and authoritative interpretation of the law with a generally binding effect. So while canon law is civil law in the sense that it restricts the power of the judges to develop the law through interpretation, it does employ the concept of a precedential interpretation, albeit reserving this function strictly to the ecclesiastical legislator himself and to those entitled by him. Canon 16 §1 CIC/1983 states, "The legislator authentically interprets laws as does the one to whom the same legislator has entrusted the power of authentically interpreting." The norm carries a voluntarist element into canonical interpretation theory, as the legislator's will is not only responsible for making the law but also remains dominant in producing its meaning. The supreme legislator in fact assigned the Pontifical Council for Legislative Texts with the task of interpreting global ecclesiastical laws authentically. To perform this task, the council is entrusted with ordinary legislative power, so when interpreting a norm, it actually acts as a legislator. The interpretations, in consequence, have the same effect as the laws to

62 Orsy, "The Interpreter and His Art," *The Jurist* 40 (1980), 41.
63 See Neudecker, *Ius sequitur vitam*, Münster, LIT, 2013.

which they relate, as canon 16 §2 half-sentence 1 CIC/1983 notes, "An authentic interpretation put forth in the form of law has the same force as the law itself and must be promulgated." As they carry the same effect as the law, the interpretations need to be officially published, something which happens in the papal law gazette, the *Acta Apostolicae Sedis*, just as it is done with global canonical laws. Yet there remains an obvious difference between a law and its interpretation, if not when it comes to its effect, at least when it comes to the genre, as emphasized by John Huels, who maintained, "The creation of law and the authentic interpretation of law are both acts of legislative power, but they are not the same. One could say that they belong to the same genus (products of legislative power), but they are different species."[64] That is surely true on a formal level, yet one may ask what difference the genre distinctions make when both genres, laws and their authentic interpretations, share the same legal effect as rules which are binding on the legal subjects. A closer look at the legal effects of authentic interpretations reveals at least slight differences. A little different from laws which regularly "regard the future, not the past, unless they expressly provide for the past" (canon 9 CIC/1983), legal effects of authentic interpretations are retroactive in some cases. Their legal effects are explicitly regulated in canon 16 §2 half-sentence 2 CIC/1983. The norm ascribes different effects to an interpretation depending on its clarifying function, "If it only declares the words of the law which are certain in themselves, it is retroactive; if it restricts or extends the law, or if it explains a doubtful law, it is not retroactive." That declarative interpretations thus have a retroactive effect does not pose a specific problem, as Huels explains, because purely declarative interpretations are in fact given to norms the meaning of which was never truly doubtful as such. Huels explicates,

> A declarative interpretation, in fact, amounts to no more than a paraphrase of the existing law. . . . The correct meaning of the law could have been determined simply by an application of the standard rules of canonical interpretation (especially cc. 17–21), perhaps with a more profound study of the law's history and related contextual information (doctrine, parallel juridical texts, canonical tradition, etc).[65]

Legal philosophers such as Andrei Marmor would therefore probably refrain from calling declarative interpretations "interpretations" at all. Interpreting, in Marmor's view, is always changing the legal text, whereas a practice that only elucidates what is already there is not interpreting.[66] His criterion fits

64 Huels, "Classifying Authentic Interpretations of Canon Law," *The Jurist* 72 (2012), 609.
65 Ibid.
66 See Marmor, *Interpretation and Legal Theory*, 2nd edn, Oxford, Hart Publishing, 2005, 165, 167.

restrictive, extensive, or explanatory interpretations as regulated in canon 16 §2 half-sentence 2 CIC/1983, where such changing actually takes place. Accordingly, a restrictive interpretation is not retroactive, as it "limits the clear meaning of the law so that it embraces fewer objects,"[67] as Huels illustrates, and thereby actually creates a new law. The same applies to extensive interpretation. It is "broadening the meaning of the law by including objects that previously did not fall within the scope of the law."[68] Neither is an explanatory interpretation retroactive, as it "declares the true meaning of a law that is objectively doubtful,"[69] Huels contends, expounding,

> The wording of the law either is not certain in itself, or its application in some cases is doubtful; or, the doubt may arise from different interpretations by authors or ecclesiastical authorities, one being correct and the other incorrect, giving rise to a need for an authoritative pronouncement of the correct interpretation.[70]

Interpretive Legal Development

This differentiation shows that restrictive, extensive, or explanatory interpretations given by the Pontifical Council for Legislative Texts are actually legislative acts, as they change the law. Huels explains this with reference to several examples of all categories. I want to mention merely one example, namely, the official and authentic interpretation of canon 917 CIC/1983.[71] The canon contained one contested word only, "*iterum*," the meaning of which was doubtful. The Latin term can mean either "again" or "a second time." The canon reads, "A person who has already received the most holy Eucharist can receive it '*iterum*' on the same day only within the Eucharistic celebration in which the person participates." If "*iterum*" is interpreted as "again," the norm allows a person to receive the Eucharist several times during the course of the day. If it means "a second time," as the Pontifical Council indeed interpreted it,[72] the person may only receive the Eucharist two times in a day. So by picking "a second time," the council delivered a specific reading of the canon and explained its meaning in a restrictive sense, thus curbing any previous practice of receiving the Eucharist several times a day. We do not know why the council determined to understand

67 Huels, "Classifying Authentic Interpretations of Canon Law," *The Jurist* 72 (2012), 610.
68 Ibid.
69 Ibid.
70 Ibid.
71 See ibid., 620–623.
72 See Pontifical Commission for Authentic Interpretation of the Code of Canon Law, "Responsa ad proposita dubia," July 11, 1984, *Acta Apostolicae Sedis* 76 (1984), 746–747.

"*iterum*" in a restrictive sense as meaning "a second time." This is because the council publishes its interpretations as responses to questions (*dubia*) issued to it by Catholic institutions and officeholders from all over the globe without giving any reasons for its decisions. It simply publishes a positive or negative response ("*affirmative*" or "*negative*") to the requests for clarification posed to it. This practice of not giving any explanatory information has met with some criticism, for instance, by canonist Hubert Socha. He quite convincingly substantiated his demand that the council should publish explanations with its decisions by citing the council's evident importance for the development of canon law.[73] In order to learn what moves the council to interpret unclear terms or phrases in the way it does and thus to develop the law in a certain direction, it would be necessary to have access to more information to understand its ruling. The council's practice is in any case nontransparent and therefore allows the legal subjects neither to anticipate nor to explain changes made to the law via authentic interpretations.

A further common complaint brought forward by canonists is the appallingly absolutist style the council adopts in imparting its conclusions, simply by waving "no" or "yes" at the petitioners without granting them an explanation. As my book is about the language of canon law and also about the style with which legal matters are communicated in the church, it is hard to overlook the discordant note that this practice of nonjustification combined with the absolutist style of conveying decisions strikes in modern ears. As we no longer live in absolutist times, it does seem rather misguided that neither the legislator nor the Pontifical Council for Legislative Texts justifies their legislative choices. One might even presume, as did one reviewer of this book, that the general absence of reasons for the laws deriving both from legislation or authentic interpretation is part of the wider problem of frustrating the comprehension of many ecclesiastical legal subjects in their understanding and reception of canon law. He or she is certainly right with this assumption that the extensive practice on nonexplanation is unacceptable for many modern Catholics and pertains to canon law in general. It becomes particularly manifest though with regard to the condescending and dismissive style in which the Pontifical Council for Legislative Texts communicates law in form of authentic interpretations.

Controlling Meaning

Besides criticizing the style in which authentic interpretations are disclosed within the church, some canonists have more generally criticized the approach

[73] See Socha, "Canon 16," in Lüdicke, ed, *Münsterischer Kommentar zum Codex Iuris Canonici* (suppl. sheets 47, February 2012), 11, no. 18d.

of entrusting the legislator and those entitled by him with interpreting the law authentically. In this vein, Ladislas Orsy remarked that "the legislator is not necessarily the best interpreter. Since he drafted the law, he is so close to it that he may not perceive its limitations and ambiguities."[74] Orsy endorses the secular concept of leaving interpretation to the courts. This would serve the rule of law, control the legislator, and, not least, save time for those who require a decision.[75] The ecclesiastical legislator's permanent control of his norms, on the contrary, could be damaging for the legitimacy and effectiveness of canon law. Orsy draws on this finding to form a favorable view of the practice of democratic legal orders leaving interpretation to the courts and other appliers of the law, as he explains with regard to secular civil law, "[I]n civil law, those who hold the power to legislate do not hold the power to interpret. The parliament makes the law, the courts determine its meaning. Once the law is born, its parent must leave it alone. The courts take care of its development."[76] The picture used by Orsy is interesting, as he compares the exclusion of the legislature from interpreting its own laws with the parental need to let go, to surrender control over the legal child to let it grow and develop independently and autonomously with the help of adjudication. It is typical of Orsy to put a very critical issue into such a charming picture, of legal "parenting" in this case. In doing so, he nevertheless also voices sharp criticism in an indirect way. In this light, legislators who extend their control to include the interpretations of their laws are actually helicopter parents refusing to cut the cord, denying their child an independent existence. The law of the church, so it seems, is never allowed to come of age. It cannot become a modern legal order as long as it is not allowed to play with other children. At the same time, the legislator expresses a deep mistrust in the ability of others to do some good to his child. The legislator's hesitation to leave the matter of interpretation solely to the ecclesiastical tribunals backs legislative power but at the same time devalues judicial power.

A Neoconservative Agenda

This concern about involving the tribunals in developing the law also sheds some more light on the motives why the supreme legislator favors textualism, as a remark by Andrei Marmor on the parallel debate in US interpretation theory helps to understand. Marmor observes that it is also part of the textualist agenda to curb the judges' authority, as he finds,

74 Orsy, "The Interpreter and His Art," *The Jurist* 40 (1980), 40.
75 See ibid., 41.
76 Ibid.

> Textualists . . . are rightly concerned about the close connection between the *how* and *who* questions—how judges determine what statutes mean significantly determines who gets to make the law. The intuitive idea is this: the more discretion or interpretative freedom judges have in statutory interpretation, the greater their role, personally and institutionally, in determining what the law is. And this is the upshot of textualism: textualists do not want judges to make the law.[77]

This textualist agenda, as Marmor states, sounds very democratic at first sight, supporting the separation of powers by leaving the task of lawmaking to the representatives of the people. However, Marmor thinks this view is deceptive. Textualism is an element of the neo-conservative political agenda, he observes, and as such is concerned less with preserving democracy and more with supporting the doctrine of the lean state, as he maintains,

> By advocating a theory of statutory interpretation that is preoccupied with literal meaning, and purportedly relies on bright-line rules or canons of statutory interpretation, textualism strives to effectuate a broader ideological agenda that seeks to reduce the state and its regulatory functions to the necessary minimum. The deep distrust of neo-conservatives is not really a distrust of judges, it is a distrust of regulation and state intervention.[78]

The analogy is not wide-ranging enough to explain the tendency in the church to curb the judges' authority across the board. But it does relate to it in parts. In contrast to secular textualists, the aim of the ecclesiastical legislator is less that of reducing the authorities' impact or reducing regulation as such, and more of securing maximum power for the legislator. It is a centralistic attempt to join the forces in Rome, giving less power to the authorities on the periphery. And it is an attempt to secure a monarchical hierarchy. It is the absolutist monarch who makes the law. And it is likewise he who explains how the law is to be interpreted. Attempting to keep control over the law not just when it comes into being but also afterward when it is applied in the local churches is a power claim that secular legislators had to give up in modernity. Yet it is evidently a staunch neoconservative move to secure centralistic power in Rome at the expense of local ecclesiastical adjudication and administration, reducing their regulatory functions to the necessary minimum, in a similar way to the conservative strategy described by Marmor.

[77] Marmor, "The Immorality of Textualism," *Loyola of Los Angeles Law Review* 38 (2005), 2064.
[78] Ibid., 2066.

8
The Language of Legal Action

The fact that the language of adjudication carries a variety of distinctive features and touches upon diverse topics of law and language has particularly attracted the attention of law and language scholars. The most prominent example of scholarship on this topic is probably Lawrence Solan's famous book *The Language of Judges*,[1] in which the author shows in a myriad of examples taken from United States jurisprudence how the terminology of legal texts, of statute law and contracts mainly, and its interpretation by judges and juries influence judicial decisions. It is here, in adjudication, where the law and its language seem to culminate in acts of institutionalized contestation. Adjudication in this sense is not merely the culmination point of the law but also of its language. The ritual of adjudication is also a liturgy of legal language, as it condenses, sacralizes, and celebrates legal communication in antagonistic constellations. Legal scholar Ralph Christensen emphasized that legal disputes embody communication in a unique way. They are a battle of words but also often represent a "battle over language,"[2] as the litigants struggle to have their interpretation of the law affirmed by the judge. This ritual dimension of adjudication and its language is coupled with a narrative dimension. Peter Tiersma alluded to the narrative nature of adjudication language by remarking, "Trials are very much about stories or narratives."[3] As stories they not only recollect events but also develop them while being told, without the end being known at the outset. Trials approach this end with the help of words—oral hearings, uttered testimonies, recorded evidence, written statements, and judicial declarations. This makes the language of law enforcement and legal action a complex bundle of texts, uttered speech and written words, outspoken language and silence. One aspect that stands out when comparing ecclesiastical adjudication with most secular systems of judicature is that the language of the judges in most modern legal systems is connected primarily with orality,[4] whereas canon law procedures are heavily textual. This is perplexing for many individuals who find themselves confronted with ecclesiastical

[1] Solan, *The Language of Judges*, Chicago, IL, The University of Chicago Press, 1993.
[2] Original quote, "Kampf um Sprache," Christensen, "Die Wortlautgrenze," in Felder/Vogel, eds, *Handbuch Sprache im Recht*, Berlin, Walter de Gruyter, 2017, 199.
[3] Tiersma, *Legal Language*, Chicago, IL, The University of Chicago Press, 1999, 147.
[4] See Hoffmann, "Mündlichkeit im Recht," in Felder/Vogel, eds, *Handbuch Sprache im Recht*, Berlin, Walter de Gruyter, 2017, 67–90.

The Language of Canon Law. Judith Hahn, Oxford University Press. © Oxford University Press 2023.
DOI: 10.1093/oso/9780197674246.003.0008

procedures, as we tend to associate legal communications in general more with orality, as Solan and Tiersma observed, "Most of the encounters that people have with the law are language events: interactions with lawyers and with the police, whether in the street, a car, or the courtroom."[5] Experiencing canon law in general and canonical adjudication in particular, though, is less influenced by orality, as legal and judicial communications in church often take on a written form. There are no face-to-face encounters with police in the church, as the church does not have a police function or other agents of law enforcement. There are usually no oral hearings before ecclesiastical tribunals; some exceptions exist, such as the oral contentious trial (see canons 1662–1667 CIC/1983), a procedure in any case which is extremely rare in practice. A tribunal does not usually collect the evidence itself, but employs an auditor to undertake that task (see canon 1428 CIC/1983), for example, by conducting oral hearings of litigants and witnesses. The evidence is documented in the acts, putting everything, including oral testimony into writing. The judges' decision is frequently based on these written acts only. Every member of a tribunal forms his or her written opinion based on the acts. Decision-making is usually a collegial act of oral consultation, discussing the written opinions with the other members of the tribunal and voting to yield a result. The decision follows the majority of votes. There is also usually no oral judgment notice in church, even though exceptions exist, for the oral contentious trial (see canon 1668 §1 CIC/1983).

8.1 Hearings and Testimonies

To learn more about the spoken language of ecclesiastical procedures, it is therefore expedient to focus on the hearings, particularly the forensic interviews of litigants and witnesses. In law and language scholarship, this subject is repeatedly addressed by forensic linguists. What they have discovered, often in empirical studies—I already referred to Luna Filipović's experiments on the recollection of English- and Spanish-speaking witnesses in chapter 6, section 6.1[6]—might go some way toward encouraging canonists to shed more light on the language of interviews in ecclesiastical settings. It is of academic interest to examine hearings as a specific form of tense, ritualized, and formalized communication. Yet knowing more about forensic speech is also of interest for ecclesiastical adjudication itself. Besides practical considerations on how to conduct good interviews which provide proof of high evidential value and are key for judicature in general,

[5] Solan/Tiersma, "Introduction," in idem, eds, *The Oxford Handbook of Language and Law*, Oxford, Oxford University Press, 2012, 5.

[6] See Filipović, "The Role of Language in Legal Contexts," in Freeman/Smith, eds, *Law and Language*, Oxford, Oxford University Press, 2013, 328–343.

ecclesiastical adjudication is reliant on how parties and witnesses experience their judicial encounters. Forensic interviews are often the only personal face-to-face encounters that the parties and witnesses have with ecclesiastical tribunals. Their negative reputation in some churches, which ecclesiastical judge Engelbert Frank witnessed in his research for Germany,[7] is not seldom the result of exactly these confrontations. So the experiences that the litigants or witnesses have in the hearings have a significant effect on public opinion regarding ecclesiastical judicature. This is of no small importance for its effectiveness, as the tribunals regularly depend on the voluntary participation of the parties and witnesses in the procedures. The church has no police; it cannot force anybody to participate in ecclesiastical processes. So it largely relies on its power of persuasion, convincing parties and potential witnesses of the merit of contributing to finding the facts. A good reputation is therefore an important precondition for the tribunals' success in unearthing the truth in ecclesiastical cases. As the interview settings are the tribunals' key points of contact with parties and witnesses, it is of academic and practical significance to give them consideration.

Complex Dialogues

The quality of evidence in a procedure in most cases depends heavily on the quality of the hearings conducted to produce proof to decide the case. Whether a judge gathers enough proof to become certain of the truth in a case often depends on the evidence taken from interviews. Interviews and hearings, in any case, are complex dialogues. They are fragile and easily obstructed by diverse factors. Even slight technical perturbations may already influence the outcome of an interview. For instance, the effect of recording hearings as a technique for documenting testimony has to be carefully examined in this respect, as forensic linguist Sonia Russell found, as it tends to distract the speakers and to shift their focus when speaking. Russell noticed, "The participants orientate to a mechanical third party, the tape, which represents a future 'referee group' . . . , the judge and jury."[8] So whenever electronic recording takes place, which is the regular way of documenting forensic interviews, also in ecclesiastical procedures, there is an invisible third party in the room, as Russell sees it, because interviewer and respondent both anticipate the judges', or in jury trials the juries', deciding the

[7] See Frank, "Die Sprache kirchlicher Ehegerichte und ihre Wahrnehmung durch Betroffene," in Puza/Weiß, eds, *Iustitia in caritate*, Frankfurt am Main, Peter Lang, 1997, 463–473; idem, "Ehenichtigkeitserklärung," in Weiß/Ihli, eds, *Flexibilitas Iuris Canonici*, Frankfurt am Main, Peter Lang, 2003, 501–514.

[8] Russell, "'Three's a Crowd,'" in Cotterill, ed, *Language in the Legal Process*, Basingstoke, Palgrave Macmillan, 2002, 116.

case afterward on the basis of the recorded evidence or of written transcripts of the records. This has to be taken into account when recording interviews and also when evaluating recorded testimony.

The quality of an interview and of the evidence derived from it also naturally depends much on the interviewer's impact on the person questioned and on his or her interview technique. Forensic linguists have contributed greatly over the past years to understanding the effect of the language used in police interviews, for example by demonstrating the effect of the interviewer's terminology and word choice on the answers given by witnesses or suspects. Alison Johnson, for instance, showed how tiny single words like "so . . . " serve to give structure to the interviews.[9] There are also cultural aspects which might influence the outcome of a hearing to a large extent. Sonia Russell characterized interview settings in this respect as complex and fragile communication situations, as she observed, "[I]t would be wrong to categorise the investigative interview as a series of simple questions and answers. It is a complex dialogue of opposing aims, realised by a variety of means."[10] This complexity of dialogue becomes even greater in cross-cultural settings. Sociolinguist Diana Eades demonstrated this in her studies on Australian cases involving Aboriginal people.[11] A particular challenge in Aboriginal witness testimony is the phenomenon of "gratuitous concurrence," a pattern in Aboriginal conversation which involves responding with "yes" to a question and with "no" to a negative question in order to express harmony between the speakers, and to do so even more when tensions between the speakers become manifest.[12] Eades unveiled with regard to a specific case of witness interrogation in court how the rising tension in the interviews caused the witnesses to express gratuitous concurrence, yet without agreeing to the allegations brought forward by the interrogators. She thus revealed that answers taken by Western listeners as consent with regard to the content of a question may not necessarily express consent to the content but rather consent to being questioned. However, as affirmative answers might also signal consent to the content, it is confusing for Western listeners to identify the actual intended meaning. From this, we learn to cast doubt on whether the question-and-answer scheme as usually used in interrogation techniques by law enforcement officers or courts is necessarily the best

[9] See Johnson, "*So . . . ?*," in Cotterill, ed, *Language in the Legal Process*, Basingstoke, Palgrave Macmillan, 2002, 91–110.

[10] Russell, "'Three's a Crowd,'" in Cotterill, ed, *Language in the Legal Process*, Basingstoke, Palgrave Macmillan, 2002, 116.

[11] See Eades, "'Evidence Given in Unequivocal Terms,'" in Cotterill, ed, *Language in the Legal Process*, Basingstoke, Palgrave Macmillan, 2002, 162–179.

[12] The term "gratuitous concurrence" was coined by Kenneth Liberman in his sociological studies on Aboriginal communication; see Liberman, *Understanding Interaction in Central Australia*, Boston, MA, Routledge & Kegan Paul, 1985, particularly 197–202.

technique to uncover the truth in all cultures.[13] In some contexts, it might in fact be more fruitful to follow a more autonomous and narrative style of conversation in interviews to allow for the parties and witnesses to reveal their knowledge in a way which suits them best. For canon law as a globally operating legal order, it might be worth keeping this in mind.

Fair Questioning

Canon law seems to be generally aware of that fact that language is highly sensitive when it comes to interview techniques. The canonical law of evidence, for instance, advises interrogators that "questions are to be brief, accommodated to the mental capacity of the person being questioned, not comprised of several points at the same time, not deceitful or deceptive or suggestive of a response, free from any kind of offense, and pertinent to the case being tried" (canon 1564 CIC/ 1983). While it is certainly hard or impossible to monitor whether the judges and auditors are actually following these rules in detail in all cases, it is still noteworthy that canon law is concerned that the interview is conducted in a fair way. Even though the interrogations serve to discover the truth in a case, this is not pursued at all costs. Overstressing, tricking, or deceiving the litigants and the witnesses to dig up the truth is not allowed, according to canon law. Forbidding deceitful, deceptive, or suggestive strategies for gaining evidence includes all tactics of deriving proof from a party or a witness by misleading them. In this respect, canon law treats litigants and witnesses not only fairly but also acts with a good degree of linguistic sophistication, as a counterexample reported by Peter Tiersma shows.[14] As a negative example of gaining evidence by deceitful and deceptive means, Tiersma referenced the *Schneckloth v. Bustamonte* case.[15] In this case, the defendant had incriminated himself by displaying proof of his involvement in a crime by opening the trunk of his car to a police officer after the officer had asked him *whether* it was possible to open the trunk. The opening of the trunk was interpreted as voluntary consent to the search, as the officer did not technically command the suspect to open his trunk but had only asked him whether the trunk opened, to which the suspect reacted by opening it. From a linguist's point of view, it is highly debatable if this event can be interpreted as a situation of consent, as Tiersma argued, as no one would understand the officer's utterance as a simple question (to which the reply would be "yes" or "no").

[13] See Eades, "'Evidence Given in Unequivocal Terms,'" in Cotterill, ed, *Language in the Legal Process*, Basingstoke, Palgrave Macmillan, 2002, 175.

[14] See Tiersma, "The Judge as Linguist," *Loyola of Los Angeles Law Review* 27 (1993), 280–283.

[15] See The United States Supreme Court, "Schneckloth v. Bustamonte," decided May 29, 1973, *United States Reports* 412 (1973), 218–291.

Instead, basically everyone would take it as a *command*, as in fact happened in the *Bustamonte* case, due to the evident power relation involved. Whether an utterance is taken as a question or as a command depends entirely on the context, Tiersma contended. If the context consists of a police officer, a state official, checking a car, the question whether the trunk opens would hardly be taken by anyone as a polite inquiry about the functionality of the car, but rather as a command requiring compliance from those addressed. The Supreme Court decision in the *Bustamonte* case, Tiersma criticized, missed this fact of linguistic pragmatics. Canon law, at least in theory, would not. Investigation technique, such as the officer's "question" technique as used in *Bustamonte*, would be regarded as deceptively suggestive and inadequate in ecclesiastical hearings.

The Right to Silence

Most interestingly, one key issue with regard to hearings and testimonies is silence, as individuals undergoing questioning in certain cases have the right to refuse active participation in an interrogation. Most legal orders provide a right to be silent, entitling the legal subjects to refuse to answer official questioning by police, law enforcement agents, or court staff under specific conditions. Most famous is the Miranda warning,[16] the obligatory notification of this right by the US police given to suspects in criminal cases. As the church does not employ police forces, it has no equivalent to the Miranda warning, but there is, in any case, the provision of an accused's right to silence in penal procedures in canon 1728 §2 CIC/1983, which reads, "The accused is not bound to confess the delict nor can an oath be administered to the accused." This right makes an exception to the rule of canon 1531 §1 CIC/1983, which regularly obliges a party who is legitimately questioned by church officials to respond and to tell the truth. Canon 1531 CIC/1983 even goes on to say in §2 that a judge is free to draw conclusions from the fact that a party refuses to respond. This norm does not apply to the defendant's refusal to testify in penal procedures, although the norm does not explicitly say so, as some canonists contend, as this would in fact undermine the right to be silent, as granted in canon 1728 §2 CIC/1983.[17] That the law is silent on this matter, in any case, and fails to note that an ecclesiastical judge may not draw negative conclusions from defendants making use of their right to refuse to give evidence is not unproblematic, as there is a natural tendency among interrogators or judges, as one may assume, to draw conclusions not only from

[16] See The United States Supreme Court, "Miranda v. Arizona," decided June 13, 1966, *United States Reports* 384 (1966), 436–545.

[17] E.g., Lüdicke, "Canon 1728," in idem, ed, *Münsterischer Kommentar zum Codex Iuris Canonici* (suppl. sheets 18, July 1992), 2, no. 2.

speech but from silence as well. In practice, silence is often interpreted as an admission of guilt, as we naturally tend to see individuals not defending themselves against accusations as tacitly affirming the charge brought against them.[18] That a judge is indeed tempted to interpret a defendant's silence to the respondent's detriment might also be down to the fact that silence is fundamentally inimical to the judge's mission to prove the facts of a case. While the right to silence itself is basically unchallenged in most legal orders, as Susan Berk-Seligson and Janet Ainsworth note, its exercise is often met with some hostility in forensic practice.[19] It is a right which, when abundantly exercised by suspects and defendants, makes it ever more difficult for the prosecution and courts to prove the facts of a case. This might provoke many judges or juries to interpret the respondent's silence to the detriment of the defendant as part of fact-finding. If canon law does not want the ecclesiastical judges to draw conclusions from the fact that a defendant does not speak up to contribute to fact-finding, it would consequently be wise if the law said so explicitly, reminding the judges to abstain from interpreting silence.

Positivizing this rule might be specifically prudent for canon law, as the canonical law of evidence is posed for a global church, as I mentioned, and is therefore being applied in the culturally diverse local churches all over the globe and in cross-cultural adjudication settings. As silence has various communicative functions in diverse cultures,[20] there are evidently different local views about silence and, as a result, presumably also different views of how to assess silence in official hearings. This might, in some cases, lead to misinterpretations, when the ecclesiastical authorities interpret silence in a distinct way which might not concord with the view of it in a particular ecclesiastical culture. This problem of the different functions of silence and the wrong conclusions drawn from it was also raised by Diana Eades in her study on Australian cases involving Aboriginal people. In Aboriginal English, Eades found, long pauses or silence "is seen as a valuable and positive part of interaction,"[21] whereas it tends to be interpreted by non-Aboriginal Australians as a sign that the individual questioned is avoiding an answer, concealing guilt, or tacitly admitting it. In forensic settings, these misunderstandings can have existential results. A cross-cultural law, such as

[18] See Ainsworth, "The Meaning of Silence in the Right to Remain Silent," in Solan/Tiersma, eds, *The Oxford Handbook of Language and Law*, Oxford, Oxford University Press, 2012, 290–298.

[19] See Berk-Seligson, "The Miranda Warnings and Linguistic Coercion," in Cotterill, ed, *Language in the Legal Process*, Basingstoke, Palgrave Macmillan, 2002, 127–143; Ainsworth, "The Meaning of Silence in the Right to Remain Silent," in Solan/Tiersma, eds, *The Oxford Handbook of Language and Law*, Oxford, Oxford University Press, 2012, 288; eadem, "Silence, Speech, and the Paradox of the Right to Remain Silent in American Police Interrogation," in Freeman/Smith, eds, *Law and Language*, Oxford, Oxford University Press, 2013, 377–381.

[20] See Krieger, "A Time to Keep Silent and a Time to Speak," *Oregon Law Review* 80 (2001), 233–235, 245, 258–259.

[21] Eades, "'Evidence Given in Unequivocal Terms,'" in Cotterill, ed, *Language in the Legal Process*, Basingstoke, Palgrave Macmillan, 2002, 164.

canon law, should be aware of this. Key penal cases, for instance, such as cases dealing with allegations of sexual abuse of minors by clerics are reserved to the Congregation for the Doctrine of the Faith and are thus transferred from the local churches to Rome.[22] Consequently, these procedures usually face the challenge of cross-cultural communication. As a result, they are especially susceptible to misinterpretations. It is therefore of major importance to clarify that judges have to abstain from interpreting silence and even more so when it results from defendants making use of their lawful right to remain silent.

Privileges in Evidence Law

Adding to the right of suspects or defendants to remain silent are some further rights which entitle witnesses not to testify under certain conditions. While witnesses questioned by an ecclesiastical judge must tell the truth, as canon 1548 §1 CIC/1983 states, there are some exemptions to that rule in §2, cases in which those questioned are not obliged to respond. The Code lists clerics who are not compelled to share knowledge gained by exercising ministerial duties, as well as civil officials, physicians, midwives, advocates, notaries, and others who are bound by professional secrecy regarding those matters subject to this secrecy. A similar list can be found in most other legal orders protecting those officeholders or professional groups who are bound by professional secrecy from violating their secrecy obligation. The solicitor-client privilege and the medical professional privilege are widespread throughout most legal orders. To these privileges of professional groups canon law adds exemptions for "those who fear that from their own testimony ill repute, dangerous hardships, or other grave evils will befall them, their spouses, or persons related to them by consanguinity or affinity" (canon 1548 §2 no. 2 CIC/1983). Compared to similar privileges that other legal orders provide, such as the spousal privilege, the canonical norm is surprisingly liberal. In fact, individuals who state reasonably that answering a question will have problematic results for themselves or for those close to them may refuse to respond to an ecclesiastical tribunal. A similar privilege can hardly be imagined in secular adjudication, as it would complicate enormously the court's effort to engage in forensic fact-finding. The generous exemption in canon law seems to concede that ecclesiastical tribunals can hardly compel anybody to answer their questions anyway, as I already mentioned. The effectiveness of ecclesiastical adjudication is heavily reliant on the voluntary participation

[22] See Congregation for the Doctrine of the Faith, "Norms regarding Delicts Reserved to the Congregation for the Doctrine of the Faith," October 11, 2021, no. 6, https://www.vatican.va/roman_curia/congregations/cfaith/documents/rc_con_cfaith_doc_20211011_norme-delittiriservati-cfaith_en.html.

of parties and witnesses. A generous exemption from the duty to respond to the court seems to acknowledge that reliance of ecclesiastical tribunals on the parties' and witnesses' free cooperation.

Witness Competence Rules

Adding to privileges in evidence law which accord certain persons the right not to testify, canon law also contains witness competence rules which disqualify certain persons from serving as witnesses. Children under the age of fourteen and mentally handicapped persons are regularly excluded as witnesses (see canon 1550 §1 CIC/1983). Also incapable of serving as witnesses are litigants in the same case and their legal representatives or legal advisers as well as the judges and their assistants entrusted with the case (see canon 1550 §2 no. 1 CIC/1983). Similar regulations can be found in most secular evidence laws as well. In canon law, priests are also incapable of giving witness testimony regarding all knowledge gained from sacramental confession (see no. 2). As canon law holds the sacramental seal to be inviolable, it is consequently forbidden to reveal any knowledge gained in the course of confession (see canon 983 §1 CIC/1983). As I said in the introduction, a priest directly breaking the seal incurs a so-called *latae sententiae* excommunication, an excommunication resulting ipso facto from committing the crime of violating the seal (see canon 1386 §1 CIC/1983). This punishment would also befall priests who reveal knowledge gained in the course of a confession in forensic contexts. Testimony about such knowledge revealed regardless of the priest's incapacity to testify is invalid as evidence.

This strict protection of the sacramental seal in canonical legislation is acknowledged by many states in granting a priest-penitent privilege to avoid conflicts between canonical and secular law. Yet while canon law renders a priest incapable of disclosing any knowledge from confession, priest-penitent privileges frequently do not see priests as incapable of testifying but simply exclude priests with regard to knowledge gained from confession from the obligation to testify in order to protect the pastoral relationship between ministers and those who seek their spiritual guidance. Priests could therefore testify, but may refuse to do so in cases protected by the privilege. This concession guaranteed by many secular states has become somewhat controversial in recent times, predominantly in the course of the sexual abuse crisis. In Australia in particular, a heated debate flared up following the Final Report of the Royal Commission into Institutional Responses to Child Sexual Abuse in 2017. One recommendation of the Royal Commission was to adjust state legislation to penalize the failure to report child abuse, even when the knowledge about the abuse resulted from a sacramental confession.[23] While accepting many other recommendations given by the commission, the Australian bishops vehemently opposed this recommendation. Most Australian state and territory jurisdictions at present are therefore hesitant to implement it, while Queensland has issued a law which obliges priests to reveal knowledge of abuse cases to state authorities, irrespective of whether this information was acquired in the course of a confession. The current Queensland Criminal Code explicitly states that adults are obliged to disclose knowledge of abuse to state authorities, while "it does not matter that the information was gained by the adult during, or in connection with, a religious confession" (section 229BC). The Australian bishops responded with outrage to this 2020 legislation. As far as I know, a concrete test case where state law and canon law collide has not yet been brought in front of a court. Should this scenario become real, it will be interesting to see how legal practice unravels the dilemma of the secular obligation to testify and the canonical duty to keep silent.

Oral Hearings, Written Acts

One challenge which confronts ecclesiastical procedures specifically due to their tendency to separate the generation of evidence from the judges' action is the transformation of recorded interviews into written text. As I said, there are frequently no oral hearings before ecclesiastical tribunals. Instead the tribunals endow auditors with the duty to collect the evidence, inter alia, by conducting oral hearings of litigants and witnesses (see canon 1428 CIC/1983). These interviews are then put into writing and become part of the written acts. This step requires a delicate change in genre, as speech as a pattern of spoken utterances and silence has to be transformed into written text. Transformation of this kind inevitably changes the testimony. It is, for instance, close to impossible to capture nonaudible events, like gestures, in the transcript; if the interview is taped, they do not even appear on the tape. And it is also virtually impossible to capture all audible events in the written texts, like hesitations or grunts. Sometimes this is at least partially done in the transcripts, albeit usually not consistently, not only because it is often hard to interpret nonverbal audible elements but also because their importance is questionable. Yet sometimes, a pause or a nonverbal utterance may have a meaning and might help to interpret a statement later on. Nevertheless, as the person writing the transcripts has a hard time deciding which nonverbal articulations to note and which to leave out, written records

[23] See Royal Commission into Institutional Responses to Child Sexual Abuse, "Final Report: Recommendations," December 15, 2017, Recommendation 35, https://www.childabuseroyalcommission.gov.au/final-report.

of interrogations always lack information, the importance of which is open to debate in any case. The process of transforming recorded interviews into written text is naturally a process in which information goes missing. This always has to be kept in mind when dealing with interview transcripts.

It was particularly the merit of forensic linguist Malcolm Coulthard to have shown how misleading written records of interrogations can be whenever bits and pieces from the original oral questioning are left out or when the style is changed, for instance, when an interrogation conducted as a question and answer interview is summed up to become a confession in monologue form.[24] Coulthard showed with regard to several British criminal convictions based on the written records of orally conducted hearings that the original statements were distorted when putting them into writing, by omitting sections or skipping the question posed by the interrogation officer. Coulthard inter alia referred to the famous Derek Bentley case from the 1950s. In this case, the defendant was convicted for his accomplice's murder of a police officer inter alia based on a statement which was interpreted as a confession that Bentley had known that his accomplice had been carrying a gun. Bentley's reference to "*the* gun" in a protocolled police interview was taken by the judge as an indication that the defendant knew about the gun. For a linguist, as Coulthard showed, it is quite obvious from the material that Bentley, when making reference to "*the* gun," must have been reacting to a previous question by a police officer which had not been written down in the interrogation record. So there is no way to be sure whether Bentley's use of the definite article was not simply a response to the officer's earlier reference to "the gun."

Now ecclesiastical procedures are hardly murder cases, hence they usually deal with less existential matters. Nevertheless, similar linguistic issues may also come up in ecclesiastical cases, depending on the way a tribunal deals with oral testimony. In the past, there was usually an actuary present during the hearings, simultaneously recording the testimony by typing it or taking it down in shorthand. This is rarely done anymore, as the presence of a third person is usually regarded as too distracting for many parties and witnesses. Today, the interviews are usually recorded electronically and transferred into written text afterward. Some tribunals record the testimonies to have them written down afterward word by word. Some tribunals do the recording but refrain from writing the statement down word by word, using shortened versions instead. Other interrogators sum up the parties' or witnesses' statement themselves and dictate them in shortened form in their own words to be put in writing. Depending on the technique used, the effects that Coulthard observed can also occur in testimonies derived from ecclesiastical hearings. It has in fact happened to me a few times that I read

[24] See Coulthard, "Whose Voice Is It?," in Cotterill, ed, *Language in the Legal Process*, Basingstoke, Palgrave Macmillan, 2002, 19–34.

a party's statement or a witness testimony in the acts and felt that something was missing, a feeling that something just did not fit very well for linguistic reasons. An incorrect reference in grammatical gender, a sudden singular or plural, an answer that in wording, grammar, or style did not seem to fit the question. This does not usually present too much of a problem, but is still noteworthy. It made me believe that the transformation of oral evidence into written form is a serious source of misunderstandings and misinterpretations. The findings of forensic linguists therefore give us substantial grounds for reflecting on whether written procedures, based purely on written acts, are the optimal way to decide a case. For ecclesiastical forensic linguistics, it is of major importance to deal with these issues to improve forensic interviews. For this reason it would be highly advisable to shed some more light on these matters with regard to the hearings conducted in ecclesiastical procedures. I will not do this here as this is not an empirical study, but I regard it as a task of importance for canon law to undertake some in-depth research in this field.

8.2 Adjudication Language

For Lawrence Solan, the most fascinating aspect of adjudication language lies in the performative consequences of the judges' speaking. I already mentioned examples of performative judicial speech in chapter 2, section 2.3. While the judges use language like anybody else, the way they make use of speech acts, particularly those with a declarative function, has consequences that differ from those of ordinary speakers, as Solan contends, observing,

> "Judges speak the same language that the rest of us speak. . . . But the consequences of how the judge understands the open issues in the language that he hears and reads, and what he says about them are frequently more awesome than the consequences of how the rest of us construe sentences and express our understandings."[25]

Existential Decisiveness

Solan underlines his observation with regard to the most radical way in which the judges' utterances can impact individual fate by referring to penal judges using declarative speech to impose a death sentence. He discerns, "We all may, in our darkest moments, wish that some evil-doer were dead. But judges are the

[25] Solan, *The Language of Judges*, Chicago, IL, The University of Chicago Press, 1993, 185.

ones who can properly use the expression, 'I hereby sentence you to death,' as a performative to sentence someone to death."[26] Of course, not all of the decisions that judges take have the drastic consequences of Solan's example. European judges, for instance, no longer impose death sentences. The last execution in the Papal States was in 1868, even though it took more than hundred years until 1969 to delete capital punishment from the penal law of the Vatican City State; that the death penalty is never acceptable from a Catholic point of view, as it violates human dignity, only just recently became part of church doctrine in 2018.[27] Nevertheless, the language of judges has tremendous power, even if it no longer includes the power to decide between life and death in many legal orders. This finding does not diminish Solan's fundamental observation about the existential consequences of judicial speech. Penal judgments of a lesser gravity usually impact the convicts' life profoundly as well. Civil sentences decide over win or loss of property, legal parenthood, or working relationships—all issues which can have crucial meaning for those involved. In church, ecclesiastical tribunals decide over the expulsion of religious from their religious institutions, the dismissal of clerics from the clerical state, or the existence of ecclesiastical marriages. These are also clearly matters which can have an existential dimension for the respective parties.

Engelbert Frank convincingly illustrated this with regard to the procedures on marriage nullity. I have already mentioned the contested terms of "nullity" and "annulment" in chapter 4, section 4.2 as expressions to which many individuals react negatively. Frank most fascinatingly describes his own encounter with tribunal language as a newly appointed judge, when he himself was appalled by the use of words like "tribunal" or "process" and avoided using them when speaking to clients, as those terms, for him as a Catholic and theologian, seemed to clash with theological ideas such as God's goodness and mercy.[28] He also observed negative reactions among his friends when speaking about his work, as the terminology of ecclesiastical tribunals moved them to show fear, guilt, or other negative feelings. Frank's first impulse was, as he expounds it, to rename the ecclesiastical procedures to address these issues on a terminological level. However, he soon found that the problems went deeper than just terminology, as he experienced parties being deeply hurt by the way they were treated within the nullity procedures.[29] Explaining the juridical terms provided little solace; in

26 Ibid.

27 See Congregation for the Doctrine of the Faith, "New Revision of Number 2267 of the Catechism of the Catholic Church on the Death Penalty," May 11, 2018, https://www.vatican.va/roman_curia/congregations/cfaith/documents/rc_con_cfaith_doc_20180801_catechismo-penadimorte_en.html.

28 See Frank, "Die Sprache kirchlicher Ehegerichte und ihre Wahrnehmung durch Betroffene," in Puza/Weiß, eds, *Iustitia in caritate*, Frankfurt am Main, Peter Lang, 1997, 463–464.

29 See ibid., 464–465.

some cases, it even exacerbated the problem. Frank outlines his learning process in which he came to understand that it is not just the mention of "tribunals" and "procedures" which terrify listeners, but rather them discovering that there are actually tribunals in church which run procedures to examine individual marriages, as they felt intimately affected by these procedures. One can take this observation as a starting point for a debate about whether there should be ecclesiastical procedures on marriage nullity. This valid question is in any case not my primary concern in this study. Instead, I want to take Frank's observation as evidence that the language of ecclesiastical tribunals still has the power to touch individuals existentially, even though in modernity it has lost its power to decide about life or death or to restrict personal and social freedom to any greater degree.

Oral Debate, Written Verdict

Ecclesiastical cases are sometimes decided by single judges. Most, in any case, are decided by a collegiate tribunal of three and sometimes five judges. A three-member tribunal is standard for the marriage nullity cases which make up for the vast majority of ecclesiastical procedures (see canon 1425 §1 no. 1 CIC/1983), and it is likewise due in penal cases which can result in the penalty of dismissal from the clerical state (see no. 2), such as the cases dealing with sexual abuse of minors. The three-member tribunal, thus, is the frequent form in which ecclesiastical adjudication and the decisive language of judges take shape. The judicial voice of the law, in any case, hardly transmits to the outside. Ecclesiastical verdicts are put in writing and sent to the parties concerned. Judicial speech in church is written text mostly. As mentioned, the tribunals do not usually collect the evidence themselves, but employ auditors to undertake that task (see canon 1428 CIC/1983). Hence, ecclesiastical judges seldom have personal contact with parties and witnesses. The evidence is documented in the acts. The judges' decisions are based on these written acts. Every member of a tribunal forms his or her opinion based on the acts and lays it down in written form. Decision-making is a collegial act of orally discussing the written opinions with the other members of the tribunal. For forensic linguistics, it would be particularly interesting to shed more light on the judges' deliberations and the language they use in them. Hardly any research has been done on that matter, as these steps are kept strictly confidential in all legal systems. The one core moment of adjudication in which the actual decision takes on its form is one of the greatest mysteries for the public and for academia, too, as we know virtually nothing about it. This is a pity, as it would be of major interest to find out how collegiate tribunals and likewise juries ensure they have heard or read all arguments, how they preserve a style of debate that allows every judge's voice to be heard adequately, and how they deal with silent and dominant voices, and timid and angry arguments.

In ecclesiastical adjudication, the decision follows the majority of votes. The majority decision of the judges is their collegial verdict (see canon 1426 §1 CIC/1983). It is regarded as the decision of the whole tribunal, thus silencing the voices of outnumbered judges vis-à-vis the parties and the public. The verdict is then put into writing by one of the judges serving as a relator (see canon 1429 CIC/1983). The relator's duty is to compose a unanimous verdict based on the judges' different opinions, by taking up the arguments supporting the ruling put forward by the judges in the deliberation. So relators when composing the sentence for a collegiate tribunal cannot simply sum up the previous debate between the judges when reaching a verdict, presenting the pros and cons for and against the ruling. They rather have to shape a conclusive argument in which the tribunal speaks with one voice. The relators' task is therefore a selective endeavor in which they collect relevant bits and pieces from the opinions of the other judges to support a conclusive argumentation in favor of the verdict. From a linguistic point of view, it would be most enlightening to shed further light on the twofold structure of taking and making a judicial decision. While it seems clear that both steps are different and follow different rationales, it still remains unclear how exactly they relate to each other.

Unassailable Speech

The verdict presents the tribunal's decision as the judges' unanimous opinion. It does so with the purpose of convincing the litigants that the ruling is indeed the only way to decide their case based on the evidence. Hence, presenting a verdict as the unified voice of a tribunal is a strategy of legitimizing the ruling. The relator therefore has to build an argument which is suitable for justifying the tribunal's decision as an inevitable conclusion based on the evidence. Through its verdict, the tribunal has to speak decisively, presenting its decision in a way that seems clear and definite to the litigants. It is the power of the courts to make use of judicial speech acts with a performative nature which places a huge responsibility on them to use their language convincingly and decisively. This has consequences for how courts and tribunals argue when giving reasons for their decisions, as Lawrence Solan discerns, writing,

> Armed with this enormous power, and faced with the responsibility of exercising it on a daily basis, judges will, at times, grab at any argument that the system accepts as legitimate in order to convince the parties and the community

> at large that the court did what it was supposed to do. After close analysis, the court was left with only a single option, the judge tells us.[30]

Hence, courts and tribunals cannot always fully disclose what has determined their decision. However, it is the duty of judges to explain their decisions to the parties concerned as well as to the public. Consequently, the language of judges is also a language of legitimization, serving to prove judicial decisions as necessary consequences of laws and facts, even though they are decisions mostly in the true sense of the word, choices between two or several plausible options. Solan calls this impossibility of being too open about the reasons that move the judges and the rationale of their decisions the "pressure on them to speak decisively."[31] Courts need to speak authoritatively and need to do so even more when the decision is not indisputable. Solan again explains this by taking up the example of a death sentence once more, maintaining,

> "'It would be very difficult for an appellate judge to say, 'I hereby affirm your death sentence, although this was a very close question, and I understand that I could just as easily have interpreted the law as requiring me to reverse your death sentence and save your life,' even if such a statement is an entirely accurate reflection of what is on the judge's mind."[32]

In consequence, judges tend to distinguish between the act of taking a decision and the act of explaining it as two different steps to their duty, as Solan explicates, "The pressure to speak with a definite voice works as a wedge, driving apart decision making on the one hand and presentation on the other."[33]

The Language of Verdicts

This need to sound authoritative and definitive results inter alia in some very distinct linguistic features which have found their way into the language of judges. The need to sound decisive and objective, for instance, has led in many judicial systems to the judges avoiding the use of the first-person perspective in their verdicts, a phenomenon to which legal scholar Lorenz Kähler has devoted some attention.[34] German judges, particularly Supreme Court judges, basically never

30 Solan, *The Language of Judges*, Chicago, IL, The University of Chicago Press, 1993, 185.
31 Ibid., 2.
32 Ibid.
33 Ibid.
34 See Kähler, "First-Person Perspectives in Legal Decisions," in Freeman/Smith, eds, *Law and Language*, Oxford, Oxford University Press, 2013, 533–556.

present themselves as an "I" or a "we." Instead they rather appear in a formal and impersonal way as "the Court." The same applies to the European Court of Justice. However, this matter is handled differently in the diverse legal cultures. While some judicial cultures never reveal the individual person, the "I" behind a decision, others are less reluctant to show that those who run adjudication are actually human beings. UK and US judges are more used to speaking in the first person, at least in individual opinions. This is much evident with the Law Lords of the United Kingdom Supreme Court, who do not usually speak in an abstract way but clearly for themselves. I cannot make a general statement for canon law worldwide, but those German decisions that I have come across were all rather impersonal, underlining the decision as an act of "the Tribunal."

Ecclesiastical verdicts, in any case, speak not merely with the authority of "the tribunal" but also draw on God's authority by speaking "in the name of the Father and of the Son and of the Holy Spirit." This is an interesting variant of the formulas common in many civil law judicatures, where verdicts often have preambles alluding to the authority from which the court draws its judicial power, by speaking "in the name of the people," "in the name of the republic," or "in the name of the Queen/King." By invocating God and referencing God as the source of ecclesiastical authority at the same time, the preamble of ecclesiastical verdicts, thus, presents an interesting genre mix in itself: a short text which is a prayer and a formula of legitimation, asking God for help and asserting the tribunal's divine authorization.

9
Conclusion

Looking back on the considerations I have assembled in this book, I find myself having collected a rather heterogeneous assemblage of theoretical approaches and practical observations, which in any case all seemed to me to be beneficial and well suited to gaining a clearer grasp of the language of canon law and to improving our understanding of how the Roman Catholic Church speaks as a legal institution. I have examined the function of language in legal communications and its sacramental—or, as one could also say, magical—functioning when generating legal effects. I have studied the character of legal language, the grammar and terminology of the law, and how it makes use of linguistic tricks and techniques to create its typical and often decisive sound. I have spoken about the comprehension difficulties that arise with ambiguities in the law, with transfer problems between legal and common language and with canon law's confusing mix of diverse genres in legal norms. I have marked these comprehension difficulties as troublesome, as they provoke the exclusion of many from the legal debates and foster an elitism which benefits those who speak Legalese; in the church, this dilemma also has a clerical coating. The antidemocratic and antimodern drift of the law is opposed by "plainers," legal experts campaigning to make the law easier to comprehend by reforming its language. I have thought about the potential consequences a plain language agenda in the church might have. It must include, as I find, a serious re-evaluation of whether dead Latin is the appropriate language for a global and cross-cultural legal order such as canon law. In its stead, I suggest that the global church develops a multi-language usage for its cross-cultural legal communications. There are several models for realizing a multi-language law. The European Union, I believe, has set the standard for how to provide a plural Union with a multi-language practice, which, while being truly challenging, is also indispensable for integrating multilingual communities into one Union. The church may learn much from this and other examples about how to approach this endeavor. I have also taken a closer look at interpreting the law and the theories used to explain how interpretation functions. The church employs a radical mix of what current interpretation theories have to offer: textualism supplemented by contextualism and intentionalism. One can find this odd or utterly pragmatic. It reveals in any case that ecclesiastical interpretation theory is well aware that interpreting the law as the core process of finding legal meaning is also one of the most delicate and difficult

The Language of Canon Law. Judith Hahn, Oxford University Press. © Oxford University Press 2023.
DOI: 10.1093/oso/9780197674246.003.0009

moments of dealing with the law. It is a matter of debate, though, whether canon law does itself any favors by attributing enormous weight to the ecclesiastical legislator in matters of interpreting the law. Canon law is evidently a highly centralistic law. Legislation is a centralist top-down endeavor. In addition, not only the law itself but also much of its meaning is currently produced in Rome. This is massively obstructing the local acceptance of global Catholic canon law. The Apostolic See's tight grip on the law and on its meaning as a strategy for preserving the uniformity of the law tends to provoke disgregation. Here, canon law can learn much from secular systems which leave interpretation issues widely to adjudication and administration. A specific field of law and language is forensic language, to which I have dedicated a whole chapter. The language of the judges and of the courts, in its difficult shifting between orality and textuality, is also a matter of specific interest for canon law and language, particularly as ecclesiastical adjudication relies heavily on the written acts to decide the cases. I have also picked up the topic of silence within forensic settings to shed some light on the fact that legal communications are about speaking and writing but also about being silent from time to time.

Summing up is always helpful when taking account of the work done, but it also begs the question of what to do with the findings and whether there is something that we can learn from them. I would like to suggest merely two points. First, instead of comprehensively dealing with the language of canon law and closing that case, my study instead reveals that it is expedient for canonists to invest more time and effort in the study of canon law and language. Second, what I have come to find when writing this book is that reforming the law of the church requires more than just a few cosmetic changes to the language of canon law. Hence, canon law and language requires more scrutiny, both academically and practically. That further research on the language of canon law is necessary has become manifest throughout my book. I have noted quite often that "one should" have a closer look at this or that, or that it would be worthwhile to devote some more study to a specific issue or topic. As I said in the introduction, I understand my own contribution merely as summing up what we may learn from the law and language debate as canonists. This does not render further investigations into the language of canon law superfluous in any way. Identifying open questions and attempting to provide an answer is a worthy academic endeavor in its own right. Adding to this, canonists who are also theologians, as I am, also study the language of canon law in the light of ecclesiological concerns. The church understands itself by its very nature as devoted to the mission of promoting the Word of God, which has embodied itself in human culture. It is therefore permanently confronted with the challenge of examining whether its message is communicated understandably and of correcting the language of its message whenever it becomes difficult to comprehend. Theologians critically reflect these processes of communicative ecclesiology. They analyze how the church speaks, not merely when it articulates itself as a community of faith, teaching and preaching and spreading the Gospel message in pastoral, liturgical, or charitable contexts, but also when it communicates with the help of the law. In recent debates in the German church, as I mentioned in the introduction, Erik Flügge has rightly criticized the church for its use of language, alluding to its pastoral sound that sometimes comes across as overly concerned, and at other times pompous and stilted. He has convincingly stressed that most Christians expect the church—the community that came into being through Christ the Word—to do better with words than it actually does. And he has initiated a debate on how to improve the language of the church. His considerations, even though they mostly focus on pastoral situations, give canonists food for thought to ponder how canon law should sound to convey the legal messages of the church in an appropriate way. For the German marriage nullity procedures, Engelbert Frank emphasized how appalled many Catholics are when confronted with tribunal speech. Admittedly, these irritations do not exclusively result from the language used in these procedures, but this often adds to many Catholics' consternation. So there are some very good reasons for thinking about the language with which canon law addresses its legal subjects. If the law is supposed to last as an effective instrument of structural value, social organization, and conflict resolution in the church, it has to start paying attention to how convincing it sounds. Ecclesiastical legislation, adjudication, and administration, which—apart from ecclesiological considerations—also operate with a low level of coercion and a high dependency on the church members' voluntary cooperation, must choose their words wisely.

Connected with this is my second suggestion, namely, that we need to make radical changes to the language of canon law. Its language is not only appalling to parties in marriage procedures but it is thoroughly out of date, as I have found in my study. It made me laugh when reading Robert Benson's passionate article "The End of Legalese: The Game is Over,"[1] in which Benson—while writing about Legalese—obviously became increasingly agitated and annoyed about it. I talked about his findings at great length in chapter 5 on the problem of legal incomprehension. It made me smile to read Benson's furious bashing of the legal profession, which he pictured as this fancy-dressed mob of "modern-day medievalists" who "seriously insist upon wearing medieval coats of armor to work,"[2] who use out-of-date language to impress the public and pompous style and prose to intimidate others. But it made me smile not only because his picture is hilarious but also because I could not stop wondering how Benson would have reacted to the language of canon law. Examining the law of the church, I can relate well

[1] Benson, "The End of Legalese," *N.Y.U. Review of Law & Social Change* 13 (1984), 519–573.
[2] Ibid., 522.

to one observation which Clifford Geertz once made when pondering some strange and exotic culture where he pictured himself "thinking of the curious mixture of borrowed fragments of modernity and exhausted relics of tradition that characterized the place, the future seemed about as remote as the past."[3] This state, being lost somewhere between the future and the past, is also what it feels like scrutinizing the church and its law. Both currently exist in an "in-between-state," lost somewhere in between the past and modernity. The language of canon law reflects this. It too is somewhere "in between." Some might find it sacred and awe-inspiring when old Latin sounds call to mind the church's mystery and glory. Yet others find it strange and outdated, even absolutistically pompous and ridiculously overstated at times. The strangest thing, as I find, is that one gets used to it. In this respect, Steven Winter once admonished his fellow lawyers that talking about the language of the law is but the first step in talking about lawyers and language. The "elephant in the room," as he called it, is the question of how law is used as a language by those who "speak it." He stated, "Instead of talking about how language functions in law, we can talk instead about how law functions as language. . . . The question is not what *language* does, but what *we* do with language."[4] One can hardly be a legal professional without becoming entrapped in the linguistic strings of legal style, as the late Peter Tiersma showed with some irony in the concluding section of his book *Legal Language*, when he remarked, "The language of the legal profession has been criticized as arcane and archaic, complex and convoluted, pompous and ponderous."[5] Clothing his own critique in this grand threefold alliteration, Tiersma alludes to serious issues of legal language, and at the very same time also to himself, the legal professional, who strikes precisely the same chord. In a similar vein, I often pass from everyday language into canon law lingo without even really noticing. But sometimes, watching myself from a distance, Robert Benson's modern-day medievalists start parading up and down before my inner eye. Then, when I find myself parading with them in medieval attire through the modern language world, I feel amused but also uncomfortable at the same time. I hope my book is of some help to those who also sense this tension and wish to address it.

[3] Geertz, "From the Native's Point of View," *Bulletin of the American Academy of Arts and Sciences* 28 (1974), 32.

[4] Winter, "Frame Semantics and the 'Internal Point of View,'" in Freeman/Smith, eds, *Law and Language*, Oxford, Oxford University Press, 2013, 126.

[5] Tiersma, *Legal Language*, Chicago, IL, The University of Chicago Press, 1999, 241.

Bibliography

Documents

Secular Law and Official Documents

The Digest of Justinian, translated by Charles Henry Monro, Cambridge, Cambridge University Press, 1904.

Parliament of England, "Declaration what Offences shall be adjudged Treason," 1351, 25 Edw 3 St 5 c 2, present text, accessed December 16, 2018, https://www.legislation.gov.uk/aep/Edw3Stat5/25/2/section/II; original French text, accessed December 16, 2018, https://www.languageandlaw.org/TEXTS/STATS/TREASON.HTM.

British North America Act 1867, royal assent March 29, 1867, commencement July 1, 1867, 30 & 31 Vict c. 3.

Deutscher Bundestag, *Basic Law for the Federal Republic of Germany*, May 23, 1949, last amended July 13, 2017, Berlin, Deutscher Bundestag, 2018.

Deutscher Bundestag, *Criminal Code*, in the version promulgated on November 13, 1998, *Federal Law Gazette* (*Bundesgesetzblatt*) I, 3322, last amended by Article 1 of the Law of September 24, 2013, *Federal Law Gazette* I, 3671 and with the text of Article 6 (18) of the Law of October 10, 2013, *Federal Law Gazette* I, 3799.

Council of the European Union, "Council Directive 2000/78/EC Establishing a General Framework for Equal Treatment in Employment and Occupation," November 27, 2000, *Official Journal of the European Union* L 303, vol. 43, December 2, 2000, 16–22.

Parliament of the United Kingdom, "Equality Act 2010," April 8, 2010, *2010 Chapter 15*, https://www.legislation.gov.uk/ukpga/2010/15.

European Court of Justice, "Rules of Procedure of the Court of Justice," September 25, 2012, *Official Journal of the European Union* L 265, vol. 55, September 29, 2012, as amended on June 18, 2013, *Official Journal of the European Union* L 173, vol. 56, July 26, 2013, 65, and on July 19, 2016, *Official Journal of the European Union* L 217, vol. 59, August 12, 2016, 69.

Royal Commission into Institutional Responses to Child Sexual Abuse, "Final Report: Recommendations," December 15, 2017, https://www.childabuseroyalcommission.gov.au/final-report.

Queensland, "Criminal Code Act 1899," current as at July 5, 2021, https://www.legislation.qld.gov.au/view/pdf/inforce/current/act-1899-009.

Ecclesiastical Law and Official Documents

Council of Trent, "Decree *Ad consummationem* on the Sacraments," seventh session, March 3, 1547, in Mansi, Giovanni Domenico et al., eds, *Sacrorum Conciliorum Nova et Amplissima Collectio*, vol. 33: Ab anno 1545, ad annum 1565, Paris, Hubert Welter, 1902, 48–60.

John XXIII, "Apostolic Constitution *Veterum sapientia* on the Promotion of the Study of Latin," February 22, 1962, *Acta Apostolicae Sedis* 54 (1962), 129–135.

Second Vatican Council, "Constitution on the Sacred Liturgy *Sacrosanctum concilium*," December 4, 1963, *Acta Apostolicae Sedis* 56 (1964), 97–138.

Second Vatican Council, "Dogmatic Constitution *Lumen gentium* on the Church," November 21, 1964, *Acta Apostolicae Sedis* 57 (1965), 5–75.

Pontifical Council for Social Communications, "Pastoral Instruction *Communio et progressio* on the Means of Social Communication," May 23, 1971, *Acta Apostolicae Sedis* 63 (1971), 593–656.

Secretariat of State, "Norms *Necessitas ipsa* on the Translation of the Code of Canon Law," January 28, 1983, *Communicationes* 15 (1983), 41.

Pontifical Commission for Authentic Interpretation of the Code of Canon Law, "Responsa ad proposita dubia," July 11, 1984, *Acta Apostolicae Sedis* 76 (1984), 746–747.

Canon Law Society of America, "Resolution 4," *Canon Law Society of America Proceedings* 45 (1984), 324–326.

Canon Law Society of America, Annulment Language Committee, *Annual Report*, October 1985 (in Archives of the University of Notre Dame, CLSA 12/28 Folder: Annulment Language Committee 1984–1986).

Canon Law Society of America, Annulment Language Committee, *Annual Report*, October 1986 (in Archives of the University of Notre Dame, CLSA 12/28 Folder: Annulment Language Committee 1984–1986).

John Paul II, "Apostolic Constitution *Pastor bonus* on the Roman Curia," June 28, 1988, *Acta Apostolicae Sedis* 80 (1988), 841–912.

Congregation for the Doctrine of the Faith, "Note on the Validity and Liceity of Administering the Sacrament of Penance via Phone," November 25, 1989, *Archiv für katholisches Kirchenrecht* 158 (1989), 484.

Pontifical Council for Legislative Texts, "Responsum ad propositum dubium," June 28, 1990, *Acta Apostolicae Sedis* 82 (1990), 845.

Congregation for Catholic Education, "Decree *Novo codice* Revising the Order of Studies in the Faculties and Departments of Canon Law," September 2, 2002, *Acta Apostolicae Sedis* 95 (2003), 281–285.

Congregation for the Doctrine of the Faith, "Responses to Questions Proposed on the Validity of Baptism Conferred with the Formulas 'I baptize you in the name of the Creator, and of the Redeemer, and of the Sanctifier' and 'I baptize you in the name of the Creator, and of the Liberator, and of the Sustainer,'" February 1, 2008, https://www.vatican.va/roman_curia/congregations/cfaith/documents/rc_con_cfaith_doc_20080201_validity-baptism_en.html.

Francis, "Apostolic Letter issued Motu proprio *La Promozione* for the Prevention and Countering of Money Laundering, the Financing of Terrorism and the Proliferation of Weapons of Mass Destruction," August 8, 2013, *Acta Apostolicae Sedis* 105 (2013), 811–813.

German Bishops' Conference, "Press Release: Die pastoralen Herausforderungen der Familie," edited by the German Bishops' Conference's Secretariat, Bonn, February 3, 2014, https://www.dbk.de/fileadmin/redaktion/diverse_downloads/presse_2014/2014-012a-Fragebogen-Die-pastoralen-Herausforderungen-der-Familie.pdf.

Francis, "Post-Synodal Apostolic Exhortation *Amoris laetitia* on Love in the Family," March 19, 2016, *Acta Apostolicae Sedis* 108 (2016), 311–446.

Congregation for Catholic Education, "Norms of Application for the Correct Implementation of the Apostolic Constitution *Veritatis gaudium*," December 27, 2017,

https://www.vatican.va/content/francesco/en/apost_constitutions/documents/papa-francesco_costituzione-ap_20171208_veritatis-gaudium.html.
German Bishops, "Aid to Orientation, Walking with Christ—Tracing Unity: Interdenominational Marriages and Sharing in the Eucharist," February 20, 2018, https://www.dbk.de/fileadmin/redaktion/diverse_downloads/dossiers_2018/Walking-with-Christ_Tracing_Unity_Arbeits%C3%BCbersetzung-der-Orientierungshilfe_ENG.pdf.
Congregation for the Doctrine of the Faith, "New Revision of Number 2267 of the Catechism of the Catholic Church on the Death Penalty," papal approval May 11, 2018, https://www.vatican.va/roman_curia/congregations/cfaith/documents/rc_con_cfaith_doc_20180801_catechismo-penadimorte_en.html.
Congregation for the Doctrine of the Faith, "Norms regarding Delicts Reserved to the Congregation for the Doctrine of the Faith," October 11, 2021, https://www.vatican.va/roman_curia/congregations/cfaith/documents/rc_con_cfaith_doc_20211011_norme-delittiriservati-cfaith_en.html.

Judicature

The United States Supreme Court, "Caminetti v. United States," argued November 13–14, 1916, decided January 15, 1917, *United States Reports* 242 (1917), 470–503.
King's Bench Division and Court of Criminal Appeal, "The King v. Casement," 1 K.B. 98, 1917, accessed December 16, 2018, http://uniset.ca/other/cs5/19171KB98.html.
United States District Court for the Northern District of Iowa, "Interstate Commerce Commission v. Allen E. Kroblin, Inc.," decided June 30, 1953, *Federal Supplement* 113 (1953), 599–631.
The United States Supreme Court, "Miranda v. Arizona," argued February 28–March 1, 1966, decided June 13, 1966, *United States Reports* 384 (1966), 436–545.
The United States Supreme Court, "Bronston v. United States," argued November 15, 1972, decided January 10, 1973, *United States Reports* 409 (1973), 352–362.
The United States Supreme Court, "Schneckloth v. Bustamonte," argued October 10, 1972, decided May 29, 1973, *United States Reports* 412 (1973), 218–291.
Bundesgerichtshof (Federal Court of Justice), January 29, 1975, file number VIII ZR 101/73, accessed September 4, 2022, research.wolterskluwer-online.de/document/c260be7a-eaf0-4a5a-b65f-5710f8ed7795.
Bundesverfassungsgericht (Federal Constitutional Court), January 10, 1995, file number 1 BvR 718/89, 1 BvR 719/89, 1 BvR 722/89, 1 BvR 723/89 ("Sitzblockaden II"), *Entscheidungen des Bundesverfassungsgerichts* 92, 1.

Dictionaries and Glossaries

Chiappetta, Luigi, *Dizionario del Nuovo Codice di Diritto Canonico: Prontuario teorico-pratico*, Naples, Dehoniane, 1986.
Corral Salvador, Carlos/De Paolis, Velasio/Ghirlanda, Gianfranco, *Nuovo Dizionario di Diritto Canonico*, Milan, San Paolo, 1993.
Corral Salvador, Carlos/Urteaga Embil, José M., *Diccionario de Derecho Cánonico*, 2nd edn, Madrid, Tecnos Universidad Pontificia Comillas, 2000.

Köstler, Rudolf, *Wörterbuch zum Codex Iuris Canonici*, Munich, Josef Kösel/Friedrich Pustet, 1927.

Ochoa, Javier, ed, *Index Verborum ac Locutionum Codicis Iuris Canonici*, Rome, Libreria Editrice Vaticana, 1983.

Pulickal, Jose, *A Dictionary of Canon Law*, Manila, Logos, 2005.

Werckmeister, Jean, *Petit Dictionnaire de Droit Canonique*, Paris, Cerf, 1993.

Zapp, Hartmut, *Codex Iuris Canonici: Lemmata, Stichwortverzeichnis*, Freiburg im Breisgau, Rombach, 1986.

Literature

Abrams, Kathryn/Keren, Hila, "Who's Afraid of Law and the Emotions?," *Minnesota Law Review* 94 (2010), 1997–2074.

Adler, Mark, "The Plain Language Movement," in Solan, Lawrence M./Tiersma, Peter M., eds, *The Oxford Handbook of Language and Law*, Oxford, Oxford University Press, 2012, 67–83.

Adler, Mark/Perry, Daphne, *Clarity for Lawyers: Effective Legal Language*, 3rd edn, London, The Law Society, 2017.

Ainsworth, Janet, "The Meaning of Silence in the Right to Remain Silent," in Solan, Lawrence M./Tiersma, Peter M., eds, *The Oxford Handbook of Language and Law*, Oxford, Oxford University Press, 2012, 287–298.

Ainsworth, Janet, "Silence, Speech, and the Paradox of the Right to Remain Silent in American Police Interrogation," in Freeman, Michael/Smith, Fiona, eds, *Law and Language* (Current Legal Issues 15), Oxford, Oxford University Press, 2013, 371–385.

Alexander, Larry/Prakash, Saikrishna, "'Is that English You're Speaking?' Why Intention Free Interpretation Is an Impossibility," *San Diego Law Review* 41 (2004), 967–995.

Allen, Jessie, "A Theory of Adjudication: Law as Magic," *Suffolk University Law Review* 41 (2008), 773–831.

Allott, Nicholas/Shaer, Benjamin, "The Illocutionary Force of Laws," *Inquiry* 61 (2018), 351–369.

Alvarez-Nakagawa, Alexis, "Law *as* Magic: Some Thoughts on Ghosts, Non-Humans, and Shamans," *German Law Journal* 18 (2017), 1247–1275.

Amann, Thomas A., "Gebot und Verbot in der Rechtssprache des CIC," in Geringer, Karl-Theodor/Schmitz, Heribert, eds, *Communio in Ecclesiae Mysterio. Festschrift für Winfried Aymans zum 65. Geburtstag*, St. Ottilien, EOS, 2001, 3–28.

Amatrudo, Anthony, "The Consumption of Legal Language: Consuming the Law," in Freeman, Michael/Smith, Fiona, eds, *Law and Language* (Current Legal Issues 15), Oxford, Oxford University Press, 2013, 386–399.

Amselek, Paul, "Philosophy of Law and the Theory of Speech Acts," *Ratio Juris* 1 (1988), 187–223.

Appleyard, Joseph A., "How Does a Sacrament 'Cause by Signifying'?," *Science et Esprit* 23 (1971), 167–200.

Atkins, William R., "Evidence—Moral Certainty—Reasonable Doubt," *Howard Law Journal* 1 (1955), 119–123.

Austin, John L., *How to Do Things with Words*, The William James Lectures delivered at Harvard University in 1955, Oxford, Oxford University Press, 1962.

Austin, John L., "Performative Utterances," in Austin, John L., *Philosophical Papers*, edited by James O. Urmson and Geoffrey J. Warnock, 3rd edn, Oxford, Clarendon Press, 1979, 233–252.

Aymans, Winfried, "Aus dem Vorwort zur ersten Auflage," in *Codex des Kanonischen Rechts*, Lateinisch-deutsche Ausgabe mit Sachverzeichnis, 7th edn, Kevelaer, Butzon & Bercker, 2012, II–III.

Aymans, Winfried, "Aus dem Vorwort zur zweiten Auflage," in *Codex des Kanonischen Rechts*, Lateinisch-deutsche Ausgabe mit Sachverzeichnis, 7th edn, Kevelaer, Butzon & Bercker, 2012, III–IV.

Aymans, Winfried, "Vorwort zur dritten Auflage," in *Codex des Kanonischen Rechts*, Lateinisch-deutsche Ausgabe mit Sachverzeichnis, 7th edn, Kevelaer, Butzon & Bercker, 2012, V–VI.

Bajčić, Martina/Martinović, Adrijana, "A Mutual Learning Exercise in Terminology and Multilingual Law," in Marino, Silvia/Biel, Łucja/Bajčić, Martina/Sosoni, Vilelmini, eds, *Language and Law: The Role of Language and Translation in EU Competition Law*, Cham, Springer Nature Switzerland, 2018, 207–223.

Bandes, Susan A./Blumenthal, Jeremy A., "Emotion and the Law," *Annual Review of Law and Social Science* 8 (2012), 161–181.

Barion, Hans, "Über doppelsprachige Konkordate: Eine konkordatsrechtliche Studie," *Deutsche Rechtswissenschaft* 5 (1940), 226–249.

Barthes, Roland, "The Death of the Author," in Barthes, Roland, *Image—Music—Text*, essays selected and translated by Stephen Heath, New York, Hill and Wang, 1977, 142–148.

Baumann, Max, "Weg vom Text—oder: Plädoyer für einen breiteren Weg vom Text zum Verstehen," in Lerch, Kent D., ed, *Recht vermitteln: Strukturen, Formen und Medien der Kommunikation im Recht* (Die Sprache des Rechts 3), Berlin/New York, Walter de Gruyter, 2005, 1–22.

Beal, John P., "Something There Is That Doesn't Love a Law: Canon Law and Its Discontents," in Lacey, Michael J./Oakley, Francis, eds, *The Crisis of Authority in Catholic Modernity*, Oxford University Press, Oxford, 2011, 135–154.

Bennett, Robert W., "Constitutional Interpretation," in Solan, Lawrence M./Tiersma, Peter M., eds, *The Oxford Handbook of Language and Law*, Oxford, Oxford University Press, 2012, 114–127.

Benson, Robert W., "The End of Legalese: The Game Is Over," *N.Y.U. Review of Law & Social Change* 13 (1984), 519–573.

Berk-Seligson, Susan, "The Miranda Warnings and Linguistic Coercion: The Role of Footing in the Interrogation of a Limited-English-speaking Murder Suspect," in Cotterill, Janet, ed, *Language in the Legal Process*, Basingstoke, Palgrave Macmillan, 2002, 127–143.

Berman, Harold J., *Law and Language: Effective Symbols of Community*, edited by John Witte, Jr., Cambridge, Cambridge University Press, 2013.

Bhatia, Vijay K., "Language of the Law," *Language Teaching* 20 (1987), 227–234.

Bix, Brian H., *Law, Language and Legal Determinacy*, Oxford, Clarendon Press, 1993.

Bix, Brian H., "Linguistic Meaning and Legal Truth," in Freeman, Michael/Smith, Fiona, eds, *Law and Language* (Current Legal Issues 15), Oxford, Oxford University Press, 2013, 34–44.

Black, Bernhard, "A Model Plain Language Law," *Stanford Law Review* 33 (1981), 255–300.

Bratschi, Rebekka/Nussbaumer, Markus, "Mehrsprachige Rechtsetzung," in Felder, Ekkehard/Vogel, Friedemann, eds, *Handbuch Sprache im Recht* (Handbücher Sprachwissen 12), Berlin/Boston, MA, Walter de Gruyter, 2017, 367–390.

Brion, Denis J., "The Ritual of the Judicial Opinion," in Lindgren, J. Ralph/Knaak, Jay, eds, *Ritual and Semiotics*, with an introduction by Roberta Kevelson (Critic of Institutions 14), New York/Washington, DC/Baltimore/Bern/Frankfurt am Main/Berlin/Vienna/Paris, Peter Lang, 1997, 1–22.

Brown, Philip J., *Canon 17 CIC 1983 and the Hermeneutical Principles of Bernard Lonergan* (Tesi Gregoriana, Serie Diritto Canonico 32), Rome, Editrice Pontifica Università Gregoriana, 1999.

Buckley, Timothy J., *What Binds Marriage: Roman Catholic Theology in Practice*, revised and expanded edition, London, Geoffrey Chapman, 2002.

Busse, Dietrich, "Was ist die Bedeutung eines Gesetzestextes? Sprachwissenschaftliche Argumente im Methodenstreit der juristischen Auslegungslehre—linguistisch gesehen," in Müller, Friedrich, ed, *Untersuchungen zur Rechtslinguistik: Interdisziplinäre Studien zu praktischer Semantik und Strukturierender Rechtslehre in Grundfragen der juristischen Methodik* (Schriften zur Rechtstheorie 133), Berlin, Duncker & Humblot, 1989, 93–148.

Busse, Dietrich, "Juristische Fachsprache und öffentlicher Sprachgebrauch: Richterliche Bedeutungsdefinitionen und ihr Einfluß auf die Semantik politischer Begriffe," in Liedtke, Frank/Wengeler, Martin/Böke, Karin, eds, *Begriffe besetzen: Strategien des Sprachgebrauchs in der Politik*, Opladen, Westdeutscher Verlag, 1991, 160–185.

Busse, Dietrich, "Rechtssprache als Problem der Bedeutungsbeschreibung: Semantische Aspekte einer institutionellen Fachsprache," *Sprache und Literatur in Wissenschaft und Unterricht* 29 (1998), 24–47.

Busse, Dietrich, "Ist die Anwendung von Rechtstexten ein Fall von Kommunikation? Rechtslinguistische Überlegungen zur Institutionalität der Arbeit mit Texten im Recht," in Lerch, Kent D., ed, *Recht vermitteln: Strukturen, Formen und Medien der Kommunikation im Recht* (Die Sprache des Rechts 3), Berlin/New York, Walter de Gruyter, 2005, 23–54.

Caron, Arthur, "The Concept of Moral Certitude in Canonical Decisions," *The Jurist* 19 (1959), 12–28.

Carroll, Lewis, *Alice's Adventures in Wonderland*, with forty-two illustrations by John Tenniel, New York, The Macmillan Company, 1920.

Castillo Lara, Rosalio J., "Die authentische Auslegung des Kanonischen Rechtes im Rahmen der Tätigkeit der Päpstlichen Kommission für die authentische Interpretation des Ius Canonicum," *Österreichisches Archiv für Kirchenrecht* 37 (1987/88), 209–228.

Cavedon, Matthew P., "Physical Presence for Court and the Catholic Church," October 2, 2020, https://canopyforum.org/2020/10/02/attention-physical-presence-for-court-and-the-catholic-church.

Charnock, Ross, "Overruling as a Speech Act: Performativity and Normative Discourse," *Journal of Pragmatics* 41 (2009), 401–426.

Charnock, Ross, "Hart as Contextualist? Theories of Interpretation in Language and the Law," in Freeman, Michael/Smith, Fiona, eds, *Law and Language* (Current Legal Issues 15), Oxford, Oxford University Press, 2013, 128–150.

Charrow, Robert P./Charrow, Veda R., "Making Legal Language Understandable: A Psycholinguistic Study of Jury Instructions," *Columbia Law Review* 79 (1979), 1306–1374.

Charrow, Veda R./Crandall, Jo Ann/Charrow, Robert P., "Characteristics and Functions of Legal Language," in Kittredge, Richard/Lehrberger, John, eds, *Sublanguage: Studies of Language in Restricted Semantic Domains*, Berlin/New York, Walter de Gruyter, 1982, 175–190.

Chauvet, Louis-Marie, *Symbol and Sacrament: A Sacramental Reinterpretation of Christian Existence*, translated by Patrick Madigan and Madeleine Beaumont, Collegeville, MN, The Liturgical Press, 1995.

Christensen, Ralph, "Die Wortlautgrenze," in Felder, Ekkehard/Vogel, Friedemann, eds, *Handbuch Sprache im Recht* (Handbücher Sprachwissen 12), Berlin/Boston, MA, Walter de Gruyter, 2017, 187–205.

Clark, Gordon H., *Language and Theology* (Trinity Paper 1), Phillipsburg, NJ, Presbyterian and Reformed Publishing, 1980.

Cohen, Mathilde, "On the Linguistic Design of Multinational Courts: The French Capture," *International Journal of Constitutional Law* 14 (2016), 498–517.

Coke, Edward, *The Selected Writings and Speeches*, vol. 1, edied by Steve Sheppard, Indianapolis, IN, Liberty Fund, 2003.

Corcos, Christine A., ed, *Law and Magic: A Collection of Essays*, Durham, NC, Carolina Academic Press, 2010.

Corcos, Christine A., "Magical Images in Law," in Wagner, Anne/Cheng, Le, eds, *Exploring Courtroom Discourse: The Language of Power and Control*, Farnham, Ashgate, 2011, 131–175.

Coughlin, John J., *Canon Law: A Comparative Study With Anglo-American Legal Theory*, Oxford/New York, Oxford University Press, 2011.

Coulthard, Malcolm, "Whose Voice Is It? Invented and Concealed Dialogue in Written Records of Verbal Evidence Produced by the Police," in Cotterill, Janet, ed, *Language in the Legal Process*, Basingstoke, Palgrave Macmillan, 2002, 19–34.

Coulthard, Malcolm/Johnson, Alison, *An Introduction to Forensic Linguistics: Language in Evidence*, Abingdon, Routledge, 2007.

Danet, Brenda, "Language in the Legal Process," *Law & Society Review* 14 (1980), 445–564.

De Sutter, Laurent, "On the Magic of Law," *Law Text Culture* 21 (2017), 123–142.

Deutsch, Andreas, "Schriftlichkeit im Recht: Kommunikationsformen/Textsorten," in Felder, Ekkehard/Vogel, Friedemann, eds, *Handbuch Sprache im Recht* (Handbücher Sprachwissen 12), Berlin/Boston, MA, Walter de Gruyter, 2017, 91–116.

Doczekalska, Agnieszka, "Legal Languages in Contact: EU Legislative Drafting and Its Consequences for Judicial Interpretation," in Marino, Silvia/Biel, Łucja/Bajčić, Martina/Sosoni, Vilelmini, eds, *Language and Law: The Role of Language and Translation in EU Competition Law*, Cham, Springer Nature Switzerland, 2018, 163–178.

Drössler, Bernd Th., "Bemerkungen zur Interpretationstheorie des CIC/1983," *Archiv für katholisches Kirchenrecht* 153 (1984), 3–34.

Duffy, Mervyn, *How Language, Ritual and Sacraments Work: According to John Austin, Jürgen Habermas and Louis-Marie Chauvet* (Tesi Gregoriana, Serie Teologia 123), Rome, Editrice Pontificia Università Gregoriana, 2005.

Dumas, Bethany K., "Reasonable Doubt about Reasonable Doubt: Assessing Jury Instruction Adequacy in a Capital Case," in Cotterill, Janet, ed, *Language in the Legal Process*, Basingstoke, Palgrave Macmillan, 2002, 246–259.

Dworkin, Ronald, *Law's Empire*, Cambridge, MA/London, Belknap Press of Harvard University Press, 1986.

Dworkin, Ronald, "Comment," in Scalia, Antonin, *A Matter of Interpretation* (New Edition): *Federal Courts and the Law*, an essay by Antonin Scalia with commentary by Amy Gutmann, Gordon S. Wood, Laurence H. Tribe, Mary Ann Glendon, Ronald Dworkin, with a new introduction by Akhil Reed Amar and a new afterword by Steven G. Calabresi, Princeton, NJ/Oxford, Princeton University Press, 1997, 115–127.

Eades, Diana, "'Evidence Given in Unequivocal Terms': Gaining Consent of Aboriginal Young People in Court," in Cotterill, Janet, ed, *Language in the Legal Process*, Basingstoke, Palgrave Macmillan, 2002, 162–179.

Ehrhardt, Sabine, "Texte als Straftat und im Straftatkontext," in Felder, Ekkehard/Vogel, Friedemann, eds, *Handbuch Sprache im Recht* (Handbücher Sprachwissen 12), Berlin/ Boston, MA, Walter de Gruyter, 2017, 547–566.

Engberg, Jan, "Word Meaning and the Problem of a Globalized Legal Order," in Solan, Lawrence M./Tiersma, Peter M., eds, *The Oxford Handbook of Language and Law*, Oxford, Oxford University Press, 2012, 175–186.

Erdő, Péter, "Expressiones obligationis et exhortationis in Codice Iuris Canonici," *Periodica de Re Morali Canonica Liturgica* 76 (1987), 3–27.

Fflur Huws, Catrin, "(Language + Law)2 = ?," in Freeman, Michael/Smith, Fiona, eds, *Law and Language* (Current Legal Issues 15), Oxford, Oxford University Press, 2013, 400–416.

Filipović, Luna, "The Role of Language in Legal Contexts: A Forensic Cross-Linguistic Viewpoint," in Freeman, Michael/Smith, Fiona, eds, *Law and Language* (Current Legal Issues 15), Oxford, Oxford University Press, 2013, 328–343.

Flügge, Erik, *Der Jargon der Betroffenheit: Wie die Kirche an ihrer Sprache verreckt*, Munich, Kösel, 2016.

Frank, David B., "Do We Translate the Original Author's Intended Meaning?," *Open Theology* 2 (2016), 653–667.

Frank, Engelbert, "Die Sprache kirchlicher Ehegerichte und ihre Wahrnehmung durch Betroffene," in Puza, Richard/Weiß, Andreas, eds, *Iustitia in caritate: Festgabe für Ernst Rößler zum 25jährigen Dienstjubiläum als Offizial der Diözese Rottenburg-Stuttgart* (Adnotationes in Ius Canonicum 3), Frankfurt am Main, Peter Lang, 1997, 463–473.

Frank, Engelbert, "Ehenichtigkeitserklärung—ein für kanonistische Laien problematisches Wort," in Weiß, Andreas/Ihli, Stefan, eds, *Flexibilitas Iuris Canonici: Festschrift für Richard Puza zum 60. Geburtstag* (Adnotationes in Ius Canonicum 28), Frankfurt am Main, Peter Lang, 2003, 501–514.

Freeman, Michael/Smith, Fiona, "Law and Language: An Introduction," in Freeman, Michael/Smith, Fiona, eds, *Law and Language* (Current Legal Issues 15), Oxford, Oxford University Press, 2013, 1–7.

Geertz, Clifford, "'From the Native's Point of View': On the Nature of Anthropological Understanding," *Bulletin of the American Academy of Arts and Sciences* 28 (1974), no. 1 (October 1974), 26–45.

Gerosa, Libero, *Grundlagen und Paradigmen der Gesetzesauslegung in der Kirche: Anregungen und Zukunftsperspektiven für die katholische Kanonistik* (Kirchenrechtliche Bibliothek 2), Münster, LIT, 1999.

Glanert, Simone/Legrand, Pierre, "Foreign Law in Translation: If Truth Be Told . . . ," in Freeman, Michael/Smith, Fiona, eds, *Law and Language* (Current Legal Issues 15), Oxford, Oxford University Press, 2013, 513–532.

Goodrich, Peter, "Rhetoric as Jurisprudence: An Introduction to the Politics of Legal Language," *Oxford Journal of Legal Studies* 4 (1984), 88–122.

Goodrich, Peter, "Legal Hermeneutics," in Craig, Edward, ed, *Routledge Encyclopedia of Philosophy*, vol. 5, London/New York, Routledge, 1998, 506–510.

Gotti, Maurizio, "Text and Genre," in Solan, Lawrence M./Tiersma, Peter M., eds, *The Oxford Handbook of Language and Law*, Oxford, Oxford University Press, 2012, 52–66.

Grabrucker, Marianne, "Sprache als Herausforderung an die Rechtsgleichheit," in Fritsch-Oppermann, Sybille, ed, *Die Rechtssprache: Fachjargon und Herrschaftsinstrument* (Loccumer Protokoll 15/97), Loccum, Evangelische Akademie, 1998, 68–79.

Grasso, Arianna, "Plain English and the EU: Still Trying to Fight the Fog?," in Marino, Silvia/Biel, Łucja/Bajčić, Martina/Sosoni, Vilelmini, eds, *Language and Law: The Role of Language and Translation in EU Competition Law*, Cham, Springer Nature Switzerland, 2018, 359–376.

Griffin, Bertram F., "Introduction to the Jargon of Canon Law," *The Jurist* 44 (1984), 19–27.

Grossi, Renata, "Understanding Law and Emotion," *Emotion Review* 7 (2015), 55–60.

Gurvitch, Georges, "Magic and Law," *Social Research* 9 (1942), 104–122.

Haering, Stephan, "Lateinische Sprache und Kanonisches Recht," *Seminarium* 43 (2003), 237–256.

Haering, Stephan, "Konziliare Ekklesiologie und kanonische Sprache," in Güthoff, Elmar/Haering, Stephan, eds, *Ius quia iustum: Festschrift für Helmuth Pree zum 65. Geburtstag* (Kanonistische Studien und Texte 65), Berlin, Duncker & Humblot, 2015, 61–80.

Haering, Stephan/Rees, Wilhelm/Schmitz, Heribert, eds, *Handbuch des katholischen Kirchenrechts*, 3rd edn, Regensburg, Friedrich Pustet, 2015.

Hahn, Judith, "Recht verstehen: Die Kirchenrechtssprache als Fachsprache—rechtslinguistische Probleme und theologische Herausforderung," in Schüller, Thomas/Zumbült, Martin, eds, *Iustitia est constans et perpetua voluntas ius suum cuique tribuendi. 20 Jahre Studiengang Lizentiat im Kanonischen Recht an der Westfälischen Wilhelms-Universität Münster—Festschrift für Klaus Lüdicke zum 70. Geburtstag* (Beihefte zum Münsterischen Kommentar 70), Essen 2014, 163–198.

Hahn, Judith, *Church Law in Modernity: Toward a Theory of Canon Law between Nature and Culture* (Law and Christianity), Cambridge, Cambridge University Press, 2019.

Hahn, Judith, "Moral Certitude: Merits and Demerits of the Standard of Proof Applied in Roman Catholic Jurisprudence," *Oxford Journal of Law and Religion* 8 (2019), 300–325.

Hahn, Judith, "Invalid Baptismal Formulas: A Critical View on a Current Catholic Concern," *Ecclesiastical Law Journal* 23 (2021), 19–33.

Hahn, Judith, *Foundations of a Sociology of Canon Law*, Cham, Springer Nature, 2022.

Halpin, Andrew, "Language, Truth, and Law," in Freeman, Michael/Smith, Fiona, eds, *Law and Language* (Current Legal Issues 15), Oxford, Oxford University Press, 2013, 62–78.

Hans, Valerie P., "Law and the Media: An Overview and Introduction," *Law and Human Behavior* 14 (1990), 399–407.

Hart, Herbert L.A., *The Concept of Law*, with a postscript edited by Penelope A. Bulloch and Joseph Raz and with an introduction by Leslie Green (Clarendon Law Series), 3rd edn, Oxford, Oxford University Press, 2012.

Heffer, Chris, "'If You Were Standing in Marks and Spencers': Narrativisation and Comprehension in the English Summing-up," in Cotterill, Janet, ed, *Language in the Legal Process*, Basingstoke, Palgrave Macmillan, 2002, 228–245.

Hibbitts, Bernard J., "Making Motions: The Embodiment of Law in Gesture," *Journal of Contemporary Legal Issues* 6 (1995), 51–81.

Hill, Claire A., "Why Are Non-US Contracts Written in US Legalese? Some Preliminary Thoughts and a Research Agenda," in Freeman, Michael/Smith, Fiona, eds, *Law and Language* (Current Legal Issues 15), Oxford, Oxford University Press, 2013, 457–465.

Hiltunen, Risto, "The Grammar and Structure of Legal Texts," in Solan, Lawrence M./ Tiersma, Peter M., eds, *The Oxford Handbook of Language and Law*, Oxford, Oxford University Press, 2012, 39–51.

Ho, Hock L., "What Does a Verdict Do? A Speech Act Analysis of Giving a Verdict," *International Commentary on Evidence* 4 (2006), 1–26.

Hoffmann, Ludger, "Mündlichkeit im Recht: Kommunikationsformen/Gesprächsarten," in Felder, Ekkehard/Vogel, Friedemann, eds, *Handbuch Sprache im Recht* (Handbücher Sprachwissen 12), Berlin/Boston, MA, Walter de Gruyter, 2017, 67–90.

Holmer, Paul L., "Language and Theology: Some Critical Notes," *The Harvard Theological Review* 58 (1965), 241–261.

Homans, George C., "Anxiety and Ritual: The Theories of Malinowski and Radcliffe-Brown," *American Anthropologist* 43 (1941), 164–172.

Huels, John M., "Interpreting Canon Law in Diverse Cultures," *The Jurist* 47 (1987), 249–293.

Huels, John M., "Classifying Authentic Interpretations of Canon Law," *The Jurist* 72 (2012), 605–640.

Jansen, Thomas, "Was ist Klerikalismus?," September 10, 2018, https://www.katholisch.de/aktuelles/aktuelle-artikel/was-ist-klerikalismus.

Johnson, Alison, "*So* . . . ?: Pragmatic Implications of *So*-Prefaced Questions in Formal Police Interviews," in Cotterill, Janet, ed, *Language in the Legal Process*, Basingstoke, Palgrave Macmillan, 2002, 91–110.

Kähler, Lorenz, "First-Person Perspectives in Legal Decisions," in Freeman, Michael/ Smith, Fiona, eds, *Law and Language* (Current Legal Issues 15), Oxford, Oxford University Press, 2013, 533–556.

Kaufhold, Hubert, "Zum ostkirchlichen Charakter der Rechtssprache des Codex Canonum Ecclesiarum Orientalium (CCEO)," in Güthoff, Elmar/Haering, Stephan, eds, *Ius quia iustum: Festschrift für Helmuth Pree zum 65. Geburtstag* (Kanonistische Studien und Texte 65), Berlin, Duncker & Humblot, 2015, 221–245.

Kibbee, Douglas A., *Language and the Law: Linguistic Inequality in America*, Cambridge, Cambridge University Press, 2016.

Klatt, Matthias, "Die Wortlautgrenze," in Lerch, Kent D., ed, *Recht verhandeln: Argumentieren, Begründen und Entscheiden im Diskurs des Rechts* (Die Sprache des Rechts 2), Berlin/New York, Walter de Gruyter, 2005, 343–368.

Koury, Joseph J., "Necessity, Utility, Scarcity: Clues to the Origins of Laws and the Process of Lawmaking," *The Jurist* 49 (1989), 95–111.

Koury, Joseph J., "From Prohibited to Permitted: Transitions in the Code of Canon Law," *Studia Canonica* 24 (1990), 147–183.

Koury, Joseph J., "The Limits of Collaboration: The New Legal Language for the Laity," *Studia Canonica* 26 (1992), 415–436.

Kowal, Wojciech, *Understanding Canon 17 of the 1983 Code of Canon Law in Light of Contemporary Hermeneutics*, New York, Edwin Mellen Press, 2000.

Kowal, Wojciech, "Some Remarks on Understanding the Concept of *Propria Verborum Significatio*," *Studia Canonica* 34 (2000), 489–504.

Kreusch, Irina M., *Der Eid zwischen Schwurverbot Jesu und kirchlichem Recht: Verehrung oder Mißbrauch des göttlichen Namens?* (Kanonistische Studien und Texte 49), Berlin, Duncker & Humblot, 2005.

Krieger, Stefan H., "A Time to Keep Silent and a Time to Speak: The Functions of Silence in the Lawyering Process," *Oregon Law Review* 80 (2001), 199–266.

Kurzon, Dennis, *It Is Hereby Performed: Explorations in Legal Speech Acts* (Pragmatics & Beyond VII:6), Amsterdam/Philadelphia, PA, John Benjamins, 1986.

Kurzon, Dennis, *Discourse of Silence*, Amsterdam/Philadelphia, PA, John Benjamins, 1998.

Lawrence, Irene, *Linguistics and Theology: The Significance of Noam Chomsky for Theological Construction*, Metuchen, NJ, Scarecrow Press, 1980.

Lederhilger, Severin, "Repetition oder Innovation? Bemerkungen zu Interpretationsgrundsätzen für den CIC/1983," *Archiv für katholisches Kirchenrecht* 172 (2003), 58–83.

Legrand, Pierre, "Foreign Law: Understanding Understanding," *Journal of Comparative Law* 6 (2011), 67–177.

Leiboff, Marett, "Theatricalizing Law," *Law and Literature* 30 (2018), 351–367.

Lerch, Kent D., "Gesetze als Gemeingut aller: Der Traum vom verständlichen Gesetz," in Lerch, Kent D., ed, *Recht verstehen: Verständlichkeit, Missverständlichkeit und Unverständlichkeit von Recht* (Die Sprache des Rechts 1), Berlin/New York, Walter de Gruyter, 2004, 225–237.

Lerch, Kent D., "Verständlichkeit als Pflicht? Zur Intransparenz des Transparenzgebots," in Lerch, Kent D., ed, *Recht verstehen: Verständlichkeit, Missverständlichkeit und Unverständlichkeit von Recht* (Die Sprache des Rechts 1), Berlin/New York, Walter de Gruyter, 2004, 239–283.

Lerch, Kent D., ed, *Recht verhandeln: Argumentieren, Begründen und Entscheiden im Diskurs des Rechts* (Die Sprache des Rechts 2), Berlin/New York, Walter de Gruyter, 2005.

Lerch, Kent D., ed, *Recht vermitteln: Strukturen, Formen und Medien der Kommunikation im Recht* (Die Sprache des Rechts 3), Berlin/New York, Walter de Gruyter, 2005.

Lerch, Kent D., "Recht vermitteln: Eine Vorbemerkung," in Lerch, Kent D., ed, *Recht vermitteln: Strukturen, Formen und Medien der Kommunikation im Recht* (Die Sprache des Rechts 3), Berlin/New York, Walter de Gruyter, 2005, XV–XXV.

Liberman, Kenneth, *Understanding Interaction in Central Australia: An Ehnomethodological Study of Australian Aboriginal People* (Studies in Ethnomethodology), Boston, MA/London/Melbourne/Henley, Routledge & Kegan Paul, 1985.

Lindbeck, George Arthur, *The Nature of Doctrine: Religion and Theology in a Postliberal Age*, Louisville, KY, Westminster John Knox Press, 1984.

Löbbert, Raoul, "Sündenbock gesucht," September 28, 2018, https://www.zeit.de/2018/40/klerikalismus-sexueller-missbrauch-selbstkritik-katholische-kirche.

Löbbert, Raoul/Löwisch, Georg, "In der Verantwortung: Der Fall des Priesters Peter H. zeigt, wie der Klerus sexuellen Missbrauch von Kindern vertuschte," *Die Zeit*, January 5, 2022, 55–56.

Loftus, Elizabeth F./Palmer, John C., "Reconstruction of Automobile Destruction: An Example of the Interaction Between Language and Memory," *Journal of Verbal Learning and Verbal Behavior* 13 (1974), 585–589.

Lötscher, Andreas, "Gesetze als Texte: Wie wird Recht in Textstrukturen gebracht?," in Lerch, Kent D., ed, *Recht vermitteln: Strukturen, Formen und Medien der*

Kommunikation im Recht (Die Sprache des Rechts 3), Berlin/New York, Walter de Gruyter, 2005, 183–207.

Lüdicke, Klaus, "Commentary on canon 1098," supplementary sheets 41, in Lüdicke, Klaus, ed, *Münsterischer Kommentar zum Codex Iuris Canonici unter besonderer Berücksichtigung der Rechtslage in Deutschland, Österreich und der Schweiz*, loose-leaf-collection, Essen, Wingen, 2006.

Lüdicke, Klaus, "Commentary on canon 1364," supplementary sheets 35, in Lüdicke, Klaus, ed, *Münsterischer Kommentar zum Codex Iuris Canonici unter besonderer Berücksichtigung der Rechtslage in Deutschland, Österreich und der Schweiz*, loose-leaf-collection, Essen, Wingen, 2001.

Lüdicke, Klaus, "Commentary on canon 1728," supplementary sheets 18, in Lüdicke, Klaus, ed, *Münsterischer Kommentar zum Codex Iuris Canonici unter besonderer Berücksichtigung der Rechtslage in Deutschland, Österreich und der Schweiz*, loose-leaf-collection, Essen, Wingen, 1992.

Luhmann, Niklas, *A Sociological Theory of Law*, translated by Elizabeth King-Utz and Martin Albrow, edited by Martin Albrow, London/New York, Routledge, 2014.

Marino, Silvia, "Introduction: The Role of the Language in EU Law," in Marino, Silvia/Biel, Łucja/Bajčić, Martina/Sosoni, Vilelmini, eds, *Language and Law: The Role of Language and Translation in EU Competition Law*, Cham, Springer Nature Switzerland, 2018, 1–6.

Marmor, Andrei A., *Interpretation and Legal Theory*, 2nd edn, Oxford/Portland, OR, Hart Publishing, 2005.

Marmor, Andrei A., "The Immorality of Textualism," *Loyola of Los Angeles Law Review* 38 (2005), 2063–2079.

Marmor, Andrei A., "Truth in Law," in Freeman, Michael/Smith, Fiona, eds, *Law and Language* (Current Legal Issues 15), Oxford, Oxford University Press, 2013, 45–61.

Martinich, Aloysius P., "Sacraments and Speech Acts," part 1 and part 2, *The Heythrop Journal* 16 (1975), 289–303 and 405–417.

Mattila, Heikki E.S., "Legal Vocabulary," in Solan, Lawrence M./Tiersma, Peter M., eds, *The Oxford Handbook of Language and Law*, Oxford, Oxford University Press, 2012, 27–38.

Mattila, Heikki E.S., *Comparative Legal Linguistics: Language of Law, Latin and Modern Lingua Francas*, 2nd edn, London/New York, Routledge, 2016.

McAuliffe, Karen, "Language and Law in the European Union: The Multilingual Jurisprudence of the ECJ," in Solan, Lawrence M./Tiersma, Peter M., eds, *The Oxford Handbook of Language and Law*, Oxford, Oxford University Press, 2012, 200–216.

McAuliffe, Karen, "Precedent at the Court of Justice of the European Union: The Linguistic Aspect," in Freeman, Michael/Smith, Fiona, eds, *Law and Language* (Current Legal Issues 15), Oxford, Oxford University Press, 2013, 483–492.

McEvoy, Sebastian, "The Grin's Cat: Language, Law, and Literature," in Freeman, Michael/Smith, Fiona, eds, *Law and Language* (Current Legal Issues 15), Oxford, Oxford University Press, 2013, 164–186.

McGinnis, John O./Rappaport, Michael B., "The Constitution and the Language of the Law," *William & Mary Law Review* 59 (2018), 1321–1411.

Mellinkoff, David, *The Language of the Law*, Boston, MA/Toronto, Little, Brown and Company, 1963.

Möllers, Christoph, *The Possibility of Norms: Social Practice beyond Morals and Causes*, Oxford, Oxford University Press, 2020.

Mörsdorf, Klaus, "Wort und Sakrament als Bauelemente der Kirchenverfassung," *Archiv für katholisches Kirchenrecht* 134 (1965), 72–79.

Mörsdorf, Klaus, *Die Rechtssprache des Codex Juris Canonici: Eine kritische Untersuchung*, 2nd edn (reprint of the 1937 edn), Paderborn, Ferdinand Schöningh, 1967.

Müller-Dietz, Heinz, "Rechtssprache: Die Macht der Sprache, die Sprache der Macht," in Fritsch-Oppermann, Sybille, ed, *Die Rechtssprache: Fachjargon und Herrschaftsinstrument* (Loccumer Protokoll 15/97), Loccum, Evangelische Akademie, 1998, 19–44.

Neudecker, Gerhard, *Ius sequitur vitam—Der Dienst der Kirchengerichte an der Lebendigkeit des Rechts: Zugleich ein Beitrag zur Vergleichung des kanonischen und staatlichen Rechtssystems* (Tübinger Kirchenrechtliche Studien 13), Münster, LIT, 2013.

Neumann, Ulfried, "Juristische Fachsprache und Umgangssprache," in Grewendorf, Günther, ed, *Rechtskultur als Sprachkultur: Zur forensischen Funktion der Sprachanalyse*, Frankfurt am Main, Suhrkamp, 1992, 110–121.

Neumann, Ulfried, "Wahrheit statt Autorität: Möglichkeit und Grenzen einer Legitimation durch Begründung im Recht," in Lerch, Kent D., ed, *Recht verhandeln: Argumentieren, Begründen und Entscheiden im Diskurs des Rechts* (Die Sprache des Rechts 2), Berlin/New York, Walter de Gruyter, 2005, 369–384.

Neuwirth, Rostam J., "Law and Magic: A(nother) Paradox?," *Thomas Jefferson Law Review* 37 (2014), 139–190.

Nobles, Richard/Schiff, David, "Legal Pluralism: A Systems Theory Approach to Language, Translation, and Communication," in Freeman, Michael/Smith, Fiona, eds, *Law and Language* (Current Legal Issues 15), Oxford, Oxford University Press, 2013, 100–114.

Nord, Christiane, "Function + Loyalty: Theology Meets Skopos," *Open Theology* 2 (2016), 566–580.

Oğlakcıoğlu, Mustafa T./Schuhr, Jan C., "Verbotene Sprache," in Felder, Ekkehard/Vogel, Friedemann, eds, *Handbuch Sprache im Recht* (Handbücher Sprachwissen 12), Berlin/Boston, MA, Walter de Gruyter, 2017, 527–546.

Ohly, Christoph, "Gravis necessitas: Erwägungen zu einem unbestimmten Begriff der kirchlichen Gesetzbücher," *Archiv für katholisches Kirchenrecht* 175 (2006), 473–485.

Ohly, Christoph, "Officium ecclesiasticum: Ein rechtssprachlicher Vorschlag," *Archiv für katholisches Kirchenrecht* 177 (2008), 56–72.

Olivecrona, Karl, "Legal Language and Reality," in Newman, Ralph A., ed, *Essays in Jurisprudence in Honor of Roscoe Pound*, Indianapolis, IN, Bobbs-Merrill, 1962, 151–191.

Olschewski, Jürgen, "Der Begriff 'iusta causa' in der kirchlichen Rechtssprache: Eine 'traditio canonica,'" in Reinhardt, Heinrich J. F., ed, *Theologia et Ius Canonicum: Festgabe für Heribert Heinemann zur Vollendung seines 70. Lebensjahres*, Essen, Wingen, 1995, 235–257.

Orsy, Ladilas M., "The Interpreter and His Art," *The Jurist* 40 (1980), 27–56.

Orsy, Ladilas M., "Models of Approaches to Canon Law and Their Impact on Interpretation," *The Jurist* 50 (1990), 83–101.

Orsy, Ladilas M., *Theology and Canon Law: New Horizons for Legislation and Interpretation*, Collegeville, MN, The Liturgical Press, 1992.

Peters, Edward N., "The Ordination of Men Bereft of Speech and the Celebration of Sacraments in Sign Language," *Studia Canonica* 42 (2008), 331–345.

Podlas, Kimberlianne, "The 'CSI Effect,'" in *Oxford Research Encyclopedia of Criminology*, August 22, 2017, DOI: 10.1093/acrefore/9780190264079.013.40.

Polvani, Carlo M., *Authentic Interpretation in Canon Law: Reflections on a Distinctively Canonical Institution* (Tesi Gregoriana, Serie Diritto Canonico 34), Rome, Editrice Pontifica Università Gregoriana, 1999.

Poscher, Ralf, "Ambiguity and Vagueness in Legal Interpretation," in Tiersma, Peter M./ Solan, Lawrence M., eds, *The Oxford Handbook of Language and Law*, Oxford, Oxford University Press, 2012, 128–144.

Poscher, Ralf, "The Hermeneutics of Law: An Analytical Model for a Complex General Account," in Forster, Michael/Gjesdal, Kristin, eds, *The Cambridge Companion to Hermeneutics*, Cambridge, Cambridge University Press, 2019, 326–353.

Posner, Eric A., "Law and the Emotions," *The Georgetown Law Journal* 89 (2001), 1977–2012.

Posner, Richard A., *Law and Literature*, 3rd edn, Cambridge, MA, Harvard University Press, 2009.

Potz, Richard, "Ökumenische Interpretation: Zur gegenwärtigen Situation der kanonistischen Auslegungslehre," *Österreichisches Archiv für Kirchenrecht* 35 (1985), 62–82.

Pree, Helmuth, *Die evolutive Interpretation der Rechtsnorm im Kanonischen Recht* (Linzer Universitätsschriften, Monographien 6), Vienna/New York, Springer, 1980.

Pyle, Ransford C., "Law, Ritual and Language," *American Legal Studies Association Forum* 8 (1984), 381–392.

Rinderknecht, Jakob K., *Mapping the Differentiated Consensus of the Joint Declaration* (Pathways for Ecumenical and Interreligious Dialogue), New York, Palgrave Macmillan, 2016.

Rodríguez, Cristina M., "Language and Participation," *California Law Review* 94 (2006), 687–767.

Russell, Sonia, "'Three's a Crowd': Shifting Dynamics in the Interpreted Interview," in Cotterill, Janet, ed, *Language in the Legal Process*, Basingstoke, Palgrave Macmillan, 2002, 111–126.

Sandrini, Peter, "Translation zwischen Kultur und Kommunikation: Der Sonderfall Recht," in Sandrini, Peter, ed, *Übersetzen von Rechtstexten: Fachkommunikation im Spannungsfeld zwischen Rechtsordnungen und Sprachen*, Tübingen, Narr, 1999, 9–43.

Šarčević, Susan, "Challenges to the Legal Translator," in Tiersma, Peter M./Solan, Lawrence M., eds, *The Oxford Handbook of Language and Law*, Oxford, Oxford University Press, 2012, 187–199.

Savigny, Friedrich Carl von, *System des heutigen Römischen Rechts*, vol. 1, Berlin, Veit und Comp., 1840.

Savoy, Bénédicte, "Property and Possession: Some Considerations on the History of Ideas Relating to a Pair of Legal Concepts," September 18, 2018, https://voelkerrechtsblog.org/property-and-possession.

Scalia, Antonin, "Common-Law Courts in a Civil-Law System: The Role of United States Federal Courts in Interpreting the Constitution and Laws," in Scalia, Antonin, *A Matter of Interpretation* (New Edition): *Federal Courts and the Law*, an essay by Antonin Scalia with commentary by Amy Gutmann, Gordon S. Wood, Laurence H. Tribe, Mary Ann Glendon, Ronald Dworkin, with a new introduction by Akhil Reed Amar and a new afterword by Steven G. Calabresi, Princeton, NJ/Oxford, Princeton University Press, 1997, 3–47.

Schane, Sanford A., "Ambiguity and Misunderstanding in the Law," *Thomas Jefferson Law Review* 25 (2002), 167–193.
Schane, Sanford A., *Language and the Law*, with a foreword by Roger W. Shuy, London/New York, Continuum, 2006.
Schmidt, Ronald, "Democratic Theory and the Challenge of Linguistic Diversity," *Language Policy* 13 (2014), 395–411.
Schreiter, Robert J., *Constructing Local Theologies*, foreword by Edward Schillebeeckx, Maryknoll, NY, Orbis Books, 1985.
Schüller, Thomas, "Auslegung von Gesetzen im Kirchenrecht: Ein rechtshistorischer und antekanonistischer Beitrag zur Debatte," in Ohly, Christoph/Rees, Wilhelm/Gerosa, Libero, eds, *Theologia Iuris Canonici: Festschrift für Ludger Müller zur Vollendung des 65. Lebensjahres* (Kanonistische Studien und Texte 67), Berlin, Duncker & Humblot, 2017, 127–138.
Searle, John R., "A Classification of Illocutionary Acts," *Language in Society* 5 (1976), 1–23.
Searle, John R., "How Performatives Work," *Linguistics and Philosophy* 12 (1989), 535–558.
Searle, John R., *Making the Social World: The Structure of Human Civilization*, Oxford, Oxford University Press, 2010.
Searle, Mark, "The Uses of Liturgical Language," *Liturgy* 4 (1985), 15–19.
Seibert, Thomas-Michael, "Semiotik im Recht," in Felder, Ekkehard/Vogel, Friedemann, eds, *Handbuch Sprache im Recht* (Handbücher Sprachwissen 12), Berlin/Boston, MA, Walter de Gruyter, 2017, 3–21.
Shaer, Benjamin, "Toward a Cognitive Science of Legal Interpretation," in Freeman, Michael/Smith, Fiona, eds, *Law and Language* (Current Legal Issues 15), Oxford, Oxford University Press, 2013, 259–291.
Shannon, Peter M., "Canon Law/Civil Law," *The Jurist* 45 (1985), 618–630.
Shapiro, Barbara J., "To A Moral Certainty: Theories of Knowledge and Anglo-American Juries 1600–1850," *The Hastings Law Journal* 38 (1986), 153–193.
Shuy, Roger W., *Language Crimes: The Use and Abuse of Language Evidence in the Courtroom*, Malden, MA/Oxford, Blackwell, 1996.
Shuy, Roger W., "To Testify or Not to Testify?," in Cotterill, Janet, ed, *Language in the Legal Process*, Basingstoke, Palgrave Macmillan, 2002, 3–18.
Simon, Heike/Funk-Baker, Gisela, *Einführung in das deutsche Recht und die deutsche Rechtssprache*, 5th edn, Munich, C.H. Beck, 2013.
Simonnæs, Ingrid, "Fachkommunikation im Recht unter Berücksichtigung der Mehrfachadressierung," in Lerch, Kent D., ed, *Recht vermitteln: Strukturen, Formen und Medien der Kommunikation im Recht* (Die Sprache des Rechts 3), Berlin/New York, Walter de Gruyter, 2005, 377–397.
Sobański, Remigiusz, "Der neue Codex des kanonischen Rechts als kirchliches und rechtliches Ereignis," *Österreichisches Archiv für Kirchenrecht* 35 (1985), 5–24.
Sobánski, Remigiusz, "Zu den Interpretationsregeln des kirchlichen Gesetzbuches," in Lüdicke, Klaus/Mussinghoff, Heinrich/Schwendenwein, Hugo, eds, *Iustus Iudex: Festgabe für Paul Wesemann zum 75. Geburtstag von seinen Freunden und Schülern* (Beihefte zum Münsterischen Kommentar 5), Essen, Wingen, 1990, 693–707.
Socha, Hubert, "Commentary on canon 16," supplementary sheets 47, in Lüdicke, Klaus, ed, *Münsterischer Kommentar zum Codex Iuris Canonici unter besonderer Berücksichtigung der Rechtslage in Deutschland, Österreich und der Schweiz*, loose-leaf-collection, Essen, Wingen, 2012.

Solan, Lawrence M., *The Language of Judges*, Chicago, IL, The University of Chicago Press, 1993.

Solan, Lawrence M., "The Clinton Scandal: Some Legal Lessons from Linguistics," in Cotterill, Janet, ed, *Language in the Legal Process*, Basingstoke, Palgrave Macmillan, 2002, 180–195.

Solan, Lawrence M., "Statutory Interpretation in the EU: The Augustinian Approach," in Olsen, Frances/Lorz, Alexander/Stein, Dieter, eds, *Translation Issues in Language and Law*, London, Palgrave Macmillan, 2009, 35–54.

Solan, Lawrence M., *The Language of Statutes: Laws and Their Interpretation* (The Chicago Series in Law and Society), Chicago, IL/London, The University of Chicago Press, 2010.

Solan, Lawrence M./Tiersma, Peter M., "Introduction," in Solan, Lawrence M./Tiersma, Peter M., eds, *The Oxford Handbook of Language and Law*, Oxford, Oxford University Press, 2012, 1–9.

Solan, Lawrence M., "Linguistic Issues in Statutory Interpretation," in Tiersma, Peter M./ Solan, Lawrence M., eds, *The Oxford Handbook of Language and Law*, Oxford, Oxford University Press, 2012, 87–99.

Sosoni, Vilelmini, "Language and Translation in EU Competition Law: Insights from English, Greek, Italian and Spanish Versions of Legislative Texts," in Marino, Silvia/ Biel, Łucja/Bajčić, Martina/Sosoni, Vilelmini, eds, *Language and Law: The Role of Language and Translation in EU Competition Law*, Cham, Springer Nature Switzerland, 2018, 179–205.

Stewart, Charlie D., "The Rhetorical Canons of Construction: New Textualism's Rhetoric Problem," *Michigan Law Review* 116 (2018), 1485–1514.

Stewen, Martin, "Klerikalismus: 'wie das Amen in der Kirche'," October 8, 2018, https:// www.feinschwarz.net/klerikalismus-wie-das-amen-in-der-kirche.

Stygall, Gail, "Textual Barriers to United States Immigration," in Cotterill, Janet, ed, *Language in the Legal Process*, Basingstoke, Palgrave Macmillan, 2002, 35–53.

Tamanaha, Brian Z., *A Realistic Theory of Law*, Cambridge, Cambridge University Press, 2017.

Taylor, Charles, *The Language Animal: The Full Shape of the Human Linguistic Capacity*, Cambridge, MA/London, The Belknap Press of Harvard University Press, 2016.

Tiersma, Peter M., "Reforming the Language of Jury Instructions," *Hofstra Law Review* 22 (1993), 37–78.

Tiersma, Peter M., "The Judge as Linguist," *Loyola of Los Angeles Law Review* 27 (1993), 269–283.

Tiersma, Peter M., *Legal Language*, Chicago, IL/London, The University of Chicago Press, 1999.

Tiersma, Peter M., "A History of the Languages of Law," in Tiersma, Peter M./Solan, Lawrence M., eds, *The Oxford Handbook of Language and Law*, Oxford, Oxford University Press, 2012, 13–26.

Tiersma, Peter M./Solan, Lawrence M., "The Language of Crime," in Tiersma, Peter M./ Solan, Lawrence M., eds, *The Oxford Handbook of Language and Law*, Oxford, Oxford University Press, 2012, 340–353.

Tran, Jonathan, "Marlo's City of Words: Tempting a Natural Theology of Language," in Tran, Jonathan/Werntz, Myles, eds, *Corners in the City of God: Theology, Philosophy, and The Wire*, Eugene, OR, Cascade Books, 2013, 59–75.

Tran, Jonathan, "Linguistic Theology: Completing Postliberalism's Linguistic Task," *Modern Theology* 33 (2017), 47–68.

Vanhoozer, Kevin J., *The Drama of Doctrine: A Canonical-Linguistic Approach to Christian Theology*, Louisville, KY, Westminster John Knox Press, 2005.

Vespaziani, Alberto, "Towards a Hermeneutical Approach to Legal Metaphor," in Bustamante, Thomas/Onazi, Oche, eds, *Human Rights, Language and Law*, Proceedings of the 24th World Congress of the International Association for Philosophy of Law and Social Philosophy, Beijing 2009, vol. 2 (Archiv für Rechts- und Sozialphilosophie, Beihefte 131), Franz Steiner Verlag/Nomos, Stuttgart, 2012, 79–92.

Vidor, Gian Marco, "Rhetorical Engineering of Emotions in the Courtroom: The Case of Lawyers in Modern France," *Rechtsgeschichte—Legal History* 25 (2017), 286–295.

Vogel, Friedemann, "Rechtslinguistik: Bestimmung einer Fachrichtung," in Felder, Ekkehard/Vogel, Friedemann, eds, *Handbuch Sprache im Recht* (Handbücher Sprachwissen 12), Berlin/Boston, MA, Walter de Gruyter, 2017, 209–232.

Wächter, Lothar, "Die Rechtssprache," in Campenhausen, Axel von/Riedel-Spangenberger, Ilona/Sebott, Reinhold, eds, *Lexikon für Kirchen- und Staatskirchenrecht*, vol. 3, Paderborn/Munich/Vienna/Zürich, Ferdinand Schöningh, 2004, 379–381.

Weber, Margit, "Rechtssprachliche Anmerkungen zur Verwendung von christifidelis, fidelis, baptizatus und christianus im CIC/1917 und im CIC/1983," in Geringer, Karl-Theodor/Schmitz, Heribert, eds, *Communio in Ecclesiae Mysterio: Festschrift für Winfried Aymans zum 65. Geburtstag*, St. Ottilien, EOS, 2001, 653–667.

Whitman, James Q., *The Origins of Reasonable Doubt: Theological Roots of the Criminal Trial*, New Haven, CT, Yale University Press, 2008.

Whorf, Benjamin L., *Language, Thought, and Reality: Selected Writings of Benjamin Lee Whorf*, edited by John B. Carroll, Cambridge, MA, The Technology Press of Massachusetts Institute of Technology, 1956.

Williams, Christopher, "Legal English and Plain Language: An Introduction," *ESP Across Cultures* 1 (2004), 111–124.

Winter, Steven L., "Frame Semantics and the 'Internal Point of View,'" in Freeman, Michael/Smith, Fiona, eds, *Law and Language* (Current Legal Issues 15), Oxford, Oxford University Press, 2013, 115–127.

Witte, John, Jr./Manzer, Christopher J., "Introduction," in Berman, Harold J., *Law and Language: Effective Symbols of Community*, edited by John Witte, Jr., Cambridge, Cambridge University Press, 2013, 1–35.

Zeller, Klaus, "Die Terminologie der kirchlichen Gesetzbücher: Versuch einer Bestandsaufnahme zur kirchlichen Rechtssprache des CIC und des CCEO," in Ohly, Christoph/Rees, Wilhelm/Gerosa, Libero, eds, *Theologia Iuris Canonici: Festschrift für Ludger Müller zur Vollendung des 65. Lebensjahres* (Kanonistische Studien und Texte 67), Berlin, Duncker & Humblot, 2017, 139–166.

Zumbült, Martin, "Ordnen—Sprache von Lehramt und Kirchenrecht," in Meyer, Guido/Wichard, Norbert, eds, *Sprachen der Kirche: Über Vielfalt und Verständlichkeit kirchlichen Sprechens*, Munich, dkv, 2018, 173–192.

Index

For the benefit of digital users, indexed terms that span two pages (e.g., 52–53) may, on occasion, appear on only one of those pages.

Aboriginal language, 188–89, 191–92
Adler, Mark, 16, 117–18
Ainsworth, Janet, 34, 190–91
annulment, 26–27, 41–42, 74–75, 99–103, 132–34, 197–99, 204–5
apostasy. *See* heresy
Aristotelian ontology, 101–2, 103, 132–34
Augustinian approach, 176–77
Austin, John L., 6–7, 41–44, 51–52, 53–57

Babel, 141–43, 176–77
bachelor(ette), 159
baptismal formula, 52–54
Barthes, Roland, 170–71
Bentley, Derek, 195
Berman, Harold J., 23–62, 70, 76–79, 110–11, 116–17
Besitz. *See* ownership
borrowing, 69–70, 76–79, 148–49
British Equality Act 2010, 61–63, 64–65
Busse, Dietrich, 14, 28, 32–33, 68–69, 72–74, 91–92, 99, 103–4, 175–76

Casement, Roger D., 97–98
Charrow, Robert P., and Charrow, Veda R., 39, 59, 61–62, 68–69, 118–19
Cheshire Cat, 102–3, 132–34
christifidelis, 94–97
Cohen, Mathilde, 143–44, 147–49
concordats, 145–46
Congregation for Catholic Education, 81–82
Congregation for the Doctrine of the Faith, 52–53, 191–92
Coulthard, Malcolm, 15, 195–96
Council of Trent, 52–53, 54–57
COVID-19, 55–57

death, 35, 72
death penalty, 97–98, 196–98, 200
declarative speech, 35, 36–38, 43–57, 72, 91, 98, 99–101, 105–6, 185–86, 196–97
defender of the bond, 74–75

dolus. *See* maliciousness
Dworkin, Ronald, 159

Eades, Diana, 188–89, 191–92
Eigentum. *See* ownership
Engberg, Jan, 129–30, 137–38, 141–42, 144, 176–77
equal authenticity, principle of, 152, 176–77
equity, 82–84
European Court of Justice, 147–48, 152, 176–77, 200–1
European Union, 20–21, 64, 85–86, 116, 141, 145–47, 149–50, 176–77, 203–4

fidelis. *See* christifidelis
Frank, David, 31–32, 168–69
Frank, Engelbert, 99–101, 186–87, 197–98, 204–5
fuzziness of terms, 162–63, 175–76

Geertz, Clifford, 138–39, 205–6
Gewalt. *See* violence
gratuitous concurrence, 188–89
grave necessity, 86–89
grave sin, 160–61

Hart, Herbert L. A., 25, 162–63, 172
heresy, 11–13, 95–97, 114
Hiltunen, Risto, 44–47, 61–62, 63
homicide. *See* murder
Huels, John M., 132–36, 138–42, 177–78, 179–82

illocutionary speech, 6–7, 42–54, 103–6
intentionalism, 29, 165, 167–71, 172–75, 203–4
International Court of Justice, 141, 144

jury instruction, 16, 33, 44–47, 59, 118–19
just cause, 88–89

Köstler, Rudolf, 79, 82–84, 93–94, 104–5

language crimes, 4–5, 6–13

Legrand, Pierre, 137–38, 140–41
lending. *See* borrowing
Lerch, Kent D., 33
linguistic relativity, 130–36
living constitutionalism, 166–67

magic, 36–40, 55–57, 111–13, 117, 203–4
maliciousness, 72–74
manslaughter. *See* murder
manufacture, 162–64, 175–76
Marmor, Andrei A., 44–47, 163–64, 180–81, 183–84
Mattila, Heikki E. S., 59, 76, 77, 82–86, 118–19
McAuliffe, Karen, 146–49, 152
medical professional privilege. *See* professional secrecy
Mellinkoff, David, 51–52, 109, 114, 126–27, 143
moral certitude, 75, 122–23
Mörsdorf, Klaus, 2–3, 12–13, 17–18, 36, 92–93, 124–25, 127–28
murder, 75, 195–96

nullity. *See* annulment

oath, 8–9, 36, 47, 190–91
Olivecrona, Karl, 23, 24–25, 35, 36–38
originalism, 166–69, 173–74
Orsy, Ladilas M., 19, 28–30, 31–32, 104–5, 106–7, 164–65, 178–79, 182–83
ownership, 31–33, 40–41, 48, 50–51, 70–72, 77, 196–97

perjury, 6–7, 8–9, 12–13
plain meaning rule, 157–63, 171–72, 173–75
possession. *See* ownership
priest-penitent privilege, 192–94
professional secrecy, 192–93
promoter of justice, 74–75
property. *See* ownership

Rechtsstaatlichkeit. *See* rule of law
right to be silent, 34–35, 190–93
Romeo and Juliet, 119
rule of law, 86, 88–89, 137–38, 182–83

sacramental seal, 10, 12–13, 193–94
Savigny, Friedrich Carl von, 173–74
Savoy, Bénédicte, 70–72
Scalia, Antonin, 166–67
Schane, Sanford A., 93–94, 97, 162–63
Schneckloth versus Bustamonte, 189–90
Schuld, 137–38
Searle, John R., 43–47, 48–52
secrecy. *See* professional secrecy
sexual abuse of minors, 1, 12–13, 84–85, 122–23, 191–92, 193–94, 198–99
ship baptism, 53–54
sign language, 55–57
Solan, Lawrence M., 6–7, 8–9, 13, 14–15, 16–17, 30, 69–70, 129, 145–46, 160–61, 162–63, 168–69, 176–77, 185–86, 196–97, 199–200
solicitation, 6–8, 12–13, 82–85
solicitor-client privilege. *See* professional secrecy
spousal privilege, 192–93
substance and accidents. *See* Aristotelian ontology

textualism, 29, 158–63, 165–67, 168–72, 173–75, 183–84, 203–4
threat, 6–8, 11–12, 42, 111–12
Tiersma, Peter M., 6–7, 8–9, 13, 14–15, 16–17, 26, 38–39, 69–70, 76–79, 114, 119–20, 129, 185–86, 189–90, 205–6
treason, 97–98

vehicles, 162–63, 175–76
Veterum sapientia, 81
violence, 73–74

whiz deletions, 64–65, 121
Whorf, Benjamin L., 132–34